SOLILOQUY!

THE SHAKESPEARE MONOLOGUES
(Men)

by William Shakespeare

Edited by Michael Earley & Philippa Keil

APPLAUSE
THEATRE BOOK PUBLISHERS

Library of Congress Cataloging-in-Publication Data

Shakespeare, William, 1564-1616.
  Soliloquy!: the Shakespeare monologues (men).

  (The Applause acting series)
  Bibliography: p.
  1. Monologues. 2. Acting. I. Earley, Michael. II. Keil, Philippa.
III. Title. IV. Title: Monologues (men) V. Series.
PR2771.E15 1988 822.3'3 87-35169
ISBN 0-936839-78-3

Applause Theatre Book Publishers
211 West 71 Street, New York, NY 10023
(212) 595-4735

Cover photo: Laurence Olivier in the role of Hamlet courtesy
               of Rank Films.

TABLE OF CONTENTS

ON ACTING SHAKESPEARE

Michael Earley

Performing a speech by Shakespeare—in an audition, rehearsal, or production—is one of the touchstone experiences of the stage. *Every* actor, no matter how experienced or confident, in the very act of mouthing the frequently quoted lines in this volume, immediately senses an instant frisson from the ghostly presence of "others": the voice prints and patterns of countless preceeding actors who have also confronted the same speeches and stamped their own personalities on the very same lines. They are not just the great "stars," like Laurence Olivier and Sarah Bernhardt who grace the covers of the men's and women's editions of *Soliloquy!*, but tens of thousands of lesser lights equally struck and captivated by the luminescence of Shakespeare's characters and his dramatic language. Like the actor looking at these speeches for the first time, like you, every past performer has picked his or her way through the same process and has wrestled with the same acting problems: how to speak the verse, how to give body and weight to character, how to communicate complex thoughts smoothly, how to sustain a long speech with ease and interest. Few traditions in the theatre that bind actors together are as common as this one. Is it any wonder that all actors, especially young ones, approach Shakespeare's soliloquies with awe, fear, and trepidation?

Yes, the Shakespeare monologues do have a reverential and monumental quality about them. They seem more *quotable* than *actable*. And they certainly are daunting histrionic challenges; deceptively natural and realistic at times, heightened and stylized at other points. Yet Shakespeare's speeches are meant to be acted and not just quoted. He never lets you forget that you are an actor on a platform stage performing. Only when the speeches are lifted off the page and become onstage events do their power, potential, and infinite variety spring to life.

It always amazes me how the *fear* of doing Shakespeare is so easily replaced by the *ease* of performing Shakespeare once actors are on their feet with the text, setting the words and ideas in motion. Without fail the speeches offer their own guidance and direction. For Shakespeare, better than any dramatist before or since, gives an actor everything he or she needs in order to do the work: clear motivations and intentions, expressive moods and emotions, precise stresses and phrasings. How he does this, and how any actor can begin probing the texts on his or her own for some of these cues, is what I want to focus on here. The "Commentaries" that follow each of the monologues in this volume continue these observations on a speech by speech basis. So let's set the stage for acting Shakespeare.

We have all been taught the same basic lesson: William Shakespeare (1564-1616) was a writer without peer. Who would even dare dispute that claim? What we have failed to learn, because it is so quickly glossed over, is the fact that Shakespeare began, continued, and ended his career in the theatre as an *actor*. His playwriting career grew out of his acting efforts, and he practiced both professions simultaneously until he retired from the theatre around 1613. Not only did he perform in his own plays (although no one is quite sure about which roles) and those of others (we do know he appeared in ones by Ben Jonson), he was also an active and principal shareholder in the best English acting company of his day: the Lord Chamberlain's Men, later called the King's Men.

When Shakespeare began to write plays, he wrote them for actors like himself. No thought was given to publishing his dramas. First editions came mainly after his death. Shakespeare's interests were fixed firmly on the stage, actors, and an audience of listeners. Just imagine for a moment, being one of those actors in the Chamberlain's/ King's Men, grappling *for the first time* with one of Shakespeare's freshly minted texts and, under the pressure and heat of a hastily rehearsed production, helping the author polish his lines to a glistening sheen of perfection. The working relationship between playwright and player must have been the same then as it still is today when dramatists and actors collaborate on a new play.

What Shakespeare must have kept squarely in mind, as he wrote his two and sometimes three plays a year, was the fact that he was writing for an actor's theatre. It was actors, after all, *not* plays, whom Elizabethan audiences flocked across the Thames to see at the Globe and other theatres which dotted London's south bank. Directors had no part in the process because they, as a profession, did not yet even exist. The art of the performer was the central focus in everyone's mind. Richard Burbage, who joined the Chamberlain's Men about the same time as Shakespeare, added to the playwright's vision by his handling of the very first performances of Richard III, Hamlet, Othello, Macbeth, and King Lear. His markings and expressive powers as an actor must certainly have found their way into the texts. And Burbage must have been just one of the many actors who inspired Shakespeare. The apprentice boy actors, still unknown to us by names, but thought to be uncommonly good performers, have equally left their traces on the great female roles: Rosalind, Beatrice, Juliet, Cleopatra, Ophelia, Desdemona, Lady Macbeth, and Lear's daughters. This kind of speculation should lead us out of the labyrinth of literary thinking by returning us to the stage and the craft of actors.

As a writer, and certainly as a performer, Shakespeare was in love with the image of acting. His characters are forever conscious of playing "roles." When faced with the reality of suicide his Juliet says, "My dismal scene I needs must act alone" (4.3.19). His Mark Antony is so skillful at manipulating a rough crowd at the funeral of Julius Caesar because he is a lover of good oratory and acting techniques. Speech after speech in Shakespeare hinges on the metaphor of theatre. Think, for instance, of the most blatant one by Jaques in *As You Like It*:

> All the world's a stage,
> And all the men and women merely players:
> They have their exits and their entrances;
> And one man in his time plays many parts,
> His acts being seven ages.
>
> (2.7.139-143)

But apart from likening the world at large to the world of the stage, Shakespeare goes further by drawing on the technical language of acting in order to get to the heart of a character's motivation, plight, and intention. Seeing a player become imaginatively overwhelmed during the delivery of a long speech, Hamlet is forced to reflect on his own weak resolve: "What would he do, had he the motive and the cue for passion that I have?" (2.2.561-563). Sometimes the motivational language in Shakespeare is so keen and sharp it verges on contemporary notions of psychological acting, as in these lines of Brutus from *Julius Caesar:*

> Since Cassius did whet me against Caesar,
> I have not slept.
> Between the acting of a dreadful thing
> And the first motion, all the interim is
> Like a phantasma or a hideous dream:
>
> (2.1.61-64)

How these abundant and useful indications of acting
filter into Shakespeare's language on a regular basis is
partly what learning to act Shakespeare is all about; particularly when an actor encounters a long soliloquy and must
work alone. In the form of a script, Shakespeare really
gives the actor a score. The beats and units of his speeches
are marked with metaphors and images, vocal sounds and
stresses, repetitions and interruptions, and pauses and silences. There is a conscious recognition on the playwright's
part that actors need these textual "cues" in order to perform words and sentences. The actor who learns to follow
Shakespeare's internal direction learns best how to act him.
We can begin the process by looking at the smallest of
these units, the blank verse line.

The medium of Shakespeare's message and the assort-
ment of acting cues he lays out for the performer are imbedded in the chain of words that make up his speeches.
When not written in straightforward prose (which accounts for about 25% of the lines), the plays are most often
written in blank verse. Blank verse is nothing more than
unrhyming verse, interrupted occasionally by rhyming
words and couplets. Blank verse is predictable and fairly
strict in its rhythmical pattern or meter: five *unstressed* or
short sounds (x) alternated or counterpointed for effect by
five *stressed* or long sounds (/). The more technical term for
this is iambic pentameter, which simply translated means
five metrical units of alternating short and long sounds
that add up to a total of ten beats:

x   / x   / x   / x   / x   /
di *dum* di *dum* di *dum* di *dum* di *dum*

In regular blank verse the stress is always placed on the
second sound, with the whole iambic pentameter line
ending in a strong (/) stress regardless of punctuation:

```
                    x   /  x   /  x  / x   / x   /
(HAMLET)            Be thou as chaste as ice, as pure as snow

                    x    /  x   /  x   /  x  / x   /
(RICHARD III)      A horse! A horse! My kingdom for a horse!

                    x  / x / x  / x  /  x   /
(DUKE ORSINO)      If music be the food of love, play on,
```

Blank verse gives the actor's speech a vocal musicality. It also makes verse sound closer to natural speech, and even today we often speak in blank verse without noticing it. It provides the performer with an efficient means of delivery and an effective tool for remembering long passages, solely through the device of repetitious rhythms. And, together with punctuation, it allows the actor wide latitude in the choice of the stress and color given certain words and phrases. Each of the above lines looks metrically the same. But the *intention* of each one is very different and alters even further when spoken by individual actors. Blank verse guides the actor without shackling his or her delivery or performance. It keeps the performer on track within the score of words, but allows him or her to endlessly invent new possibilities with the words themselves. It does not limit but, in fact, frees the performer to add emphasis to his or her role.

More often than not, Shakespeare will break the potentially singsong and monotonous cadence of regular blank verse by placing added stresses in off-beat positions:

```
                /   / x x  x   /    /   /   /   /
(HENRY V)      Once more unto the breach, dear friends, once more

                x  / x  / x  /  / x x   /  x
(HAMLET)       To be or not to be, that is the question
```

The added strong stresses in these lines from *Henry V* and *Hamlet* introduce a variety for the speaker that also underscores his dramatic intention. King Henry is urging his troops on in an assault over the sounds of battle and alarums. He must be heard above the clamor. Hamlet, who ends his line with an unstressed *eleventh* syllable (called a *feminine ending*) is pointing up a distinction between *being* and *non-being*. He strains to be as precise as possible about an abstract thought and wants the audience to take special note of it. In scanning Shakespeare's speeches for stresses, the actor enters a world of varied expressive shadings. And Shakespeare focuses the stresses to give him or her the freedom to explore the unlimited reaches of an intention.

When you look more carefully at the stressed and unstressed parts of a Shakespearean line, you become aware of the fact that Shakespeare has imbedded a subtext for the actor in the *stressed* words that clearly charts a direction that his or her acting intention might follow, often in very concrete ways. Notice how these stressed words from all the lines above indicate the characters' intentions and obsessions:

> *thou chaste ice pure snow*
> *horse horse king for horse*
> *mus*(ic) *be food love on*
> *Once more breach dear friends once more*
> *be not be that* (is) *quest*

You begin to see that Shakespeare has planted deliberate intentions for the actor that are unmistakably private bits of direction. This kind of notated shorthand, within the larger unit of a whole line, allows the actor to uncover something vital in his character. The alert actor will pick up the cues and see even more clearly what a character is really saying and doing. These hidden notes urge an actor on more specifically than the whole line might seem to be doing in a general way.

Such intentional patterns demonstrate that Shakespeare was not aimlessly writing attractive words and phrases but *loading* the words with directions for an actor's use. The meaning of the words is not so much the issue here as is the impulse they give to a performer. It is this self-directional and intentional quality in all of Shakespeare's language that help give his speeches their playable results.

Let's go further by looking at a two-line interchange from *Henry IV, Part 2*. It will take us deeper into the heart of the matter of acting Shakespeare. The lines are from the famous moment when Prince Hal, now crowned King Henry V, rejects and renunciates his old comic companion Sir John Falstaff. Falstaff begins by greeting the young King on a crowded public street near Westminster Abbey. Cathedral bells might be heard in the distance as he speaks:

```
                   x   /  x   / x   / x  / x   /
(FALSTAFF)         My king! My Jove! I speak to thee my heart!

                   x  /   x    /  /  /   / x x   /
(KING HENRY)       I know thee not, old man. Fall to thy prayers.
```

Notice immediately that Falstaff's line is in perfectly measured iambic pentameter: ten alternating stresses, grouped in four phrases separated by punctuation, and ending with a strong and telling stress on *heart*. Look at how the line colors and ornaments Falstaff's affections for Hal: abundant, elegiac, resounding, and romantic. Falstaff's line is a celebratory one; a statement of both homage and kinship. Its strong monosyllables and intentional pattern (*king Jove speak thee heart*) give the verse line a ringing quality, almost as if "fat" Jack Falstaff were one of the Westminster cathedral bells, tolling at the coronation of the new King. With a classical allusion to the god Jove, he places Hal on an Olympian plane, elevating and separating him from everyone else in the scene. The intentional stresses magnify all that is rich, generous, and fulsome in Falstaff's character. Hearing the words spoken with their exclamation points, we see that Shakespeare directs the actor to *declare* the lines in salute. We also remember that the *Henry* plays have been martial dramas, focused on soldiers and fighting. So Falstaff is also like a huge cannon firing triumphant volleys.

We can even imagine that the clamor of bells and Falstaff's words are followed by a long pause, so that the air can clear and become silent from the ringing echoes. The line is replete with the crackle of consonants: k's, j's, s's, h's, and t's. These, too, help to characterize Falstaff and affect his delivery. Some of these same consonants make up his name. With a full stop at the end of the line, the momentary pause prepares the way for Hal's reply. And it is here that the acting variety of blank verse takes a turn.

Notice, first of all, that Hal's line is *irregular*. In the way that I have scanned the line above, it is disrupted by offbeat stresses on *old* and *fall*. Rather than musically measured clusters, the King's speech is separated into two periodic units. They stress finality and, perhaps, harsh anger. *Know* and *not* sound negative. They are declarative and menacing sentences. The variety built into the off-stressed sounds suggests that an individual actor can give further readings with wholly different stresses as in the three examples on the next page.

```
 /  x    x  /  /  /   /  x  /   x
```
I know thee *not, old man. Fall* to *thy* prayers.

```
 /  /    x  /  /  /   /  x x    x
```
I know thee *not, old man. Fall* to thy prayers.

```
 /  /  /  /  /  /   /  /   /
```
I know thee not, old man. Fall to thy prayers.

In each case the tension and threat build in Hal's lines. They dramatize him. The intentional variations only accent and reinforce his role as a ruler speaking to an underling. His intention is to stop Falstaff in his tracks, and then to put him down, literally, on his knees in servitude and homage. The standing of the two characters is no longer equal. Master lords above servant. He even says he does not know Falstaff. Now very close to the end of the play, this is a climactic turning point in a relationship that has been building in complexity over the course of the two parts of *Henry IV*. After Henry finishes the rest of his speech, he will never look upon Falstaff again. In acting terms, the line is a major change and revelation for Hal's character. No longer a boisterous Prince who loved the company of carousing and familiar companions like Falstaff, Hal assumes the role of the more responsible and sober "King Henry." In this one line of verse, he firmly establishes a new character, forgetting his former self, and points us to the next play in the trilogy, *Henry V*. In order to assume his grip on majesty, Henry must cut Falstaff down to size and put him in his proper place. Falstaff is now merely an ordinary subject and no longer a boon companion.

Like Falstaff, the King uses monosyllables to parallel the appearance of Falstaff's line. The effect, however, is remarkably different. Falstaff's words reach upwards,

Henry's downwards. The King stresses vowels rather than consonants: i's, o's, e's, and a's. The rounded vocality in the o's, especially, caricature the rotundity of Falstaff. Henry's words do not ring, they pound, beating Falstaff down to his knees. The very word *Fall* is a deliberate pun on Falstaff's name as well as a command. As in all of Shakespeare's verse, the richness of sounds has a physical impact. Henry practically bludgeons Falstaff with his phrases.

We can notice even more in this simple but rich line. Through the mere pause between a comma and period, Hal isolates the phrase *old man*, both characterizing Falstaff and demeaning him in public. Falstaff's vigor and strength are deflated in this *old man*, an old man being quite distant from the *Jove*-like King. Hal's lines begin a spectacle of public humiliation, with the peers of the realm onstage and the theatre audiences as witnesses of Henry's new-found power. Henry's sentences are, indeed, a kind of "sentencing" and expulsion of Falstaff from the King's favor. Falstaff's warmth, familiarity, and openheartedness are contradicted and made antithetical by Henry's cold and banishing rebuke. These are icy sentences, frosty in their withering directness and candor. Happy Jack is sliced down to size and deflated by Hard Harry.

The irregularity in blank verse gives an actor sudden mobility and freedom. The actor playing Hal has all kinds of possible choices to aid him in his aggressive attack on Falstaff. He can deliver Hal's lines as dismissively, offhandedly, or dictatorially as he wishes. But the very structure and makeup of Shakespeare's sentences cue the actor to a specific range of intentions: ending and severing a very special kind of relationship. It is up to the actors to make that intention clear through their individual means of expression.

In this brief example, you can see both the economy and variety that Shakespeare builds into his intentional cues. And when he pits the *regularity* against the *irregularity* of his verse lines, the rich antitheses that result explode in a tense and dramatic moment. Only the acting of this exchange and not the mere reading of it can expose its theatrical impact.

The actor should take the entire structure of Shakespeare's lines very seriously. Although modern editors of his plays approach the texts differently, changing marks of punctuation and even words that differ in Quarto and Folio editions of the plays, we have arrived at some basic notions about Shakespeare's sentences. The actor does himself and herself a favor by obeying the punctuation in the speeches. Half-lines usually mean that a pause is called for; a moment is there to ponder. Here is an example from Macbeth's speech after hearing of Lady Macbeth's death:

> Life's but a walking shadow, a poor player
> That struts and frets his hour upon the stage,
> And then is heard no more. It is a tale
> Told by an idiot, full of sound and fury,
> Signifying nothing. [Here is the half-line.]
>   (*Enter a Messenger*)
> Thou com'st to use thy tongue; thy story quickly!

The half-line gives the actor time to register the emptiness of the word "nothing" before quickly responding to the Messenger.

Monosyllables and polysyllables have different weights and values. The opening Chorus speech in *Henry V*, "O for a Muse of fire," is bright and quick. But Macbeth's "Tomorrow, and tomorrow, and tomorrow" is slow and ponderous, like a dull clock ticking away the seconds of a life. But Hamlet's "O that this too, too solid flesh," although largely monosyllabic, is equally ponderous. Juliet's "Gallop apace you fiery-footed steeds" has polysyllables, but races. The actor must give the words their due recognition in the act of performing them. There are no easy and simple rules to follow except obeying Shakespeare's sound score. What you begin to notice is that Shakespeare traffics his words through their vocal colors. And he gives you paths and by-ways that lead you through a speech until you begin to act him with your own kind of courage and authority.

The Shakespeare Monologues

Soliloquies and set speeches have a pride of place in both Shakespeare's plays and those of other Elizabethan and Jacobean playwrights. The origin of the soliloquy lies in classical sources, particularly the Latin plays, poems, and orations that Shakespeare would have probably learned by heart as a schoolboy. Its roots also lie in the highly rhetorical medieval dramas that influenced the evolution of English Renaissance plays. Elizabethan society itself, with its formalities, proclamations, love of liturgy, song, poetry, and majesty was, by its nature, a world in which the soliloquy found a comfortable place. Shakespeare's society was a world of language. His vocabulary alone numbers over 30,000 words, many of them newly invented by him or others. Rarely has language undergone such an expansion as it did during the age of Shakespeare.

The true soliloquy is a speech that an actor delivers alone onstage, either to himself/herself or the audience. Its format is a convention because no actor can speak in isolation. There must be a listener, an audience. So, really, the soliloquy is always meant to be overheard by the audience. Very often in Shakespeare long speeches, or monologues, are delivered by characters to other players onstage. In both cases there is a listener, a crucial fact which must never be forgotten.

Shakespeare's monologues take many different guises. And all the speeches in this book fall into one or more of these categories: interior monologues, pitiful laments, romantic outpourings, angry harangues, confessions and asides, comic wordplays, expository and didactic lectures, rhetorical declamations, and solemn resolutions centering on death. The infinite variety of Shakespeare's monologues makes it difficult to lock them into precise categories. Often several types of monologues appear in one. Usually in the "Commentary" following each of the speeches, we have tried to tell the actor the exact kind of speech he or she is performing. Each one has its own moods and conventions, its own kind of language.

Acting a speech *solus*, alone onstage, was common in Shakespeare's day. The very notion of the Elizabethan platform stage, thrust out into the center of the audience with listeners all around it, served the actor to the audience on a plate. John Heywood, writing in 1612 in his *Apology for Actors*, graphically highlights the solo actor and his roots as orator:

> Whatsoever is commendable in the grave Orator, is most exquisitley perfect in him; for by a full and significant action of body, he charmes our attention: sit in a full Theater, and you will thinke you see so many lines drawne from the circumference of so many eares, whiles the *Actor* is the *Center*.

Heywood may have been describing Shakespeare's favorite actor, Richard Burbage, the best solo actor of his day. In *Hamlet*, Burbage was given a speech by Shakespeare that best sums up what every actor ought to know and often forgets. All great actors of Shakespeare point to this speech, again and again, as the best single source of advice for playing Shakespeare. It is also one of the best prose monologues in the plays. Here is the first part where the lesson plan is laid out:

HAMLET

    Speak the speech, I pray you, as I pronounced it to
    you, trippingly on the tongue. But if you mouth it,
    as many of your players do, I had as lief the town
    crier spoke my lines. Nor do not saw the air too
5 much with your hand, thus, but use all gently; for
    in the very torrent, tempest, and as I may say the
    whirlwind of your passion, you must acquire and
    beget a temperance that may give it smoothness.
    O, it offends me to the soul to hear a robustious,
10 periwig-pated fellow tear a passion to tatters, to
    very rags, to split the ears of the groundlings, who
    for the most part are capable of nothing but inex-
    plicable dumb shows and noise. I would have such
    a fellow whipped for o'erdoing Termagant. It out-
15 Herods Herod. Pray you avoid it. Be not too tame,
    neither. But let your own discretion be your tutor.
    Suit the action to the word, the word to the action,
    with this special observance: that you o'erstep not
    the modesty of nature. For anything so overdone is
20 from the purpose of playing, whose end, both at
    the first and now, was and is, to hold, as 'twere,
    the mirror up to nature, to show virtue her own
    feature, scorn her own image, and the very age
    and body of the time his form and pressure . . . .

(3.2.1-25)

In this monologue the actor can begin to see how Shakespeare's language works as one word and idea build to tell a story through narration. Although written in prose, notice how the patterns of the words resemble the rhythm of blank verse. Words play with and off each other in unison and opposition. Good and bad acting compete for attention. The good always comes away sounding grand and sincere, and the bad atrociously false and farcical.

Look at the emphasis Hamlet gives to certain words: "speak," "speech," "pronounced," "tongue," "mouth," "crier," and "spoke." But rather than being a lesson in elocution, Hamlet urges the actor to emphasize the *manner* in which he or she performs them so that the *matter* will come shining through. He asks the actor to focus on his instrument—body and voice—and on the best means of delivering a playwright's *intention*. Above all else, the actor's craft should strive for "temperance," "smoothness," the balance of "action" to "word" and "word" to "action." Naturalness must always temper the histrionic and stylized quality inherent in any drama. The actor, in fact, is our mirror. His acts and words are our very reflection.

Hamlet's speech is like a director giving "notes" to an actor before he or she goes onstage to perform. And that is precisely the dramatic situation at this point. The speech is casual and colloquial, even though the pattern of words is formally crafted. It breaks down any barriers between the speaker and listeners. It draws us in and takes us along as any speech from the stage should.

This second soliloquy is something altogether different. The unnatural Richard of Gloucester (later the murderous Richard III) is about as far removed from the natural Prince of Denmark as any character can be. He is, in fact, more like the Devil, the Prince of Darkness. And Richard is very much meant to be the personification of the character Vice from the medieval morality plays. He is cut from the same cloth as Iago and Macbeth. But what he shares with Hamlet, and so many other of Shakespeare's men and women, is a love of the stage and an audience. It is almost impossible to get him off it. He dominates the play from start to finish and is rarely absent for a moment. When the play opens, we see him already rooted to the stage as though he had been born on that very spot just seconds before. He beckons us into the center of his thoughts:

RICHARD OF GLOUCESTER
Now is the winter of our discontent
Made glorious summer by this son of York;
And all the clouds that loured upon our house
In the deep bosom of the ocean buried.
5 Now are our brows bound with victorious wreaths,
Our bruisèd arms hung up for monuments,
Our stern alarums changed to merry meetings,
Our dreadful marches to delightful measures.
Grim-visaged war hath smoothed his wrinkled front,
10 And now—instead of mounting barbèd steeds
To fright the souls of fearful adversaries—
He capers nimbly in a lady's bedchamber
To the lascivious pleasing of a lute.
But I, that am not shaped for sportive tricks
15 Nor made to court an amorous looking glass;
I, that am rudely stamped, and want love's majesty
To strut before a wanton ambling nymph;
I, that am curtailed of this fair proportion,
Cheated of feature by dissembling Nature,
20 Deformed, unfinished, sent before my time
Into this breathing world scarce half made up—
And that so lamely and unfashionable
That dogs bark at me as I halt by them—
Why, I, in this weak piping time of peace
25 Have no delight to pass away the time,
Unless to spy my shadow in the sun
And descant on my own deformity.
And therefore, since I cannot prove a lover
To entertain these fair well-spoken days,
30 I am determined to prove a villain
And hate the idle pleasures of these days.
Plots have I laid, inductions dangerous,
By drunken prophecies, libels and dreams,
To set my brother Clarence and the King
35 In deadly hate the one against the other.
And if King Edward be as true and just
As I am subtle, false, and treacherous,
This day should Clarence closely be mewed up
About a prophecy that says that "G"
40 Of Edward's heirs the murderer shall be.

Apart from his formal Prologues, this is the only instance where Shakespeare allows a central character to begin a play with a soliloquy. He experiments here with a dominant character beside whom all other players in the action are mere props. Richard, ugly and deformed, is a master with language. It is his major and only attraction. And here he woos us, the audience, just as he will later, outrageously, woo Lady Anne to be his wife.

Even a quick glossing of this speech, in formal blank verse, shows the excitement of acting Richard. He is unabashedly theatrical. His openly stressed "*Now*," repeated twice more in the opening section of the speech, shoots out at the audience, commanding our attention. It immediately brings us into the action. His irregular verse lines are full of mean wit and antitheses: "winter"/"summer"; "discontent"/"glorious." There is an instant pun on "son"/"sun" that pays off later on when Richard talks about spying his "shadow in the sun." The rising and falling of lines 4-5 ("clouds" to "ocean buried"), climbs up again to "victorious wreaths" and "hung up for monuments" in lines 5-6. Then two more antitheses: "stern alarums"/"merry meetings"; "dreadful marches"/"delightful measures." The balances within the sentences show what a controlling speaker Richard is. The images dance together in harmony even though opposed. War is personified (lines 9-13) as a lascivious lord and lecher, profaning the very idea of a gracious lord and courtier. The entire speech is in three parts (lines 1-13; 14-27; 28-41), this being only the first section. Most of Shakespeare's soliloquies follow this three-part structure, giving the actor the task of working on smaller "speeches" within a total unit. The speech becomes a small play of its own.

In the second part of the speech, right after he Prologue-like has set the stage for us (wartime turned to peacetime), Richard becomes uncomfortably familiar with us, switching to the personal "I." Notice how the measured phrases of the opening section suddenly give way to a catalog of Richard's deformities; all in one long sentence! The semicolons along the way let the actor rest and regain breath through the twisting narrows of Richard's serpentine thoughts. Here we understand why the character is so often portrayed as a viperous reptile. His language literally snakes across the page with its hissing consonants. He also alludes here to the actor's cosmetic art ("made up") and that "mirror" image ("looking glass") that Hamlet used so effectively in his speech. The lively action of dogs *barking* accents the fact that verbs are dominant here. The whole section ends with the polysyllabic vowels in "deformity"; a word that has a chilling echo.

Having stripped himself bare, Richard takes us into his confidence by telling us his secret plots to become King. This is where the solo actor must really work hard for a result. So insidious is Richard, he literally intends to implicate *us* in his crimes. We become part of his conspiracy because we have the knowledge (the "dramatic irony") that other characters lack. The actor, throughout the speech, feigns familiarity with us in order to *win* us over. Richard's art is the actor's art. He is a melodramatic villain to be sure, constantly in danger of "out-Heroding Herod." But he must touch us and take us along with him so that we do not betray him to others. As much as Hamlet, Richard is a master of soliloquies like this one. Through them he displays all the different vocabularies of the actor's craft. And as with any monologue, *persuasion* is the final intention.

Shakespeare's women are not given nearly the number or variety of speeches as his men. Female roles were not played by women but by boys. All accounts suggest that these boy actors were extremely good performers. We also know, from Japanese Kabuki theatre, that men in women's roles can be uncommonly effective.

Although women are not given the broad range of the men's roles, they do have a depth of emotion and, particularly, *vision* that repeats in monologue after monologue. The very limited constraints that a woman in Shakespeare's society faced—daughter, wife, mistress, mother, queen, bawd, witch, madwoman—shows the progression of his female characters. Somewhere on this spectrum each of his women finds her role. Sometimes she has a dominant part in the action, like Cleopatra or Queen Margaret; elsewhere she is subservient and a victim, like Ophelia or Desdemona. They are best when they are partners with men in the drama, like Lady Macbeth. And they excel as characters in the romantic and comic plays: Rosalind, Viola, Beatrice, Juliet, Miranda, Helena, Portia, Cressida, etc. Here is where Shakespeare's women almost eclipse the men. It is certainly in these plays that some of the best speeches are found.

To use a brief example, here is a speech by Miranda from *The Tempest*. It comes very early in the action soon after the storm has destroyed a ship at sea. Miranda speaks to her father, who may be standing somewhere above her:

MIRANDA
    If by your art, my dearest father, you have
    Put the wild oceans in this roar, allay them.
    The sky, it seems, would pour down stinking pitch
    But that the sea, mounting to the welkin's cheek,
5   Dashes the fire out. O, I have suffered
    With those that I saw suffer! A brave vessel—
    Who had no doubt some noble creatures in her—
    Dashed all to pieces! O, the cry did knock
    Against my very heart! Poor souls, they perished!
    Had I been any god of power, I would
10 Have sunk the sea within the earth or ere
    It should the good ship so have swallowed and
    The fraughting souls within her.

It is common to all of Shakespeare's women that their seer-like vision is their strongest asset. It makes up for their lack of physical strength and power. Miranda's speech, like the more famous one by Portia in *The Merchant of Venice*, is about the quality of mercy. She pleads with her father above the final roars of a storm. The lines stress her subservient position to her father, but her rich emotions free an independent life of character. Miranda is suffering because she has *seen* suffering. Without challenging her father directly (it was Prospero who caused the storm that sank the ship), she recaptures the horror of the event which creates it own kind of indictment. She has lived on this island, which she and Prospero inhabit, for most of her life, becoming a creature of nature. Fire, water, air, and earth find their way into her speech, releasing, for the actress, powers that parallel the magical strengths of her father. The speech and its words capture the sense of drowning. Miranda steps into the role as victim and helpless savior.

In a way, Miranda is the essential Shakespearean heroine. She is innocent, a daughter, eventually a lover and wife, a waif, potentially a witch, and, in moments like this, assertive. She expresses the best parts of Shakespeare's women. Her youth makes her seem like a young actress at the start of her career. Shakespeare gives her but a short speech. But the powerful potential in the words and its assertive "I" show that the intention for the actor is to grip and shake the emotions of the lines. From a bright example like this, a glint though it is, the actor sees what brilliant lights Shakespeare has in store for her in other great monologues.

Notes from the Editors

Our brief "introduction" to each speech gives the actor certain cues that will help launch him or her into the dramatic situation. Sometimes we have left in specific "cue lines" to provide more context to ignite the actor. The speeches are followed by "glossary notes" that explain difficult words and passages or highlight something the actor might want to notice in particular. The "Commentaries" try to sample some of the riches in the monologues from an acting point of view. They *do not* tell the performer "how to act" a speech, but are rather appreciations of Shakespeare's skill and ingenuity. These brief comments are merely one person's observations, and the reader is very free to argue or contradict what is said in the "Commentaries."

In the "Selected Bibliography," we refer you to some of the best of the more recent and available work written about acting Shakespeare. The literature on this topic is woefully slight, however. And probably the best "textbook" remains Shakespeare's infinite capacity to challenge and test the actor's talents through his plays.

Any reader or actor must realize that reading an isolated speech outside its rightful dramatic place smacks of artificiality. Shakespeare's lines must always be returned to the plays as quickly as possible. Yet looking at the speeches in isolation duplicates the condition of the Elizabethan actor who was given only his "part" of the play to work on alone, often without the benefit of a rehearsal with other actors. So working in isolation on a Shakespeare speech is how it all began and continues to begin for the actor.

The sampling of speeches here is but a slight gleaning

of a rich harvest. There are well over 500 such speeches in Shakespeare. If *Soliloquy!* does anything, it should challenge you, the actor, to discover Shakespeare again and again on your own.

Michael Earley
Philippa Keil

* * *

These volumes are dedicated to the fond memory of Bernard Beckerman. Our gracious thanks to our publisher Glenn Young for his support and patience during the work on these books.

ALL'S WELL THAT ENDS WELL

Parolles

Act 1, Scene 1. Roussillon (France). Bertram's palace.
Helena, a chaste gentlewoman, asks the braggart
Captain Parolles, a confidant of her love, Bertram, why
men are such enemies of virginity and how women
can guard against their assault. Parolles answers with
this discourse.

[HELENA Bless our poor virginity from underminers
120 and blowers-up. Is there no military policy° how
 virgins might blow up men?]
PAROLLES Virginity being blown down, man will
 quicklier be blown up.° Marry, in blowing him
 down again, with the breach° yourselves made, you
125 lose your city.° It is not politic° in the common-
 wealth of nature to preserve virginity. Loss of
 virginity is rational increase,° and there was never
 virgin got° till virginity was first lost. That° you
 were made of is mettle° to make virgins. Virginity,
130 by being once lost, may be ten times found;° by
 being ever kept, it is ever lost. 'Tis too cold° a
 companion; away with't!
[HELENA I will stand for't° a little, though therefore I
 die a virgin.]
PAROLLES
135 There's little can be said in't. 'Tis against the rule
 of nature. To speak on the part° of virginity is to
 accuse your mothers,° which is most infallible°
 disobedience. He that hangs himself is a virgin:°
 virginity murders itself, and should be buried in
140 highways, out of all sanctified limit, as a desperate
 offendress against nature. Virginity breeds mites,°
 much like a cheese; consumes itself to the very

1

paring, and so dies with feeding his own stomach.
Besides, virginity is peevish, proud, idle, made of
145 self-love—which is the most inhibited sin in the
canon.° Keep° it not, you cannot choose but lose
by't. Out with't! Within t'one year it will make
itself two, which is a goodly increase, and the
principal itself not much the worse. Away with't!
[HELENA
150 How might one do, sir, to lose it to her own liking?]
PAROLLES [Let me see. Marry, ill, to like him that
ne'er it likes.] 'Tis a commodity° will lose the gloss
with lying:° the longer kept, the less worth. Off
with't while 'tis vendible.° Answer the time of
155 request. Virginity, like an old courtier, wears her
cap out of fashion, richly suited but unsuitable, just
like the brooch and the toothpick,° which wear not
now. Your date° is better in your pie and your
porridge than in your cheek, and your virginity,
160 your old virginity, is like one of our French
withered pears: it looks ill, it eats drily, marry, 'tis a
withered pear—it was formerly better, marry, yet
'tis a withered pear. Will you anything with it?°

120 **policy**/strategy 122-123 **blown down...blown up**/sexual puns, i.e.,
conquered by an erection 124 **breach**/i.e., pudendum 125 **city**/i.e.,
maidenhood **politic**/expedient 127 **increase**/i.e., pregnancy 128 **got**/
begot with child **That**/that which 129 **mettle**/substance or semen 130
found/i.e., in sex or children 131 **cold**/frigid 133 **stand for't**/defend it 136
part/side 137 **accuse...mothers**/i.e., since they have lost their virginity
infallible/certain 138 **He...virgin**/i.e., the virgin and suicide are the same
141 **mites**/insects that carry disease 146 **canon**/sacred law **Keep**/hoard
152 **commodity**/valued goods 153 **lying**/sexual pleasure 154 **vendible**/
salable 157 **brooch...toothpick**/both items now out of fashion 158 **date**/
the fruit or age 163 **Will...it?**/Will you have anything to do with it?

Commentary: Parolles's name means "words" (French *paroles*),
and he is full of them. He is a boisterous, lying swaggerer;
somewhat akin to Sir John Falstaff. His didactic, three-part
monologue is full of blatant male presumptions, sexual puns and outrageous sophistry (false arguments). Parolles loves the off-color

remark (e.g., "He wears his honor in a box unseen/That hugs his kicky-wicky here at home"), relishing this chance to be lewd in front of a woman. Yet his comic language reveals a rapacious intent. Parolles is out to "murder" virginity and not just conquer it wittily and gallantly. Barring that, he would treat virginity as an object to be bought and sold and, finally, as "a withered pear": a hideous image that chimes nicely with his often repeated "with't!"

ANTONY AND CLEOPATRA

Enobarbus

Act 2, Scene 2. Rome. The house of Lepidus. The soldier Enobarbus, a close friend of Antony, gives this vivid account of the Egyptian Queen Cleopatra. He is describing her rareness to Agrippa and Maecenas, friends of Caesar. Their reactions push Enobarbus on.

ENOBARBUS
The barge she sat in, like a burnished° throne
Burned on the water. The poop° was beaten gold;
200 Purple the sails, and so perfumèd that
The winds were love-sick with them. The oars°
    were silver,
Which to the tune of flutes kept stroke, and made
The water which they beat to follow faster,
As amorous of their strokes. For her own person,
205 It beggared all description. She did lie
In her pavilion—cloth of gold, of tissue—
O'er-picturing° that Venus where we see
The fancy outwork nature. On each side her
Stood pretty dimpled boys,° like smiling Cupids,
210 With divers-colored fans whose wind did seem
To glow the delicate cheeks which they did cool,
And what they undid did.
[AGRIPPA   O, rare for Antony!]
ENOBARBUS
Her gentlewomen, like the Nereides,°
So many mermaids, tended her i'th' eyes,°
215 And made their bends adornings.° At the helm°
A seeming mermaid steers. The silken tackle°
Swell with the touches of those flower-soft hands
That yarely frame the office.° From the barge
A strange invisible perfume hits the sense

4

220 Of the adjacent wharfs. The city cast°
       Her people out upon her, and Antony,
       Enthroned i'th' market-place, did sit alone,°
       Whistling to th'air, which but for vacancy°
       Had gone to gaze on Cleopatra too,
225 And made a gap in nature.°
[AGRIPPA   Rare Egyptian!]
ENOBARBUS
       Upon her landing Antony sent to her,
       Invited her to supper. She replied
       It should be better he became her guest;
       Which she entreated. Our courteous Antony,
230 Whom ne'er the word of "No" woman heard
            speak,
       Being barbered° ten times o'er, goes to the feast,
       And for his ordinary° pays his heart
       For what his eyes eat only.
[AGRIPPA   Royal wench!
       She made great Caesar lay his sword to bed.
       He ploughed° her, and she cropped.°]
ENOBARBUS
235   I saw her once
       Hop forty paces through the public street,
       And having lost her breath, she spoke and panted,
       That she did make defect perfection,
       And breathless, pour breath forth.
[MAECENAS   Now Antony
       Must leave her utterly.
ENOBARBUS
240   Never. He will not.]
       Age cannot wither° her, nor custom° stale
       Her infinite variety. Other women cloy°
       The appetites they feed, but she makes hungry
       Where most she satisfies. For vilest° things
245 Become° themselves in her, that the holy priests
       Bless her when she is riggish.°

198 **burnished**/shiny, lustrous 199 **poop**/stern of a ship; (colloq., female genitals; infect with venereal disease) 201 **oars**/sexual pun when used with "flutes kept stroke," "beat" and "amorous" 207 **O'er-picturing**/more artfully rendered than a painting of Venus 209 **boys**/(possible theatrical pun on the fact that boys played women's roles; e.g., Cleopatra) 213 **Nereides**/sea nymphs 214 **tended...eyes**/stood within eyesight 215 **bends adornings**/bows and looks added to the grace and beauty of the scene 215 **helm**/steerage 216 **tackle**/rigging 218 **yarely...office**/nimbly perform (perhaps a sexual pun with "tackle") 220 **city cast**/i.e., like a net 222 **alone**/(a strong contrast to Cleopatra's state) 223 **but...vacancy**/because he was unoccupied 225 **And...nature**/i.e., was knocked-out by what he saw 231 **barbered**/groomed 232 **ordinary**/meal, i.e., expecting just dinner he loses his heart 234 **ploughed...cropped**/sexual acts 241 **wither**/dry up her potency **custom**/habit, sexual intercourse 242 **cloy**/satiate, sexually gratify 244 **vilest**/basest 245 **Become**/are adorned 246 **riggish**/wanton

Commentary: This panegyric (elaborate eulogy) by Enobarbus is one of the great descriptive passages in Shakespeare. Every actor adds his own touches to its delivery. The speech is full of sensuous details: a relish for words, colors and images that convey sight, sound, smell and touch. The vividness of his account is almost cinematic. Lines 205-212 capture Cleopatra in her boudoir-like stage setting where she is likened to Venus. Such classical and painterly allusions are scattered throughout the speech. Agrippa's ecstatic reactions break-up the speech into parts, allowing the actor playing Enobarbus to rest and take the speech in a new direction. Each time the subject of the speech changes, Cleopatra is transformed into something new: a sea goddess, a temptress, etc. The speech is full of sexual puns and asides. Now back in Rome, telling this speech to male dinner companions, Enobarbus obviously wants to flesh-out his tale with as much exotic and erotic detail as possible. The final part of the speech extolls Cleopatra's seductive charms and powers; the very elements that will be Antony's undoing. Cleopatra emerges as a force indomitable and immortal.

ANTONY AND CLEOPATRA

Antony

Act 4, Scene 13. A battlefield near Alexandria. His army already defeated on land, Antony's fleet has just been crushed at sea through Egyptian treachery. Antony witnesses the whole scene from shore and enters with this angry, humiliating report.

ANTONY   All is lost.

10 This foul Egyptian hath betrayèd me.
     My fleet hath yielded to the foe, and yonder
     They cast their caps up, and carouse together
     Like friends long lost. Triple-turned whore!° 'Tis thou
     Hast sold me to this novice,° and my heart
15 Makes only wars on thee. Bid them all fly;
     For when I am revenged upon my charm,°
     I have done all. Bid they all fly. Be gone.
     (Exits Scarus)
     O sun, thy uprise shall I see no more.
     Fortune and Antony part here; even here
20 Do we shake hands. All come to this? The hearts
     That spanieled me at heels,° to whom I gave
     Their wishes, do discandy,° melt their sweets
     On blossoming Caesar; and this pine is barked°
     That overtopped them all. Betrayed I am.
25 O this false soul of Egypt! This grave charm,
     Whose eye becked forth my wars and called them home,
     Whose bosom was my crownet, my chief end,
     Like a right gipsy hath at fast and loose
     Beguiled me to the very heart of loss.
     What, Eros, Eros!
     (Enter Cleopatra)

30   Ah, thou spell!   Avaunt.
[CLEOPATRA
    Why is my lord enraged against his love?]
ANTONY
    Vanish, or I shall give thee thy deserving
    And blemish Caesar's triumph. Let him take thee
    And hoist thee up to the shouting plebeians;
35 Follow his chariot, like the greatest spot°
    Of all thy sex; most monster-like be shown
    For poor'st diminutives, for dolts,° and let
    Patient Octavia° plough thy visage up°
    With her prepared nails.   (Exit Cleopatra)
                                        'Tis well thou'rt gone,
40 If it be well to live. But better 'twere
    Thou fell'st into my fury, for one death
    Might have prevented many. Eros, ho!
    The shirt of Nessus° is upon me. Teach me,
    Alcides, thou mine ancestor, thy rage.
45 Let me lodge Lichas on the horns o'th' moon,
    And with those hands that grasped the heaviest
        club
    Subdue my worthiest self. The witch shall die.
    To the young Roman boy° she hath sold me, and I
        fall
    Under this plot. She dies for't. Eros,° ho!

13 **Triple-turned   whore**/thrice faithless to former lovers: Caesar,
Pompey, now Antony 14 **novice**/young Octavius Caesar 16 **charm**/person
who casts spells 21 **spanieled...heels**/followed like dogs 22 **discandy**/
dissolve 23 **barked**/stripped of bark (also pun with "spanieled") 35
spot/blemish, disgrace 37 **diminutives...dolts**/lowest common persons or
coins 38 **Octavia**/Antony's wife back in Rome **plough...up**/scratch your
face 43 **shirt of Nessus**/myth., bloody shirt which meant protection but
caused violent pain 48 **Roman boy**/Octavius Caesar 49 **Eros**/Antony's
servant

Commentary: The themes of Antony's laments and curses are the
supposed betrayal of Cleopatra and the ingratitude of his own men.
At this point in the play his fortunes plummet: "Fortune and Antony
part here" (line 19). Having lost command of the battle and his own

forces, he has lost himself; a thought that will preoccupy him for the rest of the play and hasten his suicide. Cleopatra, Queen and lover, is transformed in Antony's speech to "whore," "gipsy," "spell" and "monster-like" witch. Full of exclamations, Antony's rage is on full display. A soldier long before he became a lover, Antony's bluntness and power return at this key moment of reversal. He will be revenged and vows to kill Cleopatra. Midway in the speech, Cleopatra enters to deliver one line (line 31). She is like a vision that only swells Antony's rage and spurs his motivation. Such a dramatic device fuels the speech and keeps it from turning into a pure rant.

ANTONY AND CLEOPATRA

Antony

Act 4, Scene 14.   Alexandria.   Cleopatra's palace at evening.   Antony has come to kill Cleopatra for her supposed treachery in battle.   Yet he stops for a moment, perhaps to reflect on the portents of a cloud.

ANTONY
> Eros,° thou yet behold'st° me?

[EROS   Ay, noble lord.]

ANTONY
> Sometime we see a cloud that's dragonish,
> A vapor° sometime like a bear or lion,
> A towered citadel, a pendent rock,
> 5 A forkèd mountain, or blue promontory
> With trees upon't that nod unto the world
> And mock our eyes with air. Thou hast seen these signs;
> They are black vesper's° pageants.°

[EROS   Ay, my lord.]

ANTONY
> That which is now a horse even with a thought
> 10 The rack° dislimns,° and makes it indistinct
> As water is in water.

[EROS   It does, my lord.]

ANTONY
> My good knave Eros, now thy captain is
> Even such a body. Here I am Antony,
> Yet cannot hold this visible shape, my knave.
> 15 I made these wars for Egypt, and the Queen—
> Whose heart I thought I had, for she had mine,
> Which, whilst it was mine, had annexed unto't
> A million more, now lost—she, Eros, has
> Packed cards° with Caesar, and false-played my glory

10

20 Unto an enemy's triumph.
Nay, weep not, gentle Eros. There is left us
Ourselves to end ourselves.

1 Eros/Antony's servant behold'st/stands by, still faithful 3 vapor/fog or
phantasm 8 black vesper's/evening pageants/i.e., illusory shows that
herald night (death) 10 rack/wind dislimns/obliterates 19 Packed
cards/stacked the deck

Commentary: Antony begins his speech with the lightest and
airiest of images: "cloud" and "vapor." But the dragon, "bear" and
"lion"—images of the warrior Antony once was—are in direct
contrast. What Antony is describing is the eclipse of his once
notable power. It is an elaborate simile for a self that is going out of
focus, and it is one of Antony's most vulnerable and knowing
speeches. Notice how painterly and impressionistic it all seems.
He feels, to change the image, that Cleopatra, like Lady Fortune,
has dealt him a false hand. By the end of the speech his intention
is to commit suicide.

AS YOU LIKE IT

Jaques

*Act 2, Scene 7. Forest of Arden. The melancholy Jaques
enters in an unusually happy mood. Even though we
do not see the scene, he has apparently met the court
fool Touchstone in the forest. He tells the Duke and
others about the encounter.*

[DUKE SENIOR
    Why, how now, monsieur, what a life is this,
10 That your poor friends must woo your company!
    What, you look merrily!]
JAQUES
    A fool, a fool! I met a fool i'th' forest,
    A motley° fool! A miserable world!
    As I do live by food, I met a fool,
15 Who laid him° down and basked him° in the sun,
    And railed on Lady Fortune in good terms,
    In good set terms,° and yet a motley fool.
    "Good morrow, fool," quoth I. "No, sir," quoth he,
    "Call me not fool till heaven hath sent me
        fortune."°
20 And then he drew a dial° from his poke,°
    And looking on it with lack-lustre eye
    Says very wisely "It is ten o'clock."
    "Thus we may see," quoth he, "how the world
        wags.
    'Tis but an hour ago since it was nine,
25 And after one hour more 'twill be eleven.
    And so, from hour° to hour, we ripe and ripe,
    And then, from hour to hour, we rot and rot;
    And thereby hangs a tale." When I did hear
    The motley fool thus moral° on the time
30 My lungs began to crow like chanticleer,°

That fools should be so deep°-contemplative,
And I did laugh sans° intermission
An hour by his dial. O noble fool,
A worthy fool! Motley's the only wear.°

13 **motley**/multi-colored garb of court fool (antithetical to the black garb usually worn by Jaques) 15 **him**/himself 17 **set terms**/strong precise phrases 19 **fortune**/fortune favors fools 20 **dial**/pocket sundial **poke**/pouch 23 **wags**/goes on 26 **hour**/a sexual pun *(whore)* when used with "wags," "ripe," "rot" and "tale" *(tail)* 29 **moral**/moralize 30 **crow...chanticleer**/laugh like a rooster 31 **deep**/profoundly 32 **sans**/without (Fr.) 34 **wear**/costume

Commentary: Jaques (pronounced *Ja'kis*) is at his melancholy best when his cynicism can be played off against some witty jesting. Touchstone the clown is the very opposite of Jaques in the same way that Feste is the opposite of Malvolio in *Twelfth Night*. In this expository monologue—which actually contains a dialogue—Jaques "plays" straight man to Touchstone's comedian. But the joke told is a dark one about the ravages of time and man's ripening and rotting. Just the sort of thing that Jaques would "laugh sans intermission" about. The subject of the speech is repeated by Jaques in his "All the world's a stage" monologue. Although he has an unsettling presence in the play, Jaques is not a comic villain; he is just gloomy, weary and out of sorts. Note the tick-tock rhythm in the verse (lines 26-28).

AS YOU LIKE IT

Jaques

Act 2, Scene 7. Forest of Arden. Jaques delivers this "set speech" to an onstage audience of the banished Duke Senior and his fellow exiles. The young Orlando has just barged in on the group and has exited to fetch his old retainer Adam. The incident prompts Jaques's commentary.

[DUKE SENIOR
    Thou seest we are not all alone unhappy.
    This wide and universal theatre
    Presents more woeful pageants than the scene
    Wherein we play in.]
JAQUES   All the world's a stage,
140 And all the men and women merely players.
    They have their exits and their entrances,
    And one man in his time plays many parts,
    His acts being seven ages. At first the infant,
    Mewling° and puking in the nurse's arms.
145 Then the whining schoolboy with his satchel
    And shining morning face, creeping like snail
    Unwillingly to school. And then the lover,
    Sighing like furnace, with a woeful ballad
    Made to his mistress' eyebrow. Then, a soldier,
150 Full of strange oaths, and bearded like the pard,°
    Jealous in honor, sudden, and quick in quarrel,
    Seeking the bubble° reputation
    Even in the cannon's mouth. And then the justice,
    In fair round belly with good capon lined,°
155 With eyes severe and beard of formal cut,
    Full of wise saws° and modern° instances;
    And so he plays his part. The sixth age shifts
    Into the lean and slippered pantaloon,°

With spectacles on nose and pouch on side,
160 His youthful hose,° well saved, a world too wide
For his shrunk shank,° and his big, manly voice,
Turning again toward childish treble, pipes
And whistles in his sound. Last scene of all,
That ends this strange, eventful history,
165 Is second childishness and mere° oblivion,
Sans° teeth, sans eyes, sans taste, sans everything.
(Enter Orlando bearing Adam)

144 **Mewling**/crying 150 **pard**/leopard (Lat., *pardus*) 152 **bubble**/empty
and insubstantial 154 **with...lined**/allusion to the practice of bribing a
judge with a capon (chicken) 156 **saws**/sayings **modern**/everyday 158
pantaloon/foolish old man (of Italian *commedia dell'arte*) 160 **hose**/
stockings 161 **shrunk shank**/thin ankles 165 **mere**/utter 166 **Sans**/
without (Fr.) (Note how it's repetition gives a funereal bell-tolling quality to
the final line.)

Commentary: Jaques (pronounced *Ja'kis*) is a world weary,
melancholic wit. A haughty lord seldom given to laughter, he is
well-seasoned in the ways of human vanity. A cynic and loner with
no major function in the play except to stand in dark contrast to the
green world of Arden, Jaques is a master of words and stories. And
this speech, like other things he says, is listened to carefully. The
monologue is typical of the way Shakespeare uses the image of the
"theatre" as an analogy for the world. In one speech of seven
distinct phases, we watch an imaginary character literally grow,
age and decline into "oblivion." Then Orlando enters with Adam to
illustrate! Jaques uses strong, actable images that can be physically
represented. Words like "mewling," "puking," "whining" and
"shining" have extraordinary sound qualities. There is a resonant
use of antithesis: entrances/exits; world too wide/shrunk shank.
Notice, finally, how the whole speech slows down at "Last scene of
all" (line 163), coming to a breathless halt at "everything."

AS YOU LIKE IT

Orlando

Act 3, Scene 2. Forest of Arden. Orlando enters with a poem in hand. He has been hanging his verses to Rosalind on every tree in the forest. As he does so with this one, he speaks the poem out loud for all to hear.

ORLANDO

    Hang there, my verse, in witness° of my love;
      And thou thrice-crownèd queen of night,° survey
    With thy chaste eye, from thy pale sphere above,
      Thy huntress' name° that my full life doth sway.
5 O Rosalind, these trees shall be my books,
      And in their barks my thoughts I'll character°
    That every eye which in this forest looks
      Shall see thy virtue witnessed° everywhere.
    Run, run, Orlando; carve on every tree
10 The fair, the chaste, and unexpressive she.°

1 **witness**/evidence 2 **queen of night**/Diana, triple goddess of the moon, the hunt and chastity 4 **huntress' name**/Rosalind, i.e., a chaste maid and follower of Diana 6 **character**/inscribe, bring to life as a character (theatrical pun) 8 **witnessed**/in evidence 10 **unexpressive she**/maid beyond words or description

Commentary: Orlando is one of Shakespeare's few ardent male lovers. Most of his men must be drawn into love, but Orlando willingly leaps right in. He is full of youth, energy and sentiment, off-setting the gloom and melancholy that veils the Forest of Arden. Although a short, compact piece of verse that ends with a pert rhyming couplet ("tree/she"), Orlando's blank verse expands from the particular poem to *all* the poems littering the forest. When he says he will "run" and "carve on every tree," we probably see him performing these actions. His "unexpressive she" is a rich and ecstatic way to end this romantic soliloquy.

CORIOLANUS

Coriolanus

Act 3, Scene 3. The Forum in Rome. Coriolanus stands before a hostile crowd of citizens to whom he has been appealing for the title of Consul. The agitated crowd asks for his banishment and Coriolanus hurls this oath at them.

[BRUTUS
    There's no more to be said, but he is banished,
    As enemy to the people and his country.
    It shall be so.
ALL (THE CITIZENS) It shall be so, it shall be so.]
CORIOLANUS
120 You common cry of curs,° whose breath I hate
    As reek o'th' rotten fens,° whose loves I prize
    As the dead carcasses of unburied men
    That do corrupt my air—I banish you!
    And here remain with your uncertainty!°
125 Let every feeble rumor shake your hearts!
    Your enemies, with nodding of their plumes,
    Fan you into despair! Have the power still°
    To banish your defenders, till at length
    Your ignorance—which finds not till it feels,°
130 Making but reservation of yourselves,°
    Still your own foes, deliver you
    As most abated° captives to some nation
    That won you without blows! Despising
    For you° the city, thus I turn my back.°
135 There is a world elsewhere.

---

120 **cry of curs**/pack of dogs 121 **fens**/marshes 124 **uncertainty**/insecurity, i.e., Coriolanus has been Rome's chief defense from barbarians 127 **still**/again and again 129 **finds...feels**/i.e., wants not until it actually needs or suffers 130 **reservation of yourselves**/i.e., exonerating

yourselves from banishment   132 **abated**/beaten   134 **For you**/on your
account   134 **turn my back**/(may indicate an action)

Commentary: Coriolanus is a proud warrior and *not* a politician.
Since returning to Rome in victory, his hatred and open disdain of
the common rabble ("the mutable rank-scented many") has inflicted
their wrath. Coriolanus's tragic flaws—the inability to adapt and
an inhuman disdain—are all distilled in this speech. The images
are vile and damning. As if using a sword, he delivers his epithets
(abusive curses) in cuts and slashes, flaying the crowd and, in the
process, severing himself from all his ties with Rome. The whole
monologue is structured like some brutal incantation, cold and hard
exclamations, that thrusts Coriolanus into the void. The final line
is remarkable by its indefiniteness. "Elsewhere" could be any-
where, or nowhere: a half-line with a long open pause to follow.

CORIOLANUS

Coriolanus

Act 4, Scene 4. Antium. In front of Aufidius's house. Banished from Rome, Coriolanus seeks refuge in the city of his enemy Aufidius, the Volscian commander. Coriolanus reflects on this ironic reversal of fortune.

CORIOLANUS

    O world, thy slippery turns!° Friends now fast
      sworn,
    Whose double bosoms seem to wear one heart,
    Whose hours, whose bed, whose meal and exercise
15 Are still together, who twin as 'twere in love
    Unseparable, shall within this hour,
    On a dissension of a doit,° break out
    To bitterest enmity. So fellest° foes,
    Whose passions and whose plots have broke their
      sleep
20 To take the one the other, by some chance,
    Some trick not worth an egg, shall grow dear
      friends
    And interjoin their issues.° So with me.
    My birthplace° hate I, and my love's upon
    This enemy town. I'll enter. If he° slay me,
25 He does fair justice; if he give me way,°
    I'll do his country service.

12 **slippery turns**/inconstancy of fortune's wheel   17 **dissension of a doit**/i.e., quarrel over pennies   18 **fellest**/fiercest   22 **issues**/actions, fortunes   23 **birthplace**/Rome   24 **he**/Aufidius   25 **way**/freedom of opportunity

Commentary: Up until this point in the play Coriolanus has not been a deep, contemplative character. Alone and banished, he can muse on his state and see how the world works by "slippery turns" (inconstant fate). The world is likened to friends or lovers; neither of which Coriolanus has had in abundance. In his speech opposites collide and change sides (i.e., lines 22-24). Once a great warrior for Rome, he is now a mere mercenary selling his services. For the first time in the action, Coriolanus seems almost calm and chastened. He is even civil to a citizen he meets in the street. He will allow Fate to do with him whatever she pleases, since he is so squarely in the midst of a contradiction.

CYMBELINE

Iachimo

Act 2, Scene 2. Britain. The chaste Imogen's bed-chamber. Iachimo, appearing from a trunk, is out to prove his boast that he can seduce Imogen. As Imogen sleeps, Iachimo slips out of hiding.

[IMOGEN

    To your protection I commend me, gods.
    From fairies and the tempters of the night
10 Guard me, beseech ye.]
    (She sleeps. Iachimo comes from the trunk)
IACHIMO
    The crickets sing, and man's o'er-labored sense°
    Repairs itself by rest. Our Tarquin° thus
    Did softly press the rushes° ere he wakened
    The chastity he wounded. Cytherea,°
15 How bravely thou becom'st thy bed! Fresh lily,
    And whiter than the sheets! That I might touch,
    But kiss, one kiss! Rubies unparagoned,°
    How dearly they do't! 'Tis her breathing that
    Perfumes the chamber thus. The flame o'th' taper°
20 Bows toward her, and would underpeep her lids,
    To see th'enclosèd lights, now canopied
    Under these windows, white and azure-laced
    With blue of heaven's own tinct.° But my
      design—
    To note the chamber. I will write all down.
    (He writes in his tables°)
25 Such and such pictures, there the window, such
    Th'adornment of her bed, the arras,° figures,°
    Why, such and such; and the contents o'th' story.°
    Ah, but some natural notes about her body
    Above ten thousand meaner movables

30 Would testify t'enrich mine inventory.
   O sleep, thou ape of death,° lie dull upon her,
   And be her sense but as a monument
   Thus in a chapel lying. Come off, come off;
   As slippery as the Gordian knot was hard.
   (He takes the bracelet from her arm)
35 'Tis mine, and this will witness outwardly,°
   As strongly as the conscience does within,
   To th' madding° of her lord. On her left breast
   A mole, cinque-spotted,° like the crimson drops
   I'th' bottom of a cowslip.° Here's a voucher°
40 Stronger than ever law could make. This secret
   Will force° him think I have picked the lock and
      ta'en
   The treasure of her honor. No more. To what
      end?
   Why should I write this down that's riveted,°
   Screwed to my memory? She hath been reading
      late,
45 The tale of Tereus.° Here the leaf's turned down
   Where Philomel gave up. I have enough.
   To th' trunk again, and shut the spring of it.
   Swift, swift, you dragons of the night, that dawning
   May bare the raven's eye! I lodge in fear.
50 Though this' a heavenly angel, hell is here.
   (Clock strikes)
   One, two, three. Time, time!
   *(Exit into the trunk. The bed and trunk are
      removed.)*

11 **o'er-labored sense**/active self 12 **Tarquin**/Roman king who raped
Lucrece 13 **rushes**/reeds strewn on the floor (also indicates that he is
walking carefully towards Imogen) 14 **Cytherea**/Venus, goddess of love 17
unparagoned/unequaled 19 **taper**/candle (sexual meaning) 21-23
underpeep...tinct/(an extended sexual image that replaces any physical
contact) 24 **tables**/notebook or palm of hand 26 **arras**/curtain tapestry
figures/statues 27 **story**/the book Imogen fell asleep reading and still
holds in her hand 31 **ape of death**/imitator of death 35 **outwardly**/to the
outside world 37 **madding**/frenzy 38 **cinque-spotted**/having five spots

39 **cowslip**/flower, a primrose **voucher**/testimony 41 **force**/compel, make
43 **riveted**/carved 45 **Tereus/Philomel**/King of Thrace who ravished his
sister-in-law, Philomele, and then cut out her tongue to prevent her from
crying out

Commentary: Iachimo is a minor Machiavellian villain, related
to Iago and Aaron the Moor. Yet he speaks more dangerously than
he acts, and, in the end, is really more impotent than destructive.
He is, however, very good with words. In one of Shakespeare's most
ingenious entrances, he appears from a trunk like a jack-in-the-box.
His soliloquy, full of description, has the same kind of miniature
motifs and grotesque images as Mercutio's "Queen Mab" speech in
Romeo and Juliet. He eases his way into the nightworld of dreams
and sounds. More a lover of heightened phrases than a love-maker,
Iachimo notes fine details with the precision of a jeweller. In fact,
he has something of the artist in him, painting word pictures in
order to best remember what he has seen. He is an aesthetic villain.
His soliloquy also captures the raptures of the voyeur in the act of
his enjoyment. Notice how he takes an "inventory" of the room and
Imogen's person, distilling his observation to her left breast and its
mole: "cinque-spotted, like the crimson drops/I'th' bottom of a
cowslip." The actor must bear in mind that Iachimo roams the room
as he makes his catalog, delivering his lines sotto voce; whispered
so that he will not awaken his quarry. At the striking of the clock,
he returns, like a vampire, to his trunk. During the rest of the play,
Iachimo will never again have a moment quite this big or
tantalizing.

Hamlet

*Act 1, Scene 2. Elsinore. The castle chamber. The King,
Queen and courtiers have just left. Hamlet has had an
angry outburst and confrontation with Claudius and
Gertrude. The strain of his grief emerges. Alone, he
now delivers his first major soliloquy.*

HAMLET
    O that this too too solid° flesh would melt,
130 Thaw, and resolve itself into a dew,
    Or that the Everlasting° had not fixed
    His canon° 'gainst self-slaughter!° O God, O God,
    How weary, stale, flat, and unprofitable
    Seem to me all the uses° of this world!
135 Fie on't, ah fie, fie! 'Tis an unweeded garden
    That grows to seed; things rank and gross in nature
    Possess it merely. That it should come to this—
    But two months dead—nay, not so much,° not
        two—
    So excellent a king, that was to this
140 Hyperion° to a satyr, so loving to my mother
    That he might not beteem° the winds of heaven
    Visit her face too roughly! Heaven and earth,
    Must I remember? Why, she would hang on him
    As if increase of appetite had grown
145 By what it fed on, and yet within a month—
    Let me not think on't; frailty, thy name is
        woman—
    A little month, or ere° those shoes were old
    With which she followed my poor father's body,
    Like Niobe,° all tears, why she, even she—
150 O God, a beast that wants discourse of reason°

Would have mourned longer!—married with
   mine uncle,
My father's brother, but no more like my father
Than I to Hercules. Within a month,
Ere yet the salt of most unrighteous tears
155 Had left the flushing° of her gallèd° eyes,
She married. O most wicked speed, to post
With such dexterity° to incestuous° sheets!
It is not, nor it cannot come to good.
But break, my heart, for I must hold my tongue.

129 **solid**/var., in Q2, *sallied*, or *sullied*, i.e., dirtied (*solid*, in F1, works much
better with the image of melting) 131 **Everlasting**/immortal God 132
canon/Christian law **self-slaughter**/suicide 134 **uses**/habits 138 **not so
much**/(realizes less then two months have passed) 140 **Hyperion**/sun god
141 **beteem**/allow 147 **ere**/before 149 **Niobe**/who so cried over her
children's death that she turned into a fountain 150 **wants...reason**/
lacking in reason 155 **flushing**/redness **gallèd**/inflamed 157 **dexterity**/
nimbleness **incestuous**/(canon law deemed as incestuous a widow's
marriage to a deceased husband's brother)

Commentary: Hamlet's only other statement up to this point in
the play has been a curt, angry reply to his mother about his dark
mood. Now he can finally begin expressing all his interior grief and
melancholy. And he does so in fits and starts and stops, evidenced in
all the incomplete sentences. In the second line the word "resolve"
appears. The resolve to take action is one of Hamlet's most vexing
problems. The theme of the first part of the soliloquy is suicide
("self-slaughter"). The rankness and grossness of the world is very
like the current state of Denmark. The greater portion of the speech
dwells on the speedy marriage of Gertrude to Claudius ("within a
month"). Hamlet's painful jealousy surfaces, counterpointing the
loving memory of his dead father. Discourse on this topic results in
the exclamation "incestuous sheets!" All of the major themes of
Hamlet's motivational quandary are sounded in this speech:
suicide, sex and sin; the state of Denmark; lack of resolve; heated
imagination; father, mother, uncle; and time. The triple negative of
line 158 sounds a portent of disaster to come.

HAMLET

Polonius

Act 1, Scene 3. Elsinore castle. Polonius's quarters.
Polonius bids a final rushed farewell to Laertes before
his son's departure for France. He imparts some
paternal wisdom in the few moments remaining.

POLONIUS
55 Yet here, Laertes? Aboard, aboard, for shame!
     The wind sits in the shoulder of your sail,
     And you are stayed for.° There°—my blessing with
          thee,
     And these few precepts in thy memory
     See thou character.° Give thy thoughts no tongue,
60 Nor any unproportioned° thought his act.
     Be thou familiar,° but by no means vulgar.°
     The friends thou hast, and their adoption tried,°
     Grapple them to thy soul with hoops of steel,
     But do not dull thy palm° with entertainment
65 Of each new-hatched unfledged comrade. Beware
     Of entrance to a quarrel, but being in,
     Bear't° that th'opposèd may beware of thee.
     Give every man thine ear but few thy voice.
     Take each man's censure,° but reserve thy
          judgement.
70 Costly° thy habit° as thy purse can buy,
     But not expressed in fancy; rich not gaudy;
     For the apparel oft proclaims the man,
     And they in France of the best rank and station
     Are of all most select and generous chief° in that.
75 Neither a borrower nor a lender be,
     For loan oft loses both itself and friend,
     And borrowing dulls the edge of husbandry.°
     This above all—to thine own self be true,

And it must follow, as the night the day,
80 Thou canst not then be false to any man.
Farewell—my blessing season° this in thee.

57 **stayed for**/detained **There**/(indicates an action, perhaps an embrace)
59 **character**/inscribe (theatrical meaning: bring to life) 60 **unproport-
ioned**/unbalanced 61 **familiar**/sociable **vulgar**/common with everyone
62 **adoption tried**/association tested and proved worthy 64 **dull thy
palm**/tarnish thy openness with just anyone 67 **Bear't**/manage it 69
censure/opinion 70 **Costly**/lavish **habit**/dress 74 **generous chief**/
eminently noble 77 **husbandry**/thrift 81 **season**/mature, ripen

Commentary: The comic irony that runs through Polonius's
didactic monologue is that his incessant verbosity is keeping Laertes
behind. Perhaps Polonius's intention is to hold onto his son just that
much longer. His talk is a series of homilies: small lectures on
moral conduct and behavior. Polonius is a lover of the run-on
sentence. Just when Laertes thinks one has ended, Polonius
manufactures a new one. Each of his "buts" keeps the embers of his
speech from dying out. The actor must remember that to Polonius all
that is said sounds wise, sage and valuable. Although not an old
man (40-50), Polonius speaks as if he were the ancient soul of
experience. This is probably why he is typically played as a man of
60 or 70.

HAMLET

Hamlet

Act 2, Scene 2. Elsinore castle. Hamlet has welcomed a troupe of traveling players to Elsinore. And he has just heard a moving monologue from the lead player: Aeneas's tale to Dido about the slaughter of the Trojans. Here Hamlet compares the player's over-whelming belief in his role to his own lack of resolve.

HAMLET

550   Now I am alone.

    O, what a rogue and peasant slave am I!
    Is it not monstrous that this player here,
    But in a fiction, in a dream of passion,°
    Could force his soul so to his own conceit°
555 That from her working all his visage wanned,°
    Tears in his eyes, distraction in his aspect,°
    A broken voice, and his whole function suiting°
    With forms to his conceit? And all for nothing.
    For Hecuba!°
560 What's Hecuba to him,° or he to Hecuba,
    That he should weep for her? What would he do
    Had he the motive and the cue° for passion
    That I have? He would drown the stage with tears,
    And cleave the general ear with horrid speech,
565 Make mad the guilty and appal the free,°
    Confound° the ignorant, and amaze indeed
    The very faculty of eyes and ears. Yet I,
    A dull and muddy-mettled° rascal, peak°
    Like John-a-dreams,° unpregnant of my cause,
570 And can say nothing—no, not for a king
    Upon whose property and most dear life
    A damned defeat° was made. Am I a coward?
    Who calls me villain, breaks my pate° across,

Plucks off my beard and blows it in my face,
575 Tweaks me by th' nose, gives me the lie i'th' throat
As deep as to the lungs? Who does me this?°
Ha? 'Swounds, I should take it; for it cannot be
But I am pigeon-livered° and lack gall°
To make oppression° bitter, or ere this
580 I should 'a' fatted all the region kites°
With this slave's offal.° Bloody, bawdy villain!
Remorseless, treacherous, lecherous, kindless
    villain!
O, vengeance!—°
Why, what an ass am I? Ay, sure, this is most
    brave,°
585 That I, the son of a dear father murdered,
Prompted° to my revenge by heaven and hell,
Must, like a whore, unpack my heart with words
And fall a-cursing like a very drab,°
A scullion!° Fie upon't, foh!—About, my brain.
590 I have heard that guilty creatures sitting at a play
Have by the very cunning° of the scene
Been struck so to the soul that presently°
They have proclaimed their malefactions;°
For murder, though it have no tongue, will speak
595 With most miraculous organ.° I'll have these
    players
Play something like the murder of my father
Before mine uncle. I'll observe his looks,
I'll tent° him to the quick. If a° but blench,°
I know my course. The spirit° that I have seen
600 May be the devil, and the devil hath power
T'assume a pleasing shape; yea, and perhaps,
Out of my weakness and my melancholy—
As he is very potent with such spirits—
Abuses me to damn me. I'll have grounds°
605 More relative° than this. The play's the thing
Wherein I'll catch° the conscience of the King.

553 **dream of passion**/imagined emotion 554 **conceit**/imagination, will
555 **visage wanned**/appearance went pale 556 **aspect**/look 557 **function
suiting**/physical actions followed suit 559 **Hecuba**/Priam's wife who
mourned the defeat and slaughter of the Trojans (Note: there is a long
pause after this partial line.) 560 **him**/the player 562 **motive...cue**/
motivation and prompting (theatrical meaning) 565 **free**/innocent 566
Confound/confuse 568 **muddy-mettled**/lacks spunk **peak**/mope,
premature ejaculation 569 **John-a-dreams**/ a limp, dreamy fellow (a
string of sexually impotent puns in this and "muddy-mettled," "peak," and
"unpregnant") 572 **defeat**/destruction 573 **pate**/head 576 **this**/(the string
of preceeding lines refers to a farce or puppet character) 578 **pigeon-
livered**/meek **gall**/bitterness 579 **oppression**/distress 580 **fatted**...
kites/fed birds of prey 581 **offal**/innards, guts 583 **O, vengeance!**/
(another long pause, as after line 559 above, to renew energy for final third
of speech) 584 **brave**/handsome, seemly 586 **Prompted**/(theatrical
image) 588 **drab**/lowly prostitute 589 **scullion**/menial servant; var., Q2,
stallion, or male prostitute 591 **cunning**/skill, ingenuity 592 **presently**/
instantly 593 **malefactions**/crimes 595 **organ**/voice, i.e., vocal organ 598
tent/probe **if a**/if he **blench**/flinch 599 **spirit**/ghost of his father 604
grounds/evidence 605 **relative**/substantial 606 **catch**/snare, trap

Commentary: Hamlet's interior soliloquy is another in a growing
string of self-rebukes for his lack of action. A player in a play or
role ("in a fiction, in a dream of passion") has more commitment to
his intention than does Hamlet, who certainly has the greater
motivation (lines 561-563). There is a crucial little acting lesson
here: concentrating on Hecuba, the actor focuses on the single *image*
of his grief. One of Hamlet's problems as an "actor" is that he has
too many focuses; one is always blocking the other. Hamlet's self-
reproval turns impotent and maudlin (lines 568-580). Yet notice that
when the image of Claudius ("villain!") comes into focus at line 581
and grows (581-582), the cue "vengeance" (583) soon follows. Then,
finally, Hamlet hatches the plot (589-606) that will be the basis of
his revenge action. Through watching the player play, Hamlet
himself has learned how to act his role as avenger. Written in
three parts, this soliloquy is one of Shakespeare's most emotionally
taxing speeches. But there are places to pause at lines 559 and 583.

HAMLET

Hamlet

Act 3, Scene 1. Elsinore castle. With Claudius and Polonius hidden from view, Hamlet enters to continue his reflections on action and inaction, being and non-being. This famous soliloquy is on a higher philosophical and metaphysical plane than all his others. It comes halfway in the play.

HAMLET

55   To be, or not to be; that is the question:
      Whether 'tis nobler in the mind to suffer
      The slings and arrows of outrageous° fortune,
      Or to take arms against a sea of troubles,
      And, by opposing, end them. To die, to sleep—
60   No more°—and by a sleep to say we end
      The heartache and the thousand natural shocks
      That flesh is heir to—'tis a consummation°
      Devoutly to be wished. To die, to sleep.—
      To sleep, perchance° to dream. Ay, there's the rub,°
65   For in that sleep of death what dreams may come
      When we have shuffled off° this mortal coil°
      Must give us pause.° There's the respect°
      That makes calamity° of so long life,
      For who would bear the whips and scorns of time,
70   Th'oppressor's wrong, the proud man's
         contumely,°
      The pangs of disprized° love, the law's delay,
      The insolence of office, and the spurns
      That patient merit of th'unworthy takes,
      When he himself might his quietus° make
75   With a bare bodkin?° Who would these fardels°
         bear,
      To grunt and sweat under a weary life,

31

But that the dread of something after death,
The undiscovered country from whose bourn°
No traveller returns, puzzles° the will,
80   And makes us rather bear those ills we have
Than fly to others that we know not of?
Thus conscience° does make cowards of us all,
And thus the native hue° of resolution
Is sicklied o'er with the pale cast° of thought,
85   And enterprises of great pitch° and moment°
With this regard their currents° turn awry,
And lose the name of action.

57 **outrageous**/unrestrained, excessive 60 **No more**/(the isolation of the phrase between pauses should be noted and used) 62 **consummation**/end 64 **perchance**/perhaps **rub**/problem, impediment 66 **shuffled off**/freed ourselves of **mortal coil**/life's tensions, upheavals 67 **pause**/moment to consider **respect**/consideration 68 **calamity**/ distress, misery 70 **contumely**/contempt 71 **disprized**/scorned 74 **quietus**/settling of an account 75 **bare bodkin**/naked dagger **fardels**/burdens 78 **bourn**/boundary, region 79 **puzzles**/bewilders 82 **conscience**/being, self-consciousness 83 **native hue**/complexion 84 **sicklied...cast**/covered with a faint hue 85 **pitch**/loftiness, in Q2 *pith* or gravity **moment**/cause 86 **currents**/sense of direction

Commentary: This is perhaps Hamlet's greatest interior monologue. Weighing the infinitives "To be or not to be," Hamlet starts this speech with abstractions. Positive and negative values—being and nonbeing—are pitted against each other. Unlike in his previous soliloquies, the personal "I" is never mentioned. Hamlet talks about himself in the abstract, giving an almost clinical diagnosis of his problem. The theme of the soliloquy is destruction and suicide. Arriving at a decision is the intention of the speech. Much less intense and more general than the previous "O what a rogue and peasant slave am I" soliloquy, Hamlet is able to go into elaborate detail about death because he is so focused on its image. The speech has such celebrated perfection partly because it builds so evenly and progressively towards its final word—action. It is also Hamlet's greatest moment in the role of thinker. From this point on in the play he enters the role of doer.

HAMLET

Hamlet

Act 3, Scene 2. Elsinore castle. Hamlet meets with the players to quickly rehearse the script he has written for them to perform in front of Gertrude and Claudius. He gives them "notes" on how to act the material, laying down observances that all actors can still follow.

(*Enter Prince Hamlet and two or three of the Players*)
HAMLET
    Speak the speech, I pray you, as I pronounced it to
    you, trippingly° on the tongue. But if you mouth°
    it, as many of your players do, I had as lief° the
    town-crier had spoke my lines. Nor do not saw the
5   air too much with your hand, thus,° but use all
    gently; for in the very torrent, tempest, and as I may
    say the whirlwind of your passion, you must
    acquire and beget a temperance that may give it
    smoothness. O, it offends me to the soul to hear a
10 robustious,° periwig-pated° fellow tear a passion to
    tatters, to very rags, to split the ears of the
    groundlings,° who for the most part are capable of
    nothing but inexplicable dumb shows and noise.° I
    would have such a fellow whipped for o'erdoing
15 Termagant.° It out-Herods Herod.° Pray you avoid
    it.
[A PLAYER I warrant your honor.]
HAMLET
    Be not too tame, neither. But let your own
    discretion° be your tutor. Suit the action to the
20 word, the word to the action, with this special
    observance: that you o'erstep not the modesty of
    nature.° For anything so overdone is from° the
    purpose of playing, whose end, both at the first and

now, was and is to hold, as 'twere, the mirror up to
25 nature, to show virtue her own feature, scorn her
own image, and the very age and body of the time
his form and pressure.° Now this overdone, or
come tardy° off, though it makes the unskillful
laugh, cannot but make the judicious grieve; the
30 censure° of the which one must in your allowance°
o'erweigh a whole theatre of others. O, there be
players that I have seen play, and heard others
praise, and that highly, not to speak it profanely,°
that neither having the accent of Christians nor the
35 gait° of Christian, pagan, nor no man, have so
strutted and bellowed that I have thought some of
nature's journeymen° had made men, and not
made them well, they imitated humanity so
abominably.
40
[A PLAYER I hope we have reformed that indifferently
         with us, sir.
HAMLET
   O, reform it altogether.] And let those that play
   your clowns speak no more than is set down for
   them; for there be of them° that will themselves
45 laugh to set on some quantity of barren° spectators
   to laugh too, though in the mean time some
   necessary question of the play be then to be
   considered. That's villainous, and shows a most
   pitiful ambition° in the fool that uses it. Go make
50 you ready.   (Exeunt Players.)

2 trippingly/nimbly and fluently mouth/exaggerated and declaimed 3
lief/soon 5 thus/(performs the action) 10 robustious/boisterous
periwig-pated/wigged 12 groundlings/audience that stood in the pit
nearest the front of the playhouse stage 12-13 who...noise/uneducated
audience fit for only mime shows and sounds of fury 15 Termagant/a
ranting tyrant in medieval plays Herod/King of the Jews, a blustering
villain in the mystery play of the same title (like Claudius, a slaughterer of
innocents) 19 discretion/inclination, choice 21-22 modesty of
nature/natural moderation and measure 22 is from/opposite to 27

34

pressure/image, impress 28 **tardy**/inadequately 30 **censure**/judgement
allowance/estimates   33 **profanely**/too harshly 35 **gait**/walk   37
journeymen/second level craftsmen   44 **of them**/among them   45
barren/empty headed 49 **ambition**/selfishness, pretension (clowns would
often expand on a scene)

Commentary: Hamlet's didactic speech is all in prose. It is also
one of the most durable critiques of acting. Its rhythms are quite
natural, colloquial and contemporary. The speech asks the actor to
strive for balance and harmony in delivery and performance. The
words themselves, like "robustious, periwig-pated fellow tear a
passion to tatters, to very rags," sound out and reproduce Hamlet's
criticisms of ranting rhetoric. Other words like "smoothness" or
"mirror up to nature" have a simplicity that captures natural,
effortless acting at its best. Contrasting these antithetical styles is
Hamlet's purpose. He speaks like a director and probably focuses
different parts of the speech on different actors in the troupe. There
is a wonderful bit of criticism (lines 38-45) of clowns who try and
steal the show with their improvisations. Since Hamlet's script is
crucial to his plot to indict Claudius, it is vital that his actors
convey his intentions perfectly.

HAMLET

Claudius

Act 3, Scene 3. Elsinore castle. The King's chamber. Polonius has just told Claudius that Hamlet is on his way to visit Gertrude. After having seen Hamlet's play performed, the shaken Claudius begins to suffer guilt for the murder of his brother, King Hamlet.

KING CLAUDIUS

O, my offence is rank! It smells to heaven.
It hath the primal eldest curse° upon't,
A brother's murder. Pray can I not.
Though inclination° be as sharp as will,
40   My stronger guilt defeats my strong intent,
And like a man to double business bound°
I stand in pause where I shall first begin,
And both neglect. What if this cursèd hand
Were thicker than itself with brother's blood,
45   Is there not rain enough in the sweet heavens
To wash it white as snow? Whereto serves mercy
But to confront the visage of offence?°
In the corrupted currents of this world
And what's in prayer but this twofold force,
To be forestallèd° ere we come to fall,
50   Or pardoned being down? Then I'll look up.
My fault is past. But O, what form of prayer
Can serve my turn?° "Forgive me my foul
    murder?"
That cannot be, since I am still possessed
Of those effects° for which I did the murder—
55   My crown, mine own ambition, and my queen.
May one be pardoned and retain th'offence?
In the corrupted currents of this world
Offence's gilded° hand may shove by° justice,
And oft 'tis seen the wicked prize itself

36

60 Buys out the law. But 'tis not so above.°
There is no shuffling,° there the action lies
In his true nature, and we ourselves compelled
Even to the teeth and forehead of our faults
To give in evidence. What then? What rests?
65 Try what repentance can. What can it not?
Yet what can it when one cannot repent?
O wretched state, O bosom black as death!
O limèd° soul that, struggling to be free,
Art more engaged! Help, angels! Make assay.°
70 Bow, stubborn knees; and heart with strings of
      steel,
Be soft as sinews of the new-born babe.
All may be well.
(He kneels.)

37 **primal eldest curse**/i.e., Cain's murder of his brother Abel   39
inclination/desire   41 **double business bound**/committed to deceit,
double dealing   46-47 **Whereto...offence**/i.e., what other purpose has
mercy but to confront sin   49 **forestalled**/pardoned in advance   52 **serve
my turn**/do the trick (Claudius is not a convincing prayer, still too devious)
54 **effects**/property, gains   58 **gilded**/bribing **shove by**/push past   60
above/in heaven   61 **shuffling**/evasion   68 **limèd**/ensnared   69 **assay**/
attempt (he is attempting to kneel down and pray)

Commentary: Claudius reflects on his villainy and directs his
speech to heaven. But he cannot pray and that is part of Claudius's
sin: he lacks remorse. His language is full of criminal phrases (i.e.,
line 56-60). His desire to be King is his "strong intent." A desire for
Gertrude is part of this, too. The whole speech is about the *effort* to
confess and pray. Set in the center of the soliloquy are the tangible
prizes that stop prayer: "My crown, mine own ambition, and my
queen." "the wicked prize itself/Buys out the law." Realizing his
immorality, Claudius spends the rest of the speech (lines 60-72)
wrestling with the darker motivations in his nature. And the way
the words scan suggest some measure (lines 69-72) of real struggling
rages within him. Notice how he fights to kneel.

HAMLET

Hamlet

Act 4, Scene 4. The Danish coast near Elsinore. On his way to exile in England, Hamlet sees Fortinbras lead his army across the stage. The resolute hero (Fortinbras) momentarily confronts the irresolute hero (Hamlet). Hamlet reflects on the encounter and its ironic parallels.

HAMLET
How all occasions° do inform against° me
And spur° my dull revenge! What is a man
If his chief good and market° of his time
35 Be but to sleep and feed?—A beast, no more.
Sure, he that made us with such large discourse,°
Looking before and after, gave us not
That capability and god-like reason
To fust° in us unused. Now, whether it be
40 Bestial oblivion,° or some craven° scruple
Of thinking too precisely on th'event—
A thought which, quartered, hath but one part
    wisdom
And ever three parts coward—I do not know
Why yet I live to say "This thing's to do,"°
45 Since I have cause, and will, and strength, and
    means,
To do't. Examples gross° as earth exhort me,
Witness this army of such mass and charge,°
Led by a delicate and tender prince,
Whose spirit with divine ambition puffed
50 Makes mouths at° the invisible event,°
Exposing what is mortal and unsure
To all that fortune, death, and danger dare,
Even for an eggshell.° Rightly to be great

38

Is not to stir without great argument,
55 But greatly to find quarrel in a straw°
When honor's at the stake. How stand I, then,
That have a father killed, a mother stained,
Excitements of my reason and my blood,
And let all sleep while, to my shame, I see
60 The imminent° death of twenty thousand men
That, for a fantasy and trick of fame,
Go to their graves like beds, fight for a plot
Whereon the numbers cannot try the cause,°
Which is not tomb enough and continent
65 To hide the slain. O, from this time forth
My thoughts be bloody or be nothing worth!

32 occasions/course of events inform against/accuse 33 spur/kick, urge
34 market/profit 36 discourse/understanding 39 fust/coarsen, mold 40
oblivion/forgetfulness craven/cowardly 44 Why...do/why I still have to
do what I should have done earlier 46 gross/obvious 47 mass and
charge/size and weight 50 Makes mouths at/makes faces at invisible
event/unseen encounter 53 eggshell/worthless object 55 straw/a trifle
60 imminent/approaching 62-63 plot...cause/piece of land not large
enough to fight upon

Commentary: Hamlet has still not acted against Claudius. As he
is literally exiting from Denmark, a more active prince (Fortinbras)
is entering. Everything ("all occasions") is sending Hamlet clear
signals about what to do. Yet he is still a character of divided and
precise reason and not bestial brawn. But *doing* and committing an
act long overdue is still Hamlet's deepest problem. "Even for an
eggshell" Fortinbras would dare any danger to complete his task.
This final bit of war-like proof braces Hamlet to think "bloody
thoughts." Yet he is leaving for England. A long time will pass
before he has the chance to make good on this pact. And then he
will finally act. Like so many other active and ripe moments for
Hamlet, the time is always out of joint with the occasion.

HENRY IV, Part 1

King Henry

Act 1, Scene 1. London. King's palace chamber. King Henry delivers the opening speech of the play to his assembled lords. The troubles that plagued the action of the previous play, Richard II, *are still present: England is under threat of civil rebellion, and Henry's planned crusade to the Holy Land has been postponed. The mood is dark and cheerless.*

KING HENRY
So shaken as we° are, so wan° with care,
Find we a time for frighted peace to pant°
And breathe short-winded accents° of new broils
To be commenced in strands afar remote.°
5   No more the thirsty entrance° of this soil
Shall daub° her lips with her own children's blood.
No more shall trenching° war channel her fields,
Nor bruise her flow'rets° with the armèd hoofs
Of hostile paces. Those opposèd° eyes,
10   Which, like the meteors of a troubled heaven,
All of one nature, of one substance bred,
Did lately meet° in the intestine shock°
And furious close° of civil butchery,
Shall now in mutual well-beseeming° ranks
15   March all one way, and be no more opposed
Against acquaintance, kindred, and allies.
The edge of war, like an ill-sheathèd knife,
No more shall cut his master. Therefore, friends,
As far as° to the sepulchre of Christ°—
20   Whose soldier now, under whose blessèd cross
We are impressèd° and engaged° to fight—
Forthwith a power° of English shall we levy,
Whose arms were molded in their mothers' womb

To chase these pagans in those holy fields
25 Over whose acres walked those blessèd feet°
Which fourteen hundred years ago were nailed,
For our advantage,° on the bitter cross.
But this our purpose now is twelve month old,
And bootless° 'tis to tell you we will go.
30 Therefor we meet not now.° Then let me hear
Of you, my gentle cousin Westmorland,
What yesternight our Council did decree
In forwarding this dear expedience.°

1 **we**/royal "we", i.e., Henry and England **wan**/pale, diminished in size 2 **Find...pant**/peace searches for a breathing spell 3 **accents**/words 3-4 **new...remote**/turmoil in the Holy Land 5 **thirsty entrance**/mouth 6 **daub**/paint 7 **trenching**/cutting, feeding 8 **flow'rets**/flowers 9 **opposed**/enemy 12 **lately meet**/recently fought **intestine shock**/domestic battle, i.e., civil feud 13 **close**/pen 14 **well-beseeming**/handsome 19 **As far as**/turning our attention to **sepulchre of Christ**/Jerusalem 21 **impressed**/drafted **engaged**/pledged 22 **power**/army 25 **blessèd feet**/Christ 27 **advantage**/benefit, sake 29 **bootless**/pointless 30 **Therefor...now**/not the purpose of this meeting 33 **dear expedience**/urgent undertaking

Commentary: Henry's expository speech updates events from the close of *Richard II*. It also tells us what kind of king Henry has become: a troubled and brooding one far from his former courageous self as Henry Bolingbroke. Kingship weighs heavily upon him. Henry's guilt is compounded by the knowledge that he is not a lawful, hereditary king. He is also burdened by his earlier command to have Richard murdered. The crusade to the Holy Land would have expiated that guilt. And, ironically, a similar holy war is underway in England over a ruler. The speech is full of forebodings and sickly, war-like images: "Shaken," "wan," "pant," "thirst," "broils," "blood," "trenching," etc. Even the tomb of Christ (analogous to the throne of the earthly king) is under seige. The King is a victim in his own kingdom. Line 28 tells us that this summary has already been told. But Henry tells it again, for our sake, we assume, and also to bear his "bitter cross" once more. Here we see one of Shakespeare's shaken rulers at the early stages of his uneasy reign.

HENRY IV, Part 1

Prince Harry (Hal)

Act 1, Scene 2. London. Prince Harry's quarters in Eastcheap. Just having plotted some criminal mischief with Falstaff and Poins, Hal is left alone to deliver his first soliloquy. He bears his true identity to the audience in place of the one we have just seen.

PRINCE HARRY

195 I know you° all, and will a while uphold
    The unyoked° humor of your idleness.
    Yet herein° will I imitate the sun,
    Who doth permit the base contagious clouds
    To smother up his beauty from the world,
200 That when he please again to be himself,
    Being wanted,° he may be more wondered at
    By breaking through the foul and ugly mists
    Of vapors that did seem° to strangle him.
    If all the year were playing holidays,°
205 To sport would be as tedious as to work;
    But when they seldom come, they wished-for
        come,
    And nothing pleaseth but rare accidents.°
    So when this loose behavior I throw off
    And pay the debt I never promisèd,
210 By how much better than my word I am,
    By so much shall I falsify men's hopes;°
    And like bright metal on a sullen ground,°
    My reformation, glitt'ring o'er my fault,
    Shall show more goodly° and attract more eyes
215 Than that which hath no foil° to set it off.
    I'll so offend to make offence a skill,
    Redeeming time° when men think least I will.

195 **you**/ i.e., Falstaff and company 196 **unyoked**/undisciplined 197 **herein**/within myself 201 **wanted**/needed 203 **seem**/appear 204 **playing holidays**/vacations 207 **rare accidents**/unexpected events 211 **hopes**/expectations (of me) 212 **sullen ground**/dark background 214 **goodly**/pleasingly 215 **foil**/contrasting background 217 **Redeeming time**/making amends

Commentary: Hal's hidden qualities emerge in this disarming soliloquy. The King his father, the Court, Falstaff and all his cronies believe that Prince Harry is an idle, wayward rogue, unfit for lofty responsibility. But Hal lets us know right away that his "idleness" is a disguise, and that he will "imitate the sun" (with a pun on "Son of God") when the "redeeming time" pleases him. He is, in a sense, on vacation from responsibility. Throughout the two parts of *Henry IV* and then *Henry V*, Prince Harry will gradually emerge as a true redeemer; restoring the monarchy to position, quelling riots, and leading England to victory over France. But before he can embark on that serious quest, Hal must spend time with comic fools like Falstaff in order to learn how best to handle greater fools. The speech is full of masking devices: "clouds," "mists," etc. The life in Eastcheap with Falstaff is simply a cocoon from which the Prince will emerge, like "bright metal," "glittering o'er my fault." Reformation and redemption are his planned intention.

HENRY IV, Part 1

Hotspur

*Act 1, Scene 3. London. King Henry's palace chamber.
The King is surrounded by the nobles who will betray
him. Young Henry Percy (Hotspur) is one. Here he
defends himself to the King on the subject of hostages
taken in a recent battle.*

HOTSPUR *(to the King)*
    My liege, I did deny no prisoners;
    But I remember, when the fight was done,
30   When I was dry with rage and extreme toil,
    Breathless and faint, leaning upon my sword,
    Came there a certain lord, neat° and trimly°
      dressed,
    Fresh as a bridegroom, and his chin, new-reaped,°
    Showed like a stubble-land at harvest-home.
35   He was perfumèd like a milliner,
    And 'twixt his finger and his thumb he held
    A pouncet-box,° which ever and anon
    He gave his nose and took't away again—
    Who° therewith angry, when it next came there
40   Took it in snuff°—and still he smiled and talked;
    And as the soldiers bore dead bodies by,
    He called them untaught° knaves, unmannerly
    To bring a slovenly unhandsome corpse
    Betwixt the wind and his nobility.°
45   With many holiday° and lady° terms
    He questioned me; amongst the rest demanded
    My prisoners in your majesty's behalf.
    I then, all smarting° with my wounds being cold—
    To be so pestered with a popinjay!°—
50   Out of my grief and my impatience
    Answered neglectingly, I know not what—

He should, or should not—for he made me mad
To see him shine so brisk, and smell so sweet,
And talk so like a waiting gentlewoman
55 Of guns, and drums, and wounds, God save the
         mark!°
And telling me the sovereign'st thing on earth
Was parmacity° for an inward bruise,
And that it was great pity, so it was,
This villainous saltpetre° should be digged
60 Out of the bowels of the harmless earth,
Which many a good tall fellow had destroyed
So cowardly, and but for these° vile guns
He would himself have been a soldier.
This bald unjointed° chat of his, my lord,
65 Made me to answer indirectly,° as I said,
And I beseech you, let not his report
Come current° for an accusation
Betwixt my love and your high majesty.

32 **neat**/clean, without battle stains **trimly**/smartly 33 **new-reaped**/
shaven 37 **pouncet-box**/perfume box 39 **Who**/i.e., his nose 40 **Took...
snuff**/snuffed it up or, perhaps, took as an offense 42 **untaught**/
uneducated 44 **nobility**/i.e., nose 45 **holiday**/pleasant **lady**/ladylike 48
smarting/stinging, hurting 49 **popinjay**/parrot 55 **God...mark!**/an angry
oath 57 **parmacity**/spermaceti, from a sperm whale 59 **saltpetre**/
potassium nitrate, used in making gunpowder 62 **but for these**/except for
these 64 **unjointed**/disconnected 65 **indirectly**/offhandedly 67 **Come
current**/be acceptable

Commentary: Hotspur, as his nickname implies, is fierce and
hotheaded. He barks words *at* the King with the same kind of
fearless and reckless abandon he pursues in battle. His monologue,
in defense of his action denying Scottish prisoners to an officer of
King Henry, is full of bragging, masculine pride. What it lacks are
the calculating refinements we find in the language of his opposite
and close rival, Prince Harry. Hotspur is not a poet. All of the
"rage," "toil," "faint" and "breathless" physical sensations of
battle fatigue are in his speech, together with a sneering comic
portrait of a nameless prissy lord who came to demand Hotspur's
prisoners. This is Harry Percy's indirect way of spurning and
challenging King Henry. He tells his side of the story in such a way

45

that we know he is physically aping and caricaturing the "popinjay" lord's mannerisms. He literally begins fulminating at lines 50-55, indicating the speed at which he speaks his lines.

HENRY IV, Part 1

Falstaff

Act 2, Scene 4. London. The Boar's Head Tavern in Eastcheap. The King has just summoned Prince Harry to the palace. Harry and Sir John Falstaff stage a mock performance of what that encounter will be like. The drunken Falstaff takes the role of the sober King.

[HOSTESS
395 O Jesu, he doth it as like one of these harlotry°
    players as ever I see!]
SIR JOHN
    Peace, good pint-pot; peace, good tickle-brain.—
    Harry, I do not only marvel where thou spendest
    thy time, but also how thou art accompanied. For
400 though the camomile,° the more it is trodden on,
    the faster it grows, yet youth, the more it is wasted,
    the sooner it wears.° That thou art my son I have
    partly thy mother's word, partly my own opinion,
    but chiefly a villainous trick° of thine eye, and a
405 foolish° hanging of thy nether° lip, that doth
    warrant° me. If then thou be son to me, here lies
    the point: why, being son to me, art thou so
    pointed at?° Shall the blessed sun° of heaven
    prove a micher,° and eat blackberries?°—A
410 question not° to be asked. Shall the son of England
    prove a thief, and take purses?—A question to be
    asked. There is a thing, Harry, which thou hast
    often heard of, and it is known to many in our land
    by the name of pitch.° This pitch, as ancient writers
415 do report, doth defile. So doth the company thou
    keepest. For, Harry, now I do not speak to thee in
    drink, but in tears; not in pleasure, but in passion;°
    not in words only, but in woes also. And yet there
    is a virtuous man whom I have often noted in thy

420 company, but I know not his name.

[PRINCE HARRY What manner of man, an it like your
    majesty?]

SIR JOHN

A goodly, portly° man, i'faith, and a corpulent;° of a
cheerful look, a pleasing eye, and a most noble

425 carriage;° and, as I think, his age some fifty, or, by'r
Lady, inclining to threescore.° And now I
remember me, his name is Falstaff. If that man
should be lewdly given,° he deceiveth me; for,
Harry, I see virtue in his looks. If, then, the tree

430 may be known by the fruit, as the fruit by the tree,
then peremptorily° I speak it—there is virtue in
that Falstaff. Him keep° with; the rest banish.

396 **harlotry players**/whorish actors 400 **camomile**/aromatic herb that
grows like a weed 399-402 **For...wears**/typical euphuism (see
Commentary below) 404 **trick**/peculiar feature, habit (also sexual pun)
405 **foolish**/idiotic **nether**/lower 406 **warrant**/assure 408 **pointed
at**/singled out, derided **sun**/i.e., Jove and son of God (future king) 409
micher/truant **blackberries**/i.e., go blackberrying or on holiday 410 **not**/
better not 414 **pitch**/something foul; also the height a falcon soars to
before dropping on its prey 417 **passion**/sorrow 423 **portly**/stately or fat
corpulent/well filled out or obese 425 **carriage**/bearing 426 **threescore**/sixty 428 **lewdly given**/inclined to evil doing 431 **peremptorily**/
decisively 432 **keep**/stay

Commentary: Falstaff addresses Harry in his best mock-
rhetorical style. He uses language he thinks a king would use, with
all the flourishing "thees" and "thous." The exaggerated pomp and
hyperbolic majesty elevates Falstaff over Harry, and Sir John is
probably sitting above him. The irony is that Falstaff does a better
job of playing the king than the weak King Henry does in the real
role. "King" Falstaff's favored rhetorical device is the euphuism:
an elegant Elizabethan literary style marked by excessive use of
balance, antithesis and alliteration, and by the frequent use of
similes drawn from classical mythology and natural sciences. Yet
his speech also parodies that style with the injection of rude puns
and bawdy suggestions. Falstaff relishes the role and the chance it
gives him to command the stage from an even greater height. The
speech also gives him the opportunity to exaggerate the size (lines
423-432) of his own "virtue."

HENRY IV, Part 1

Prince Harry (Hal)

Act 3, Scene 2. London. King Henry's chamber. In a long emotional speech, the King has just accused himself and his son Harry of grievious faults and cowardice. Critical threats to the kingdom by Henry Percy and the rebels have made it a time to act. The Prince must answer his accusers and show his true self by becoming a leader.

PRINCE HARRY

Do not think so; you shall not find it so.
130 And God forgive them that so much have swayed
Your Majesty's good thoughts away from me.
I will redeem all this on Percy's° head,
And in the closing of some glorious day
Be bold to tell you that I am your son;
135 When I will wear a garment all of blood,°
And stain my favors° in a bloody mask,
Which, washed away, shall scour my shame with
   it.
And that shall be the day, whene'er it lights,°
That this same child of honor and renown,
140 This gallant Hotspur,° this all-praisèd knight,
And your unthought-of Harry chance to meet.
For every honor sitting on his helm,
Would they were multitudes, and on my head
My shames redoubled! For the time will come
145 That I shall make this northern youth exchange
His glorious deeds for my indignities.°
Percy is but my factor,° good my lord,
To engross° up glorious deeds on my behalf;
And I will call him to so strict account
150 That he shall render every glory up—

49

Yea, even the slightest worship of his time°—
Or I will tear the reckoning° from his heart.
This, in the name of God, I promise here,
The which if he be pleased I shall perform,
155 I do beseech your majesty may salve°
The long-grown wounds of my intemperature;
If not, the end of life cancels all bands;°
And I will die a hundred thousand deaths
Ere break the smallest parcel° of this vow.

132 **Percy**/Harry Percy (Hotspur)   135 **garment...blood**/i.e., sign of a
warrior or redeemer   136 **favors**/features   138 **lights**/dawns, comes to light
140 **Hotspur**/Harry Percy, Prince Hal's nemesis   146 **indignities**/shames
147 **factor**/agent   148 **engross**/hoard or gather   151 **worship...time**/glory
gained in his lifetime   152 **reckoning**/payment   155 **salve**/soothe, remedy
157 **bands**/debts   159 **parcel**/part

Commentary: This resolution speech marks a turning point for
Hal. It is notable for its emphatic control, working through a series
of promises that end in a major vow (lines 153-159). Words are
clipped, severe and sarcastic. Harry's determined "shalls" and
"wills" ring with authority and resolution, erasing all doubts about
his princely mettle. His avowed intention is to win praise and
credibility from his father and the court who has "swayed" the
King's belief in him. And he means to carry out this intention by
defeating Hotspur: "I will redeem all this on Percy's head." By
setting up Hotspur as a despised adversary who will "pay the
price," Harry intends to make his antagonist the agent ("factor") of
his ultimate victory and vindication. The prize in this conflict is
"honor." It's helpful to compare this speech with Hal's earlier one
(1.2:195-217). Both speeches are about unmasking a truer, redeeming
self. Now the time is right for Hal to become Prince Harry. His
monologue has a finality that leaves nothing in doubt.

HENRY IV, Part 1

Falstaff

Act 5, Scene 1. King Henry's camp near Shrewsbury Field. A decisive battle is about to take place and the courage of the troops has been rallied. Falstaff stops to consider the value of honor when weighed against the greater fear of death.

[FALSTAFF I would 'twere bed-time, Hal, and all well.
PRINCE HARRY Why, thou owest God a death. *(Exit)*]
FALSTAFF

'Tis not due° yet. I would be loath to pay him
before his day. What need I be so forward with him
that calls not on me? Well, 'tis no matter; honor
130 pricks° me on. Yea, but how if honor prick me off°
when I come on? How then? Can honor set-to a
leg?° No. Or an arm? No. Or take away the grief
of a wound? No. Honor hath no skill in surgery,
then? No. What is honor? A word. What is in
135 that word "honor"? What is that "honor"? Air. A
trim reckoning!° Who hath it? He that died o'°
Wednesday. Doth he feel it? No. Doth he hear it?
No. 'Tis insensible° then? Yea, to the dead. But
will it not live with the living? No. Why?
140 Detraction° will not suffer it. Therefore I'll none of
it. Honor is a mere scutcheon.° And so ends my
catechism.°

---

127 **due**/i.e., as in a promissory note that is due for payment 130 **pricks**/
urges me against my will **prick me off**/pick me off (like a target) (also a
sexual pun with "come on") 131-132 **Can...leg?**/i.e., does honor have the
power to fix a broken leg? 136 **trim reckoning**/neat sum **o'**/on 138
insensible/makes no sense 140 **Detraction**/slander, bad reputation 141
scutcheon/funeral shield bearing the heraldic emblem of the deceased
warrior (also a short tail, with sexual overtones) 142 **catechism**/oral
instruction in the form of questions and answers that tests belief and
doctrine

Commentary: This is a prose soliloquy in which Falstaff's lust for life duels with and defeats any desire for immortal honor. His monologue is put into the form of a dialogue: a series of mock-Platonic questions and answers in the style of a catechism (see glossary above). "Honor" and "no," the two most rounded words befitting a characterization of Falstaff, are the most prominent sounds in the speech, and have great playing values. The word "none" is Falstaff's conclusion.

HENRY IV, Part 2

Rumor

Induction. The play begins with Rumor, dressed in a grotesque robe painted full of tongues. The character recounts the closing action of the first part of Henry IV and sets the stage for this second part. This is the character's only appearance.

RUMOR

Open your ears; for which of you will stop
The vent° of hearing when loud Rumor speaks?
I from the orient to the drooping west,°
Making the wind my post-horse,° still° unfold
5 The acts° commencèd on this ball of earth.°
Upon my tongues continual slanders ride,
The which in every language I pronounce,
Stuffing the ears of men with false reports.
I speak of peace, while covert° enmity
10 Under the smile of safety wounds the world;
And who but Rumor, who but only I,
Make fearful musters° and prepared defence
Whiles the big° year, swoll'n with some other
    griefs,
Is thought with child by the stern tyrant war,
15 And no such matter?° Rumor is a pipe
Blown by surmises,° Jealousy's conjectures,°
And of so easy and so plain a stop°
That the blunt monster with uncounted heads,
The still-discordant wav'ring multitude,
20 Can play upon it. But what need I thus
My well-known body to anatomize°
Among my household? Why is Rumor here?
I run before King Harry's victory,
Who in a bloody field by Shrewsbury
25 Hath beaten down young Hotspur and his troops,

Quenching the flame of bold rebellion
Even with the rebels' blood. But what mean I
To speak so true at first?° My office is
To noise abroad° that Harry Monmouth° fell
30 Under the wrath of noble Hotspur's sword,
And that the King before the Douglas' rage
Stooped his anointed head as low as death.
This have I rumored through the peasant towns
Between that royal field of Shrewsbury
35 And this° worm-eaten hold of raggèd stone,
Where Hotspur's father, old Northumberland,
Lies crafty-sick. The posts° come tiring° on,
And not a man of them brings other news
Than they have learnt of me. From Rumor's
tongues
40 They bring smooth comforts false, worse than true
wrongs.

2 **vent**/opening, freedom from restraint 3 **I...west**/i.e., from sunrise to sunset 4 **post-horse**/mail carrier **still**/continually, without stop 5 **acts**/actions (theatrical meaning, i.e., earlier acts of *Henry IV*) **ball of earth**/globe 9 **covert**/secret 12 **musters**/gathering of an army 13 **big**/ pregnant 15 **no such matter**/i.e., not at all true 16 **surmises**/speculations conjectures/evil suspicions 17 **stop**/finger hole that alters a pipe's pitch and sound 21 **anatomize**/lay bare, interpret 27-28 **But...first?**/i.e., "but why am I telling you the truth when I should be spreading lies?" 29 **noise abroad**/spread rumors **Harry Monmouth**/Prince Harry, the victor over Hotspur 35 **this**/the setting (character is probably indicating the stage set) 37 **posts**/reports **tiring**/feeding ravenously

Commentary: Rumor's soliloquy is pure exposition and mood setting. It starts in motion the string of lies and deceits in the play to follow. Rumor doesn't have much in the way of character. What he/she does have is an arsenal of attention-grabbing devices. "Open your ears," immediately commands the audience's attention, as it is meant to do. An allegorical figure in a costume covered in tongues (perhaps a monster because rumors are ugly), Rumor speaks in an elaborate rhetorical style that is rich with similes and metaphors: "Rumor is a pipe/Blown by surmises, Jealousy's conjectures," etc. At line 22 Rumor finally gets down to business and provides the audience with a resumé of action since the close of

Henry IV, Part 1. Because Rumor is a bearer of confused and conflicting reports ("Upon my tongues continual slanders ride"), the character probably projects a crafty, malicious villainy to match his/her rumor-mongering calumny.

HENRY IV, Part 2

King Henry

Act 3, Scene 1. London. The King's palace at night.
King Henry enters in a dressing gown with dispatches
in his hand. He cannot sleep. He is disheartened by the
rebellion throughout his kingdom, and wishes he
could get some rest and comfort from kingly cares. His
soliloquy opens the act.

KING HENRY *(giving letters)*
    [Go call the Earls of Surrey and of Warwick.
    But ere they come, bid them o'er-read these letters
    And well consider of them. Make good speed.
                           Exit page]
    How many thousand of my poorest subjects
5   Are at this hour asleep? O sleep,° O gentle sleep,
    Nature's soft nurse, how have I frighted thee,
    That thou no more wilt weigh my eyelids down
    And steep° my senses in forgetfulness?
    Why rather, sleep, liest thou in smoky cribs,°
10   Upon uneasy pallets° stretching thee,
    And hushed with buzzing night-flies to thy
      slumber,
    Than in the perfumed° chambers of the great,
    Under the canopies of costly state,
    And lulled with sound of sweetest melody?
15   O thou dull god, why li'st thou with the vile
    In loathsome beds, and leav'st the kingly couch
    A watch-case,° or a common 'larum-bell?°
    Wilt thou upon the high and giddy mast
    Seal up the ship-boy's eyes, and rock his brains
20   In cradle of the rude imperious surge,
    And in the visitation of the winds,
    Who take the ruffian billows by the top,

Curling their monstrous heads, and hanging them
With deafing° clamor in the slippery clouds,
25 That, with the hurly,° death itself awakes?
Canst thou, O partial° sleep, give thy repose
To the wet sea-boy in an hour so rude,
And in the calmest and most stillest night,
With all appliances° and means° to boot,
30 Deny it to a king? Then happy low, lie down.
Uneasy lies the head that wears a crown.

5 sleep/(personified here in order to give the speaker a partner to address)
8 steep/soak 9 smoky cribs/beds in chimneyless hovels 10 pallets/a
humble bed 12 perfumed/i.e., to keep out stale air 17 watch-case/sentry
box 'larum-bell/alarm bell 24 deafing/deafening 25 hurly/hurlyburly,
confusion 26 partial/choosy 29 appliances/expedients, remedies
means/interventions, agents

Commentary: This is one of the greatest of Shakespeare's kingly
laments. The poetry is full of beautiful images and control, spoken
in the quiet of the night. Its confessional solitude marks why so
many of the great soliloquies are spoken at night. The King is
doubly depicted as watchman or shepherd over his ship or flock of
subjects, keeping a vigilant eye out for catastrophe. The monologue
is composed as an elaborate apostrophe to sleep. Henry broods
openly because he is alone, comparing his antithetical states of
anxiety and comfort to the more enviable condition of a peasant in a
lowly hovel. The simile then changes to that of a ship-boy keeping
watch at sea for a storm. In the latter case Henry envies the boy his
ability to sleep through a storm. The actor must not forget that the
King is also sick, growing more so as the play progresses. So sleep is
also like a yearning for the comfort of death. As head of state,
Henry's mind is racked with turmoil. Yet this is his most quiet
moment in the play; the one moment, ironically, when he most
resembles the poetic Richard II, the rightful king whom Henry
deposed and had murdered. Compare this monologue to a similar
speech by another King—Henry VI (below 2.5: 1-54).

HENRY IV, Part 2

Falstaff

*Act 4, Scene 3. Yorkshire. A battlefield near the Forest
of Gaultree. With the battle won and the rebels routed,
Sir John Falstaff asks Prince John (Prince Henry's
younger brother) if he might have leave to return
home. John grudgingly agrees.*

[PRINCE JOHN
    Fare you well, Falstaff. I in my condition
    Shall better speak of you than you deserve.]
    (Exeunt all but Falstaff)

FALSTAFF
    [I would you had but the wit; 'twere better than
    your dukedom.] Good faith, this same young sober
85 blooded boy doth not love me, nor a° man cannot
    make him laugh. But that's no marvel;° he drinks
    no wine. There's never none of these demure°
    boys come to any proof;° for thin drink doth so
    overcool their blood, and making many fish meals,
90 that they fall into a kind of male green-sickness;°
    and then, when they marry, they get wenches.°
    They are generally fools and cowards—which some
    of us should be too, but for inflammation. A good
    sherry-sack hath a two-fold operation in it. It
95 ascends me into the brain, dries me there all the
    foolish and dull and crudy° vapors° which environ
    it, makes it apprehensive, quick, forgetive, full of
    nimble, fiery, and delectable shapes, which,
    delivered o'er to the voice, the tongue, which is the
100 birth, becomes excellent wit.° The second property
    of your excellent sherry is the warming of the
    blood, which, before cold and settled, left the liver°

white° and pale, which, is the badge of
pusillanimity° and cowardice. But the sherry
105 warms it, and makes it course° from the inwards to
the parts' extremes; it illuminateth the face, which,
as a beacon, gives warning to all the rest of this
little kingdom,° man, to arm; and then the vital
commoners and inland petty spirits muster me all
110 to their captain, the heart; who, great and puffed up
with his retinue, doth any deed of courage. And
this valor comes of sherry. So that skill in the
weapon is nothing without sack, for that sets it a-
work; and learning a mere hoard of gold kept by a
115 devil, till sack commences° it and sets it in act and
use. Hereof° comes it that Prince Harry is valiant;
for the cold blood he did naturally inherit of his
father he hath, like lean, sterile, and bare land,
manured, husbanded, and tilled, with excellent
120 endeavour of drinking good, and good store of
fertile sherry, that he is become very hot and
valiant. If I had a thousand sons, the first human
principle I would teach them should be to forswear
thin potations,° and to addict themselves to sack.

85 **a**/any 86 **marvel**/surprise, wonder 87 **demure**/grave, serious 88
proof/testing, strength 90 **green-sickness**/anemia given to young girls 91
wenches/girl children rather than boys 92 **inflammation**/i.e., of the
spirits with drink (also sexual meaning) 96 **crudy**/crude **vapors**/injurious
secretions of the body and mind 100 **wit**/intelligence, good cheer 102
liver/supposed seat of love and violent passion 103 **white**/cowardly 104
pusillanimity/extreme timidity 105 **course**/flow 108 **kingdom**/(notice
how the speech moves from the body of Falstaff to the whole body politic of
England) 115 **commences**/graduates (i.e., commencement to a higher
degree) 116 **Hereof**/(Falstaff turns from the general to the particular
proof, Prince Harry) 124 **thin potations**/weak drinks

Commentary: Falstaff's prose soliloquy to the glory of sherry-
sack and manliness begins with a thumbnail sketch of Prince John, a
sober and efficient soldier who makes a few brief appearances in the
tetralogy. But it's all a set-up for Falstaff's extravagant com-
parison between sullen sobriety and the warm excesses of drink.

Falstaff's speech is intoxicating comic sophistry (outrageous justification). After all the battles and treacheries witnessed in the play so far, this is a light moment that illuminates the action. The speech is also something of a victory celebration. England is at last triumphant and free of threat.   Now, with fiery sack flowing through the bloodstream of the kingdom, England can become as "hot and valiant" as Prince Harry. Like all of Falstaff's monologues, this is an ode to life and the living. And it is ultimately a long extended "toast" to Prince Harry who, ironically, will renounce Falstaff in the coming act and turn as "sober-blooded" and treacherous towards Sir John as did Prince John towards the rebel nobles.

HENRY IV, Part 2

Prince Harry (Hal)

Act 4, Scene 5. London. The King's chamber at Westminster. The sick King Henry, after hearing of the rebels' defeat, succumbs to exhaustion and falls asleep. His crown lies on the pillow beside his head. Prince Harry, his son, thinking his father is dead, picks up the crown and all it symbolizes. Music is playing through speech.

[CLARENCE
    Let us withdraw into the other room.
WARWICK
    Will't please your grace to go along with us?]
PRINCE HARRY
    No, I will sit and watch here by the King.
    (Exeunt all but the King and Prince Harry)
20   Why doth the crown lie there upon his pillow,
    Being so troublesome a bedfellow?
    O polished perturbation!° Golden care!
    That keep'st the ports° of slumber open wide
    To many a watchful night!—Sleep with it now!
25   Yet not so sound, and half so deeply sweet,
    As he whose brow with homely biggen° bound
    Snores out the watch of night. O majesty!°
    When thou dost pinch thy bearer, thou dost sit
    Like a rich armor worn in heat of day,
30   That scald'st with safety.°—By his gates of breath°
    There lies a downy feather which stirs not.
    Did he suspire,° that light and weightless down
    Perforce must move.—My gracious lord, my
        father!°—
    This sleep is sound indeed. This is a sleep
35   That from this golden rigol° hath divorced

61

So many English kings.—Thy due from me
Is tears and heavy sorrows of the blood,°
Which nature, love, and filial tenderness
Shall, O dear father, pay thee plenteously.
40   My due° from thee is this imperial crown,
Which, as immediate from° thy place and blood,°
Derives° itself to me.
(He puts the crown on his head)

Lo, where it sits,
Which God shall guard; and put° the world's
          whole strength
Into one giant arm, it shall not force
45   This lineal° honor from me. This from thee
Will I to mine° leave, as 'tis left to me. *(Exits)*
(Music ceases.   The King awakes.)

22 **perturbation**/disturbance   23 **ports**/city gates, eyes   26 **biggen**/
nightcap   27 **majesty**/i.e., the crown   30 **scald'st...safety**/burns while
protecting **gates of breath**/mouth   32 **suspire**/breathe   33 **My...father!**/
(calls out to the King)   35 **rigol**/ring, crown   37 **blood**/i.e., seat of passion   40
due/right, i.e., birthright   41 **as...from**/as next to (in line of succession)
place and blood/hereditary   42 **Derives**/delivers   43 **and put**/and if you
put   45 **lineal**/natural lineage   46 **mine**/descendant (i.e., first born)

Commentary: Harry begins his soliloquy as the King's servant,
sitting by his side, and ends standing as King himself—if only for
the moment.   The strong visual prop of the crown gives the
monologue focus and power.   And the whole speech is delivered as
an apostrophe to the crown itself.   The King as vigilant watchman
whose fortress head is encircled by the walls of the crown is the
soliloquy's most striking path of imagery.   "Scald'st with safety"
adds an antithetical touch to a speech so full of such contrasts.   The
attraction/rejection of the crown itself by Harry is a strong
motivation for the actor.   But notice that once Harry firmly seizes
the crown and places it on his head, he is instantly transformed into
an imperial ruler (lines 40-46).   Fortune's circle has crowned a new
lineal subject, wiping away the sins of unnatural succession that
have plagued both parts of *Henry IV*.   Kingship is back on the track
of natural hereditary succession.   The crowning irony is that King
Henry is sill alive and wakes up after Harry leaves the stage at the
end of his speech.   The play is full of such rude, black jokes.

HENRY IV, Part 2

King Harry

Act 5, Scene 5. London. On route to the palace at Westminster. Prince Harry, upon the death of his father, takes on the "new and gorgeous garment, majesty," and is crowned King Henry V. As the new King and his retinue cross the stage they encounter Sir John Falstaff and his cronies. The young King rejects Falstaff and puts him in his place. This is the closing moment of the play.

[FALSTAFF
    My king, my Jove, I speak to thee, my heart!]
KING HARRY
    I know thee not,° old man. Fall° to thy prayers.
    How ill white hairs becomes a fool and jester!
50   I have long dreamt° of such a kind of man,
    So surfeit-swelled,° so old, and so profane;
    But being awake, I do despise my dream.
    Make less thy body hence,° and more thy grace.
    Leave gormandizing; know the grave doth gape
55   For thee thrice wider than for other men.
    Reply° not to me with a fool-born jest.
    Presume not° that I am the thing I was,
    For God doth know, so shall the world perceive,
    That I have turned away my former self;
60   So will I those that kept me company.
    When thou dost hear I am as I have been,
    Approach me, and thou shalt be as thou wast,
    The tutor° and the feeder of my riots.
    Till then I banish thee, on pain of death,
65   As I have done the rest of my misleaders,°
    Not to come near our person by ten mile.
    For competence of life I will allow you,

That lack of means enforce you not to evils;°
And as we hear you do reform yourselves,
70 We will, according to your strengths and qualities,°
Give you advancement. *(To Lord Chief Justice)* Be
    it your charge, my lord,
To see performed the tenor° of our word. *(To his
    train)*
Set on! *(Exeunt King Harry and his train.)*

48 **I...not**/c.f., New Testament, *Matthew 25:10-12* **Fall**/(action implied) 50 **dreamt**/(Earlier, in the first part of *Henry IV*, Harry was hiding out in a dream of riotous youth.) 51 **surfeit-swelled**/swollen from overindulgence 53 **hence**/henceforth, from this moment 56 **Reply**/(perhaps the actor playing Falstaff attempts to reply here) 57 **Presume not**/dare not suppose 63 **tutor**/mentor 65 **misleaders**/deceivers 67-68 **For...evils**/For life's necessities only you may have what you need, but no more that could lead you to evil 70 **qualities**/attainments through good deeds 72 **tenor**/importance

Commentary: King Harry uses this opportunity to reject his wild youth by publicly humiliating Falstaff and likening the sins of the past to a despised "dream." Falstaff was Harry's surrogate father and boisterous role model while Prince Hal was in hiding from his responsibility. Now Falstaff is treated like the Devil and banished along with Harry's former self (lines 57-60). Charged with the weight and crown of hereditary kingship, Harry uses that "bright metal" to cut down all pretenders. His monologue is full of pounding, commanding sentences that not only renounce Falstaff but diminish him in size and capacity. One injunction after another is laden on Falstaff (e.g., line 53). Harry first forces Falstaff to his knees and then further reduces him to a "fool," "jester" and "old man." All that is vital about Sir John—food, drink, rioting—is indicted as sinful. Harry's tones are wrathful and biblical. While the young King's monologue is mean, cold, calculating and holier-than-thou, the actor playing Harry must remember that if he is to establish strong rule, he must first weed-out the misrule in his kingdom. Carousing cowards and fools like Sir John Falstaff are the lords of misrule. By strong necessity and example, King Harry sets "strength and quality" above girth and jests. As King, Harry no longer has friends but only subjects.

HENRY IV, Part 2

Epilogue

*Epilogue. The stage has been cleared. The epilogue is
spoken by a dancer to the audience.*

EPILOGUE
First my fear,° then my curtsy,° last my speech.
    My fear is your displeasure;° my curtsy, my duty;
and my speech to beg your pardons. If you look for
a good speech now, you undo° me; for what I have
5 to say is of mine own making,° and what indeed I
should say will, I doubt, prove mine own marring.°
But to the purpose, and so to the venture. Be it
known to you, as it is very well, I was lately here in
the end of a displeasing play,° to pray your patience
10 for it, and to promise you a better. I did mean
indeed to pay you with this; which, if like an ill
venture° it come unluckily home,° I break,° and
you, my gentle creditors, lose. Here I promised you
I would be, and here I commit my body to your
15 mercies. Bate° me some, and I will pay you some,
and, as most debtors do, promise you infinitely.
    If my tongue cannot entreat you to acquit° me,
will you command me to use my legs? And yet
that were but light payment, to dance out of your
20 debt. But a good conscience will make any possible
satisfaction, and so would I. All the gentlewomen
here have forgiven me; if the gentlemen will not,
then the gentlemen do not agree with the gentlewomen, which was never seen before in such an
25 assembly.
    One word more, I beseech you. If you be not too
much cloyed° with fat meat, our humble author

will continue the story with Sir John in it, and
make you merry with fair Katherine of France;°
30 where, for anything° I know, Falstaff shall die of a
sweat°—unless already a be killed with your hard
opinions. For Oldcastle° died a martyr,° and this is
not the man. My tongue is weary; when my legs
are too, I will bid you good night, and so kneel
35 down before you—but, indeed, to pray for the
Queen.
     (He dances, then kneels for applause. Exit.)

1 fear/(perhaps pretended stagefright) **curtsy**/bow, courtesy 2 **My...
displeasure**/i.e., that you did not like the play or a part of it 4 **undo**/ruin 5
mine own making/i.e., actor's speech and not the playwright's 6
marring/spoiling (pun on "making") 9 **displeasing play**/(presumably a
previous, but unnamed, play in the same theatre booed by the audience)
12 **venture**/business venture **unluckily home**/prove disastrous **break**/
go bankrupt 15 **Bate**/quarrel or debate (also a wordplay on *bait*, to hurl
abuse or attack with dogs) 17 **acquit**/prove innocent and set free 27
cloyed/satiated, full 27-29 **author...France**/i.e., highlights of *Henry V* 30
anything/all 31 **sweat**/the sweating plague 32 **Oldcastle**/Sir John
Oldcastle, the character upon whom Shakespeare based Falstaff
martyr/(or so some sources say)

Commentary: In strong contrast to the sneering Induction spoken
by Rumor, the Epilogue of *Henry IV* has a festive quality. The
former character was all tongues, the latter is both tongue and legs.
The speech dances with simple merry things: nonsense sayings and
doggerel. Its chief purpose is to put the audience in a good mood,
especially after they have just seen a popular character like
Falstaff literally put down. At the end of the speech, Epilogue
kneels, reminding us of Falstaff's forced kneeling to King Harry. But
Epilogue's prayer is to Queen Elizabeth. It's likely that the line,
"for what I have to say is of mine own making," shows that the
clown speeches of Shakespeare allowed for improvisations by the
actor. The words are only a pretext for a little cabaret turn while
the audience leaves the theatre. And it also prepares for the play
they will next see; a kind of coming attractions for *Henry V*.

HENRY V

Prologue

Prologue. Empty stage. The Chorus enters as Prologue to set both the scene of the play's action and the audience's imagination to work.

CHORUS

O for a Muse of fire,° that would ascend
The brightest heaven of invention:°
A kingdom for a stage, princes to act,
And monarchs to behold the swelling scene.°
5 Then should the warlike Harry, like himself,
Assume the port° of Mars, and at his heels,
Leashed in like hounds, should famine, sword, and
    fire
Crouch for employment. But pardon, gentles all,
The flat unraisèd spirits° that hath dared
10 On this unworthy scaffold° to bring forth
So great an object.° Can this cock-pit° hold
The vasty fields of France? Or may we cram
Within this wooden O° the very casques°
That did affright the air at Agincourt°?
15 O pardon: since a crookèd figure may
Attest in little place a million,°
And let us, ciphers° to this great account,
On your imaginary forces work.
Suppose within the girdle° of these walls
20 Are now confined two mighty monarchies,°
Whose high uprearèd and abutting fronts°
The perilous narrow ocean° parts asunder.
Piece out our imperfections° with your thoughts:
Into a thousand parts divide one man,
25 And make imaginary puissance.°
Think, when we talk of horses, that you see them,
Printing° their proud hoofs i'th' receiving earth;

67

For 'tis your thoughts that now must deck° our
    kings,
Carry them here and there, jumping o'er times,°
30 Turning th'accomplishment of many years
Into an hourglass—for the which supply,
Admit me Chorus to this history,°
Who Prologue-like your humble patience pray
Gently to hear, kindly to judge, our play.

1 fire/a shot or volley 2 invention/poetic invention 1-4 O...scene/i.e., if
this play could rise above poetic limitations then this limited stage would be
a genuine kingdom and real princes and monarchs would replace mere
actors 6 port/visage 9 flat unraisèd spirits/dull aspiring actors 10
scaffold/raised stage 11 object/objective, presentation cock-pit/theatre
(meaning had been transferred from gaming bird arena to the theatre) 13
wooden O/circular theatre built of wood, Elizabethan playhouse
casques/helmets 14 Agincourt/French city that is scene of decisive
English victory in Henry V 15-16 since...million/a zero or low sum in place
of a million; i.e., one actor for many armies 17 ciphers/nonentities 19
girdle/belt, circuit 20 monarchies/i.e., England and France 21 fronts/
cliff frontiers 22 ocean/i.e., English Channel 23 imperfections/i.e., that
which the stage cannot represent 25 puissance/troops, strength 27
Printing/stamping, implanting 28 deck/dress 29 times/i.e., the exigen-
cies of plot, time and place 31-32 for...history/i.e., the Chorus will act as
guide in the story and narrate unrepresented events before each new act

Commentary: This expository soliloquy is aimed directly at the
audience. It includes some of Shakespeare's most memorable verse
lines and is one of his great homages to the power of the theatre.
Like Rumor in Henry IV, Part 2, Prologue tells the audience what it
will see and hear in the action ahead. The character previews
things to come. Unlike Rumor's monologue, Prologue's soliloquy is
much more glorious because Henry V is a more glorious and
heightened play. The monologue is given epic, Homeric dimensions:
"Then should the warlike Harry, like himself,/Assume the port of
Mars," etc. "Ascend" is truly an operative word in this speech. For
words and images attain a height of poetry here that is rare.
Prologue is most accomplished and inventive when telling an
audience how to view the world of the stage: "Into a thousand parts
divide one man;" "Think, when we talk of horses, that you see
them." The imaginative conviction that it takes to watch and
listen to drama are here addressed: the audience must merge with
the actor into a common experience of fictional event.

HENRY V

Chorus

Act 3. The Chorus begins each of the five acts of Henry V.

CHORUS
    Thus with imagined wing° our swift scene flies
    In motion of no less celerity°
    Than that of thought. Suppose that you have seen
    The well-appointed° king at Dover pier°
5   Embark his royalty,° and his brave fleet
    With silken streamers the young Phoebus°
       fanning.
    Play with your fancies,° and in them behold
    Upon the hempen tackle° ship-boys climbing;
    Hear the shrill whistle, which doth order give
10 To sounds confused; behold the threaden sails,
    Borne with th'invisible and creeping wind,
    Draw the huge bottoms° through the furrowed sea,
    Breasting the lofty surge. O do but think
    You stand upon the rivage° and behold
15 A city° on th'inconstant billows dancing—
    For so appears this fleet majestical,
    Holding due course to Harfleur.° Follow, follow!
    Grapple your minds to sternage° of this navy,
    And leave your England, as dead midnight still,
20 Guarded with grandsires, babies, and old women,
    Either past or not arrived to pith and puissance.°
    For who is he, whose chin is but enriched
    With one appearing hair, that will not follow
    These culled and choice-drawn° cavaliers to
       France?
25 Work, work your thoughts, and therein see a siege.
    Behold the ordnance° on their carriages,

With fatal mouths gaping on girded° Harfleur.
Suppose th'ambassador from the French comes
   back,
Tells Harry that the King doth offer him
30 Catherine his daughter, and with her, to dowry,°
Some petty and unprofitable dukedoms.
The offer likes not, and the nimble gunner
With linstock° now the devilish cannon touches,
(Alarum, and chambers go off)
35 And down goes all before them. Still be kind,
And eke out° our performance with your mind.

1 **imagined wing**/flights of imagination   2 **celerity**/speed   4 **well-appointed**/well armed   **Dover pier**/i.e., embarkation point for France (earlier the Prologue had fixed this action at Southampton, causing a discrepancy in the text) 5 **royalty**/nobles 6 **Phoebus**/sun god who controls winds 7 **fancies**/imaginations 8 **tackle**/ropes, lines 12 **bottoms**/ ships' hulls 14 **rivage**/shore 15 **city**/i.e., fleet 17 **Harfleur**/French port at the mouth of Seine 18 **sternage**/sterns 21 **pith and puissance**/strength and battle age 24 **culled and choice-drawn**/select, cream of the crop 26 **ordnance**/cannons, guns 27 **girded**/fortified 30 **to dowry**/added to her dowry 33 **linstock**/torch 35 **eke out**/supplement, draw out

Commentary: The Chorus, who delivered the Prologue, continues his/her narrative soliloquies by again provoking the audiences' imagination. Here the character gives us a bird's eye view, as if from on high, of the English preparations and departure for France. The intention of the Chorus is to have the audience imagine the transitions between acts, especially the massive movements of troops from one country to another. The effect is cinematic and the words convey sound and movement.

HENRY V

King Harry

Act 3, Scene 1. France. During the seige of the fortified Port of Harfleur. Alarums and confusion all around. King Harry urges his army into another storming encounter.

(Alarum. Enter King Harry and the English army, with scaling ladders.)

KING HARRY

Once more° unto the breach, dear friends, once
    more,
Or close° the wall up with our English dead.
In peace there's nothing so becomes a man
As modest stillness and humility,
5 But when the blast of war blows in our ears,
Then imitate the action° of the tiger.
Stiffen the sinews, conjure up the blood,
Disguise fair nature with hard-favored° rage.
Then lend the eye a terrible aspect,°
10 Let it pry through the portage° of the head
Like the brass cannon, let the brow o'erwhelm° it
As fearfully as doth a gallèd° rock
O'erhang and jutty his confounded° base,
Swilled° with the wild and wasteful ocean.
15 Now set° the teeth and stretch the nostril wide,
Hold hard the breath, and bend up every spirit
To his full height. On, on, you noblest English,
Whose blood is fet° from fathers of war-proof,
Fathers that like so many Alexanders°
20 Have in these parts from morn till even° fought,
And sheathed their swords for lack of argument.
Dishonor not your mothers; now attest
That those whom you called fathers did beget you.°
Be copy now to men of grosser° blood,

25   And teach them how to war. And you, good
      yeomen,°
    Whose limbs were made in England, show us here
    The mettle° of your pasture; let us swear
    That you are worth your breeding—which I doubt
      not,
    For there is none of you so mean and base°
30   That hath not noble lustre in your eyes.
    I see you stand like greyhounds in the slips,°
    Straining upon the start. The game's afoot.
    Follow your spirit, and upon this charge
    Cry, "God for Harry! England and Saint George!°"
    (Alarum, and chambers° go off. Exeunt.)

1 **Once more**/once again (a repeated action) 2 **close**/seal (i.e., the breach in the wall) 6 **imitate the action**/take on the character (he then goes on to detail those characteristics) 8 **hard-favored**/hard featured 9 **aspect**/look 10 **portage**/port holes 11 **o'erwhelm**/overhang (i.e., furrowed with rage) 12 **gallèd**/i.e., worn into a crag by salt water 13 **confounded**/ruined 14 **Swilled**/washed repeatedly 15 **set**/clench 18 **fet**/derived (note the sound string with "from fathers") 19 **Alexanders**/the great conquerer, King of the Macedons 20 **even**/evening 22-23 **Dishonor...you**/i.e., declare yourselves legitimate men 24 **grosser**/fuller, coarser 25 **yeoman**/sturdy, freemen 27 **mettle**/breeding, sperm, stock 29 **base**/lowly 31 **slips**/leashes 34 **Saint George**/patron saint of England who killed the dragon SD **chambers**/small cannon fire

Commentary: "Once more" lets us know that this speech stands for many others before it. Harry's battle cry is full of urges and courage-boosting phrases. What he describes here is the face of war: its eyes, head, brow, teeth, breath and spirit. It is equally a portrait of the soldier's anatomy as well as acting tips on how to play a tiger. Since the monologue is delivered in the midst of a swirling battle, it must be heard above the on-stage sounds. Words like "tiger," "blood," "rage," "brow," "rock," "on, on," are meant to conquer the hubbub. Harry becomes a kind of cheerleader as well as commander, and he probably goes from man to man with his words. His language mingles with the clash of sounds and swords. Two animal images, "tiger" and "greyhound," are used. Like the scaling ladders brought on-stage, Harry's speech climbs the scales of courage, ending in the triumphant breakthrough of the final line. The discharge of gunfire is a final mark of punctuation.

HENRY V

Boy

Act 3, Scene 2. France. Battle of Harfleur. A boy, servant to the three buffoons Nym, Bardolph and Pistol, stops to address the audience. This is a moment of comic relief from the fighting.

BOY

As young as I am, I have observed° these three
30   swashers.° I am boy° to them all three, but all they
three, though they should serve me, could not be
man° to me, for indeed three such antics° do not
amount to a man. For Bardolph, he is white-
livered° and red-faced—by the means whereof a
35   faces it out,° but fights not. For Pistol, he hath a
killing tongue° and a quiet sword—by the means
whereof a breaks words,° and keeps whole
weapons. For Nim, he hath heard that men of few
words are the best men, and therefore he scorns to
40   say his prayers, lest a should be thought a coward.
But his few bad words are matched with as few
good deeds—for a never broke any man's head but
his own, and that was against a post, when he was
drunk. They will steal anything, and call it
45   "purchase." Bardolph stole a lute case,° bore it
twelve leagues, and sold it for three halfpence.
Nim and Bardolph are sworn brothers in filching,°
and in Calais° they stole a fire shovel.° I knew by
that piece of service the men would carry coals.°
50   They would have me as familiar with men's
pockets° as their gloves or their handkerchiefs—
which makes° much against my manhood,° if I
should take from another's pocket to put into
mine, for it is plain pocketing up° of wrongs. I

55   must leave them, and seek some better service.
      Their villainy goes against my weak stomach, and
      therefore I must cast it up.°

29 **observed**/watched and humored 30 **swashers**/swaggerers, idiots
boy/servant 32 **man**/man servant, as much a man **antics**/clowns, grotesque buffoons 33-34 **white-livered**/cowardly, i.e., lily-livered 34-35 **a...
out**/is brazen only in appearance 36 **killing tongue**/words are mightier
than his sword 37 **breaks words**/quarrels 45 **lute case**/(he stole the case
but not the more valuable lute) 47 **filching**/stealing 48 **Calais**/English
port **fire shovel**/i.e., worthless object 49 **carry coals**/i.e., do dirty work 50-
51 **familiar...pockets**/learn to pickpocket (also sexual meaning) 52
makes/interferes **manhood**/proper development (sexual meaning) 54
pocketing up/receiving 57 **cast it up**/give it up or vomit it up

Commentary: The Boy delivers a soliloquy on the subject of
villainy and gross cowardice. This little set speech is in contrast to
the greater patriotic soliloquies of King Harry where courage and
honor are the themes. Delivered in prose, the speech is rough,
colloquial and rich with puns. But it also imparts observed wisdom
about petty criminality. The Boy's motivation is escape from such
ill use. And, indeed, he becomes physically ill by the end of the
speech as a way of punctuating his dilemma. Exposed to petty
crimes and stupidities, the Boy maintains an innocence and morality
in the midst of his immoral education.

HENRY V

King Harry

Act 4, Scene 1. France. The English camp on the night before the decisive Battle of Agincourt. The restless King Harry, in disguise, roams about the camp unrecognized. He has just spoken to a group of gruff soldiers who tell him that all responsibility hangs upon the King.

KING HARRY
Upon the King.
"Let us our lives, our souls, our debts, our care-full°
    wives,
Our children, and our sins, lay on the King."
230 We° must bear all. O hard condition,°
Twin-born with greatness, subject to the breath
Of every fool whose sense no more can feel
But his own wringing.° What infinite heart's ease
Must kings neglect that private men enjoy?
235 And what have kings that privates° have not too,
Save ceremony, save general ceremony?
And what art thou, thou idol Ceremony?°
What kind of god art thou, that suffer'st more
Of mortal griefs than do thy worshippers?
240 What are thy rents?° What are thy comings-in?°
O Ceremony, show me but thy worth!
What is thy soul of adoration?
Art thou aught else° but place,° degree, and form,
Creating awe and fear in other men?
245 Wherein thou art less happy, being feared,
Than they in fearing.
What drink'st thou oft, instead of homage sweet,
But poisoned flattery? O be sick, great greatness,
And bid thy Ceremony give thee cure!

250 Think'st thou the fiery fever will go out
    With titles blown° from adulation?
    Will it give place to flexure° and low bending?
    Canst thou, when thou command'st the beggar's
        knee,
    Command the health of it? No, thou proud
        dream°
255 That play'st so subtly with a king's repose;
    I am a king that find thee,° and I know
    'Tis not the balm,° the sceptre, and the ball,°
    The sword, the mace, the crown imperial,
    The intertissued° robe of gold and pearl,
260 The farcèd° title running 'fore the king,
    The throne he sits on, nor the tide° of pomp
    That beats upon the high shore of this world—
    No, not all these, thrice-gorgeous ceremony,
    Not all these, laid in bed majestical,
265 Can sleep so soundly as the wretched slave
    Who, with a body filled and vacant mind,
    Gets him to rest, crammed with distressful° bread;
    Never sees horrid night, the child of hell,
    But like a lackey° from the rise to set
270 Sweats in the eye of Phoebus,° and all night
    Sleeps in Elysium;° next day, after dawn
    Doth rise and help Hyperion° to his horse,
    And follows so the ever-running year
    With profitable labor to his grave.
275 And, but for ceremony, such a wretch,
    Winding up° days with toil and nights with sleep,
    Had° the forehand° and vantage of a king.
    The slave, a member of the country's peace,
    Enjoys it; but in gross brain little wots°
280 What watch° the King keeps to maintain the peace,
    Whose hours the peasant best advantages.°

228 **care-full**/anxious   230 **We**/royal "we," the King **condition**/rank, privilege   233 **wringing**/suffering   235 **privates**/common soldiers   237 **Ceremony**/sacred symbols and signs of greatness or majesty   240 **rents**/revenues   **comings-in**/income   243 **aught else**/anything else   **place**/rank   251 **blown**/cooled or puffed-up   252 **flexure**/bowing   254 **dream**/illusion   256 **find thee**/exposes you   257 **balm**/consecrating oil   **ball**/orb   259 **intertissued**/interwoven   260 **farced**/inflated   261 **tide**/flow   267 **distressful**/hard-earned   269 **lackey**/menial servant   270 **eye of Phoebus**/in the sun   271 **Elysium**/fields of paradise   272 **Hyperion**/sun god   276 **Winding up**/filling   277 **Had**/would have   **forehand**/upper hand, advantage   279 **wots**/knows   280 **watch**/guard (note the sound string "wots, what, watched")   281 **best advantages**/benefits most

Commentary: King Harry is a genuinely likeable and heroic character. His lonely soliloquy nicely balances both his kingly majesty and cares for the common man. Although something of a lament—he fears the coming battle at dawn—it is nothing like the laments of Richard II or Harry's father, Henry IV. Harry's troops are outnumbered and feel abandoned. They look to the King. The theme of his speech is the cares thrust "upon the King." And the great centerpiece of the monologue is his interrogation of "Ceremony." Harry questions the *stagecraft* of kingship and the trappings of glory. Sleep, a repeated concern in these types of lamenting soliloquies, is also addressed. By an honest humbling of himself, Harry's genuine greatness shows through. The speech maintains such a clear focus on thinking, and the language comes in such waves of understated grandeur (see lines 256-274), that we can't help but feel and hear that streak of common sympathy that has always been a part of Harry's character. Finally, he puts himself directly in touch with the audience: an honest King confesses his doubts to his subjects.

HENRY V

King Harry

Act 4, Scene 3. France. The English camp at dawn of the decisive Battle of Agincourt. Woefully outnumbered, the nobles and troops prepare for battle, wishing that those still asleep in England could join their force. King Harry arrives and delivers this famous rousing speech to bolster their courage.

(Enter King Harry, behind)

[WARWICK   O that we now had here
But one ten thousand of those men in England
That do no work today.]

KING HARRY   What's° he that wishes so?
My cousin Warwick? No, my fair cousin.
20   If we are marked to die, we are enough
To do our country loss; and if to live,
The fewer men, the greater share of honor.
God's will, I pray thee wish not one man more.
By Jove, I am not covetous for gold,
25   Nor care I who doth feed upon my cost;°
It ernes° me not if men my garments wear;
Such outward things dwell not in my desires.
But if it be a sin to covet honor
I am the most offending soul alive.
30   No, faith, my coz, wish not a° man from England.
God's peace, I would not lose so great an honor
As one man more methinks would share from me
For the best hope I have. O do not wish one more.
Rather proclaim it presently° through my host°
35   That he which hath no stomach to this fight,
Let him depart. His passport shall be made
And crowns for convoy put into his purse.
We° would not die in that man's company

That fears his fellowship to die with us.
40   This day is called the Feast of Crispian.°
He that outlives this day and comes safe home
Will stand a-tiptoe° when this day is named
And rouse him at the name of Crispian.
He that shall see this day° and live t'old age
45   Will yearly on the vigil feast his neighbors
And say, "Tomorrow is Saint Crispian."
Then will he strip his sleeve and show his scars
And say, "These wounds I had on Crispin's day."
Old men forget; yet all shall be forgot,
50   But he'll remember, with advantages,
What feats he did that day. Then shall our names,
Familiar in his mouth as household words—
Harry the King, Bedford and Exeter,
Warwick and Talbot, Salisbury and Gloucester—
55   Be in their flowing cups° freshly remembered.
This story shall the good man teach his son,
And Crispin Crispian shall ne'er go by
From this day to the ending of the world
But we in it shall be rememberèd,
60   We few, we happy few, we band of brothers.
For he today that sheds his blood with me
Shall be my brother; be he ne'er so vile,°
This day shall gentle his condition.
And gentlemen in England now abed°
65   Shall think themselves accursed° they were not
      here,
And hold their manhoods cheap whiles any speaks
That fought with us upon Saint Crispin's day.
(Enter the Earl of Salisbury)
[SALISBURY
My sovereign lord, bestow yourself with speed.
The French are bravely in their battles set
And will with all expedience charge on us.

79

18 **What's**/who's   25 **cost**/wealth   26 **ernes**/grieves   30 **a**/one   34 **presently**/immediately   **host**/army   38 **We**/royal "we"   40 Feast of **Crispian**/October 25 (Crispin and Crispinian, patron saints of shoemakers, were early Christian martyrs. Ironically, they are French saints and not English.)   42 **stand a-tiptoe**/stand-up proudly   44 **see this day**/i.e., live to see the end of the day   55 **flowing cups**/drinks, toasts   62 **be...vile**/i.e., if ever once evil   64 **abed**/in bed   65 **accursed**/cursed

Commentary: Harry's patriotic exhortations, delivered as an oration to an audience of troops, is an all too familiar soliloquy. Making it fresh and memorable is a challenge for the actor. Notice how simple the words are: "We few, we happy few, we band of brothers". There are no complex ideas at work here other than the subjects of honor, martyrdom and immortal fame for those who will fight this day. The verse is rather strict and balanced, binding the listeners into a common sense of purpose. Like Antony, in *Julius Caesar*, Harry touches the heart and passions of the common man. He also bribes them a bit with a promise of immortalization for generations to come. In some ways, the cadence of the soliloquy has the flavor of a biblical sermon by Christ to his disciples. Harry would be aware of that kind of effect.

HENRY VI, Part 2

Young Clifford

Act 5, Scene 2. A battlefield near St. Albans. A decisive battle has just taken place, resulting in heavy losses. John Clifford, a young follower of King Henry, enters to find the dead body of his father, Lord Clifford, lying on stage. He was slain by Richard, Duke of York.

(Alarums. They fight. York kills Clifford.)
[YORK

Now, Lancaster, sit sure—thy sinews shrink.
Come, fearful Henry, grovelling on thy face—
30   Yield up thy crown unto the prince of York. *Exit.*]
(Alarums, then enter Young Clifford)
YOUNG CLIFFORD

Shame and confusion! All is on the rout!°
Fear frames° disorder, and disorder wounds
Where it should guard. O, war, thou son of hell,
Whom angry heavens do make their minister,
35   Throw in the frozen° bosoms of our part°
Hot coals of vengeance! Let no soldier fly!
He that is truly dedicate° to war
Hath no self-love; nor he that loves himself
Hath not essentially, but by circumstance,°
The name of valor.
(He sees his father's body)
40   O, let the vile world end,
And the premisèd° flames of the last day
Knit earth and heaven together.
Now let the general trumpet blow his blast,
Particularities° and petty sounds
45   To cease! Wast thou ordainèd,° dear father,
To lose thy youth in peace, and to achieve
The silver livery of advisèd° age,
And in thy reverence and thy chair-days, thus

To die in ruffian battle? Even at this sight
50 My heart is turned to stone, and while 'tis mine
It shall be stony. York not our old men spares;
No more will I their babes. Tears virginal
Shall be to me even as the dew° to fire,
And beauty that the tyrant oft reclaims
55 Shall to my flaming wrath be oil and flax.
Henceforth I will not have to do with pity.
Meet I an infant of the house of York,
Into as many gobbets° will I cut it
As wild Medea young Absyrtus° did.
60 In cruelty will I seek out my fame.
Come, thou new ruin of old Clifford's house,°
(He takes his father's body up on his back)
As did Aeneas old Anchises bear,
So bear I thee upon my manly shoulders.
But then Aeneas bare a living load,
65 Nothing so heavy as these woes of mine.

31 **rout**/riot 32 **frames**/shapes 35 **frozen**/cowardly **part**/side, i.e., troops
37 **dedicate**/dedicated 39 **circumstance**/conditions, i.e., war creates
conditions for valor that would otherwise not be there 41 **premisèd**/
promised 44 **Particularities**/trifles 45 **ordainèd**/destined 47 **advisèd**/
wise 53 **dew**/(dew was believed to make fires burn hotter) 58 **gobbets**/
pieces of raw flesh 59 **Absyrtus**/the brother who Medea hacked into
pieces to halt the pursuit of her father 61 **new...house**/i.e., old Clifford's
dead body

Commentary: Although not a major character in the action, Young
Clifford's lament and vow of vengeance is a powerful indictment of
war and its sufferings. Delivering his speech over the dead body of
his father adds impact to Clifford's grief and tears. It also provides
the actor with a strong focus. His revenge is not only against the
Duke but the entire House of York—those living and those yet to be
born (lines 57-59). This moment and the curse it engenders is of particular importance, because in *Henry VI, Part 3*, Clifford will be a
principal agitator of King Henry and the first man to stab York.
Here he finds the motivation for actions yet to come. Young Clifford
enters the speech in confusion and leaves in resolution. Entering as
young Clifford, he exits as *Lord* Clifford, carrying his ancestry on
his back.

HENRY VI, Part 3

King Henry

Act 2, Scene 5. A battlefield near York. In the midst of a raging and bloody battle, King Henry takes a brief respite from the fighting to contemplate a different sort of life. This quiet soliloquy is set between two particularly vicious scenes of combat. Its power comes from that juxtaposition.

KING HENRY
    This battle fares like to the morning's war,°
    When dying clouds contend with growing light,
    What time the shepherd, blowing of his nails,°
    Can neither call it perfect day nor night.
5   Now sways it this way, like a mighty sea
    Forced by the tide to combat with the wind;
    Now sways it that way, like the selfsame sea
    Forced to retire by fury of the wind.
    Sometime the flood prevails, and then the wind;
10 Now one the better, then another best;
    Both tugging to be victors, breast to breast,
    Yet neither conqueror nor conquerèd.
    So is the equal poise° of this fell° war.
    Here on this molehill° will I sit me down.
15 To whom God will, there be the victory.
    For Margaret my queen, and Clifford too,
    Have chid° me from the battle, swearing both
    They prosper best of all when I am thence.
    Would I were dead, if God's good will were so,
20 For what is in this world but grief and woe?
    O God! methinks it were a happy life
    To be no better than a homely swain;°
    To sit upon a hill, as I do now,
    To carve out dials° quaintly,° point by point,°

25 Thereby to see the minutes how they run—
    How many makes the hour full complete,
    How many hours brings about the day,
    How many days will finish up the year,
    How many years a mortal man may live;
30 When this is known, then to divide the times—
    So many hours must I tend my flock,
    So many hours must I take my rest,
    So many hours must I contemplate,°
    So many hours must I sport° myself;
35 So many days my ewes have been with young,
    So many weeks ere the poor fools will ean,°
    So many months ere I shall shear the fleece.
    So minutes, hours, days, weeks, months, and years,
    Passed over to the end they were created,
40 Would bring white hairs unto a quiet grave.
    Ah, what a life were this! how sweet, how lovely!
    Gives not the hawthorn bush a sweeter shade
    To shepherds looking on their seely° sheep
    Than doth a rich embroidered canopy
45 To kings that fear their subjects' treachery?
    O yes, it doth, a thousandfold° it doth.
    And to conclude, the shepherd's homely curds,°
    His cold thin drink out of his leather bottle,
    His wonted° sleep under a fresh tree's shade,
50 All which secure and sweetly he enjoys,
    Is far beyond a prince's delicates,°
    His viands sparkling in a golden cup,
    His body couchèd in a curious° bed,
    When care, mistrust, and treason waits on him.

1 This...war/i.e., the battle can be compared to the creation *(war)* of
daybreak 3 of his nails/on his fingers 13 poise/balance fell/fierce 14
molehill/fig., little ridge of earth 17 chid/driven away with scolding 22
swain/shepherd, person of lowly rank 24 dials/pocket sundials quaintly/
skillfully point by point/(might imitate the action of carving) 33 contem-
plate/meditate, pray 34 sport/amuse 36 ean/bring forth (lambs) 43
seely/var., "silly" helpless 46 thousandfold/thousand times 47 curds/

thickened part of milk 49 **wonted**/accustomed 51 **delicates**/delicacies 53 **curious**/elaborate

Commentary: From the start of the action, nothing goes right for Henry. He is a suffering monarch who uses every opportunity to deliver a litany of his grief. Here he does it in the middle of a swelling battle. King since the age of nine, Henry has only known how to play the King's part. Here, in a disarming moment of vulnerability, he wonders just what it would be like to be transformed into a shepherd and to lead a lowly pastoral life; to surrender his crown and live according to nature's clock and rule. Notice how Henry survives the metaphorical storm (the wind and tide of war) in the opening third of the speech, emerging newly born into the realm of the "happy life." Now his language is full of common touches, far removed from royal rhetoric. The reason that Henry has fled combat is apparent from lines 15-20: he is useless as a leader and warrior. Sitting on his "molehill" this mountain of a monarch can deliver his lament to no one but the empty fields. Yet it is, of course, meant for the audience. After a string of humble sentiments and lulling repetitions, marked by "How many" and "So many," Henry snaps out of his reverie. In the final line he is forced to return to the treacheries of kingship and the alarums of warfare, where "care, mistrust, and treason waits on him."

HENRY VI, Part 3

Clifford

Act 2, Scene 6. A battlefield near York. The forces of Lancaster and York are locked in a deadly struggle. Lord Clifford, who has killed Richard, Duke of York and pretender to the throne, is himself killed in this scene. Here is his death speech.

(*A loud alarum. Enter Lord Clifford, wounded with an arrow in his neck*)

CLIFFORD

Here burns my candle° out—ay, here it dies,
Which, whiles it lasted, gave King Henry light.
O Lancaster,° I fear thy overthrow
More than my body's parting with my soul!
5   My love and fear° glued many friends to thee—
And, now I fall, thy tough commixture° melts,
Impairing Henry, strength'ning misproud York.°
The common people swarm like summer flies,
And whither fly the gnats° but to the sun?
10   And who shines now but Henry's enemies?
O Phoebus,° hadst thou never given consent
That Phaëton° should check thy fiery steeds,
Thy burning car never had scorched the earth!
And, Henry, hadst thou swayed° as kings should
     do,
15   Or as thy father and his father did,
Giving no ground unto the house of York,
They never then had sprung like summer flies;
I and ten thousand in this luckless realm
Had left no mourning widows for our death;
20   And thou this day hadst kept thy chair° in peace.
For what doth cherish weeds, but gentle air?

86

And what makes robbers bold, but too much
    lenity?°
Bootless° are plaints,° and cureless are my wounds;
No way to fly, nor strength to hold out flight;
25   The foe is merciless and will not pity,
For at their hands I have deserved no pity.
The air hath got into my deadly wounds,
And much effuse° of blood doth make me faint.
Come York and Richard, Warwick and the rest—
30   I stabbed your fathers' bosoms; split my breast.
(He faints.)

1 **candle**/light, life 3 **Lancaster**/House of Lancaster, i.e., King Henry, *et al*
5 **My...fear**/My obedience to and fear of your rightful position 6
commixture/mingling of love and fear 7 **misproud York**/arrogant,
usurping House of York 9 **gnats**/i.e., Yorkists 11 **Phoebus**/sun god 12
Phaeton/son of Phoebus who died driving sun's chariot out of control
across sky 14 **swayed**/ruled, held sway 20 **chair**/throne 22 **lenity**/
lenience 23 **Bootless**/useless **plaints**/complaints 28 **effuse**/lose, pouring
out

Commentary: A soliloquy of grief and woe, Clifford has trouble
delivering his speech for obvious reasons. A staunch defender of the
weak King Henry, since the second part of *Henry VI* Clifford has
become a kind of avenging angel, wreaking havoc on the House of
York. His speech and unfortunate physical condition show how
faithful men are used as battle's fodder: new generations filling in
as feed when others fall. The sheer strenuousness of delivery gives
this monologue theatrical urgency. A few moments later, Clifford's
enemies will find and behead him. But Clifford's dying speech is as
stirring as his previous speech over the body of his father (see
above *2 Henry VI*, 5.2: 28-65).

HENRY VI, Part 3

Richard, Duke of Gloucester

Act 3, Scene 2. London. Palace of Henry VI. Richard of Gloucester, later the infamous Richard III, unveils his dark side in this soliloquy. He lays bare his plan to steal the crown for himself. This is the second half of a longer soliloquy.

RICHARD OF GLOUCESTER
Well, say there is no kingdom° then for Richard—
What other pleasure can the world afford?
I'll make my heaven in a lady's lap,
And deck my body in gay ornaments,°
150 And 'witch° sweet ladies with my words and looks.
O, miserable thought! And more unlikely
Than to accomplish twenty golden crowns.
Why, love forswore° me in my mother's womb,
And, for° I should not deal in her soft laws,
155 She did corrupt frail nature with some bribe
To shrink mine arm up like a withered shrub,°
To make an envious mountain° on my back—
Where sits deformity to mock my body—
To shape my legs of an unequal° size,
160 To disproportion me in every part,
Like to a chaos,° or an unlicked bear whelp
That carries no impression like the dam.°
And am I then a man to be beloved?
O, monstrous fault, to harbor such a thought!
165 Then, since this earth affords no joy to me
But to command, to check,° to o'erbear° such
As are of better person than myself,
I'll make my heaven to dream upon the crown,
And whiles I live, t'account this world but hell,
170 Until my misshaped trunk that bears this head

Be round impalèd with a glorious crown.
And yet I know not how to get the crown,
For many lives stand between me and home.
And I—like one lost in a thorny wood,°
175 That rends the thorns and is rent with the thorns,
Seeking a way and straying from the way,
Not knowing how to find the open air,
But toiling desperately to find it out—
Torment myself to catch the English crown.
180 And from that torment I will free myself,
Or hew my way out with a bloody axe.
Why, I can smile, and murder whiles I smile,
And cry "Content!" to that which grieves my heart,
And wet my cheeks with artificial tears,
185 And frame° my face to all occasions.
I'll drown more sailors than the mermaid shall;
I'll slay more gazers than the basilisk;°
I'll play the orator as well as Nestor,
Deceive more slyly than Ulysses could,
190 And, like a Sinon, take another Troy.
I can add colors to the chameleon,
Change shapes with Proteus for advantages,
And set the murderous Machiavel to school.
Can I do this, and cannot get a crown?
195 Tut, were it farther off, I'll pluck it down.

146 Well...kingdom/i.e., let's suppose the crown is out of reach 149
ornaments/attire 150 'witch/bewitch 153 forswore/abandoned 154
for/so that 156 To...shrub/(Richard has a deformed and useless arm) 157
envious mountain/detestable humpback 159 unequal/one shorter than
the other 161 chaos/shapeless lump 162 dam/mother bear (bear cubs
were thought born as shapeless lumps and then licked into a shape by their
mothers) 166 check/rebuke o'erbear/dominate (pun on "bear") 174
thorny wood/thicket 185 frame/change 187 basilisk/a serpent whose
look kills

Commentary: Richard, from this first moment, is a supremely
monologous character. He goes on at considerable length about
motivations and intentions. His reasoning for why he is the way he

is goes all the way back to the womb (line 153). All of Richard's best soliloquies feature a sketch of his crookback appearance (lines 156-158). He uses the audience like a mirror. As a certified loner, Richard is ripe for plotting. Denied love and attraction, he really has no interests other than getting power. What we see here is Richard at the start of his campaign, just as he is putting on his makeup and preparing a face to meet other faces. A superb actor, Richard's speeches always talk about role playing (lines 180-193). One curious thing to note is the part of the speech where he gets lost in a thicket (lines 174-179). He almost seems to suffocate in its density.

HENRY VIII

Cardinal Wolsey

Act 3, Scene 2. London.   The palace of Henry VIII.
Cardinal Wolsey has opposed the King's marriage to
Anne Bullen.   It has also been discovered that Wolsey
has amassed a large fortune.   In retaliation, the King
orders him stripped of state power and his possessions.

[NORFOLK *(to Wolsey)*
    And so we'll leave you to your meditations
    How to live better. For your stubborn answer
    About the giving back the great seal to us,
    The King shall know it and, no doubt, shall thank
       you.
350 So fare you well, my little good lord Cardinal.]
    (Exeunt all but Wolsey)
CARDINAL WOLSEY
    So farewell—to the little good you bear me.
    Farewell, a long farewell, to all my greatness!
    This is the state of man. Today he puts forth
    The tender leaves of hopes; tomorrow blossoms,
355 And bears his blushing° honors thick upon him;
    The third day comes a frost, a killing frost,
    And when he thinks, good easy° man, full° surely
    His greatness is a-ripening, nips° his root,
    And then he falls, as I do. I have ventured,
360 Like little wanton° boys that swim on bladders,°
    This many summers in a sea of glory,
    But far beyond my depth;° my high-blown pride
    At length broke under me,° and now has left me
    Weary, and old with service, to the mercy
365 Of a rude° stream that must for ever hide me.
    Vain pomp and glory of this world, I hate ye!
    I feel my heart new opened. O, how wretched

Is that poor man that hangs on princes' favors!
There is betwixt that smile we would aspire° to,
370 That sweet aspect° of princes, and their ruin,°
More pangs and fears than wars or women have,
And when he falls, he falls like Lucifer,
Never to hope again.

355 **blushing**/glowing 357 **easy**/easygoing **full**/very 358 **nips**/cuts 360
wanton/playing **bladders**/inflated pig's bladders used for swimming 362
far...depth/out of my depth 362-363 **my...me**/i.e., like a burst bladder 365
rude/rough 369 **aspire**/rise 370 **aspect**/look **their ruin**/i.e., the ruin they
cause

Commentary: Cardinal Wolsey's farewell soliloquy is about the
tenuousness of earthly power. The entire monologue is written as a
gradual descent from greatness, as Wolsey slides back down the
route of his ascent like Lucifer from God's heaven. The speech is a
lament and also a recognition of sins: "high-blown pride," "Vain
pomp and glory." There is surprisingly little of the religious in
Wolsey's words. So much of his power has been material from a
combination of politics and worldly wealth. And this is where he
feels the greatest loss. Once again, Fortune has found a victim.

JULIUS CAESAR

Cassius

Act 1, Scene 2. Rome. A public street. Cassius speaks to Brutus about Caesar's growing ambitions to become emperor. It is important that Cassius involve Brutus in the republican plot to assassinate Caesar. Here he begins to plant doubts in Brutus' mind about Caesar by portraying his weaknesses.

CASSIUS

90 I know that virtue° to be in you, Brutus,
As well as I do know your outward favor.°
Well, honor is the subject of my story.
I cannot tell what you and other men
Think of this life; but for my single self,
95 I had as lief not be,° as live to be
In awe of such a thing as I myself.°
I was born free as Caesar, so were you.
We both have fed as well, and we can both
Endure the winter's cold as well as he.
100 For once upon a raw and gusty day,
The troubled Tiber chafing with her shores,°
Said Caesar to me "Dar'st thou, Cassius, now
Leap in with me into this angry flood,
And swim to yonder point?" Upon the word,°
105 Accoutred° as I was I plungèd in,
And bade him follow. So indeed he did.
The torrent roared, and we did buffet° it
With lusty sinews,° throwing it aside,
And stemming° it with hearts of controversy.°
110 But ere° we could arrive the point proposed,°
Caesar cried "Help me, Cassius, or I sink!"
Ay, as Aeneas our great ancestor
Did from the flames of Troy upon his shoulder

93

The old Anchises bear, so from the waves of Tiber
115 Did I the tirèd° Caesar. And this man
Is now become a god, and Cassius is
A wretched creature, and must bend° his body
If Caesar carelessly but nod on him.
He had a fever when he was in Spain,
120 And when the fit° was on him, I did mark°
How he did shake. 'Tis true, this god did shake.
His coward lips did from their color fly;°
And that same eye whose bend° doth awe the
        world
Did lose his lustre. I did hear him groan,
125 Ay, and that tongue of his that bade the Romans
Mark him and write his speeches in their books,
"Alas!" it cried, "Give me some drink, Titinius,"
As a sick girl. Ye gods, it doth amaze° me
A man of such a feeble temper should
130 So get the start° of the majestic world,
And bear the palm° alone!

90 **virtue**/honor 91 **favor**/appearance 95 **had...be**/would just as soon not
be alive (note sound play of *lief not be* and *live to be*) 96 **such...myself**/a
mortal man like me (not a god) 101 **chafing...shores**/i.e., struggling to
overflow shore's limits 104 **word**/command 105 **Accoutred**/laden with
equipment 107 **buffet**/fight 108 **sinews**/muscle, strength 109 **stemming**/
pressing forward **hearts of controversy**/in keen competition 110 **ere**/
before **point proposed**/i.e., finish line 115 **tired**/exhausted 117 **bend**/
bow, supplicate 120 **fit**/extreme pain **mark**/notice 122 **color fly**/go pale,
i.e., to flee like a coward in battle 123 **bend**/glance 128 **amaze**/greatly
bewildered 130 **get the start**/have the advantage 131 **palm**/victor's prize

Commentary: Cassius' story of Caesar is full of jealousy and
competition. It is said in counterpoint to the cheers that Caesar is
receiving at a ceremony in the distance. It is fitting that while
Caesar is off in the distance watching footraces, Cassius tells Brutus
about a swimming race he was dared into by Caesar. The intention
of the speech is to make Caesar appear weak and frail rather than
divine; not at all the stuff of a leader. Not only, in Cassius' story, is
Caesar a poor swimmer, he is a cowardly and simpering patient
when sick. All his stoical Roman values are here undercut,
especially in the last three lines where majesty and competitive

racing join images, antithetically, under Caesar's "feeble temper." Although this monologue is delivered for Brutus' benefit, the actor cannot avoid the urge to mix political calculation with Cassius' stronger motivations of rivalry and envy toward Julius Caesar.

JULIUS CAESAR

Cassius

Act 1, Scene 2. Rome. A public street. In the distance, a crowd cheers and implores Julius Caesar to take the emperor's crown. Cassius continues to woo Brutus into a plot to assassinate Caesar and proclaim him a tyrant.

(Flourish and shout within)
[BRUTUS Another general shout!
    I do believe that these applauses are
    For some new honors that are heaped on Caesar.]
CASSIUS
135 Why, man, he doth bestride° the narrow world
    Like a Colossus,° and we petty men
    Walk under his huge legs, and peep about
    To find ourselves dishonorable graves.
    Men at sometime° were masters of their fates.°
140 The fault, dear Brutus, is not in our stars,°
    But in ourselves, that we are underlings.
    Brutus and Caesar: what should be in that
      "Caesar?"
    Why should that name be sounded° more than
      yours?
    Write them together: yours is as fair a name.
145 Sound them: it doth become the mouth° as well.
    Weigh them: it is as heavy. Conjure° with 'em:
    "Brutus" will start a spirit as soon as "Caesar."
    Now in the names of all the gods at once,
    Upon what meat doth this our Caesar feed
150 That he is grown so great? Age,° thou art shamed.
    Rome, thou hast lost the breed of noble bloods.°
    When went there by an age since the great flood,°
    But it was famed with° more than with one man?

When could they say till now, that talked of Rome,
155 That her wide walls encompassed but one man?
Now is it Rome indeed, and room° enough
When there is in it but one only man.
O, you and I have heard our fathers say
There was a Brutus once° that would have
      brooked°
160 Th'eternal devil to keep his state in Rome
As easily as° a king.

135 **bestride**/stand over 136 **Colossus**/100 foot high statue of Apollo
striding the harbor at Rhodes and later destroyed in an earthquake
(portent of Caesar's destruction) 139 **at sometime**/once **fates**/destiny
140 **stars**/fortunes, i.e., astrology 143 **sounded**/pronounced and
resounded 145 **become the mouth**/i.e., has a pleasant ring 146 **Conjure**/
perform magic (which cannot be done because both are men not gods) 150
Age/i.e., time in which we live 151 **breed...bloods**/race of great men 152
great flood/destruction of the earth by Zeus, leaving only Deucalion and
his wife, Pyrrha 153 **famed with**/notable for 156 **room**/(rhymed with
Rome) 159 **a Brutus once**/Junius Brutus, who fought and drove away the
Tarquin from Rome **brooked**/tolerated 161 **As easily as**/more readily
than (as a republican, Cassius is bitterly opposed to emperors)

Commentary: This monologue continues Cassius' rendering of
Caesar as a mere mortal rather than a god (see previous soliloquy).
His tack now shifts to focus on Brutus. He flatters Brutus by putting
him before Caesar. Notice how he places a great deal of weight on
balancing the names of "Brutus" and "Caesar" (lines 142-147). He
tries to touch an ambitious chord in Brutus, searching for the right
motivation that will win Brutus to the conspirators' cause. Cassius
is a master politician and strategist. He needs noble Brutus to act as
a kind of front man for the cause, knowing that Brutus is an
"honorable" man. Cassius also knows that the people respond to
symbols. Notice how he singles out the statues of the Colossus and
the lost "breed of noble blood." His intention is to transform Brutus
into just such a symbol.

JULIUS CAESAR

Julius Caesar

Act 1, Scene 2. Rome. A public street. Caesar returns from watching the festive games, passing Cassius and Brutus. He has a troubled look on his face and speaks to Mark Antony.

CAESAR
> Let me have men about me that are fat,
> Sleek-headed° men, and such as sleep a-nights.
195 Yon Cassius has a lean and hungry look.
> He thinks too much. Such men are dangerous.

[**ANTONY**
> Fear him not, Caesar, he's not dangerous.
> He is a noble Roman, and well given.°]

CAESAR
> Would he were fatter! But I fear him not.
200 Yet if my name° were liable to fear,
> I do not know the man I should avoid
> So soon as that spare° Cassius. He reads much,
> He is a great observer, and he looks
> Quite through the deeds of men.° He loves no
>   plays,°
205 As thou dost, Antony; he hears no music.
> Seldom he smiles, and smiles in such a sort°
> As if he mocked himself, and scorned his spirit
> That could be moved to smile at anything.
> Such men as he be never at heart's ease°
210 Whiles they behold a greater than themselves,
> And therefore are they very dangerous.
> I rather tell thee what is to be feared
> Than what I fear, for always I am Caesar.
> Come on my right hand, for this ear is deaf,°
215 And tell me truly what thou think'st of him.

194 **Sleek-headed**/smooth-haired, groomed 198 **given**/disposed 200 **my name**/i.e., my great name, I 202 **spare**/lean, to be avoided 203-204 **He...men**/i.e., Cassius can distinguish between appearance and reality; he observes motives **plays**/theatre 206 **sort**/manner, i.e., sneers 209 **heart's ease**/satisfied, contented 214 **deaf**/(confirms Cassius' weak opinion of Caesar and ironically undercuts the greatness sounded in the line before)

Commentary: Caesar's speech is an extended aside to Antony. Since being approached by the Soothsayer on his way to the games ("Beware the Ides of March"), we can assume that Caesar is troubled. Like all men in power, Caesar is ripe for a fall. He wants to gather the faithful around him like bodyguards (lines 193-194). All men are suspicious, especially "lean," "hungry" and "spare" men like Cassius. *Realpolitiks* is Caesar's strength. But his dead spot is that noble men like Antony (and Brutus) do not bear watching. The noblest men are closer to the hearts and minds of the people and should be watched and listened to most keenly. His imperfect hearing signals a major flaw. When he says, "for always I am Caesar," he touches on an arrogance which is another central flaw. No man can "always" be.

JULIUS CAESAR

Brutus

*Act 2, Scene 1. Rome. Brutus' garden. Late at night,
before the assassination of Julius Caesar. Brutus has
not slept, and is pondering the decision to act against
Caesar.*

BRUTUS

10   It must be by his death. And for my part
     I know no personal cause to spurn° at him,
     But for the general.° He would be crowned.°
     How that might change his nature, there's the
          question.°
     It is the bright day° that brings forth the adder,°
15   And that craves° wary walking. Crown him: that!°
     And then I grant we put a sting° in him
     That at his will he may do danger with.
     Th'abuse of greatness is when it disjoins°
     Remorse° from power. And to speak truth of
          Caesar,
20   I have not known when his affections swayed°
     More than his reason. But 'tis a common proof°
     That lowliness° is young ambition's ladder,
     Whereto the climber-upward turns his face;
     But when he once attains the upmost round,°
25   He then unto the ladder turns his back,
     Looks in the clouds, scorning the base degrees°
     By which he did ascend. So Caesar may.
     Then lest he may, prevent.° And since the quarrel
     Will bear no color for the thing he is,
30   Fashion it thus: that what he is, augmented,
     Would run to these and these extremities;°
     And therefore think him as a serpent's egg,

Which, hatched, would as his kind° grow
    mischievous,
And kill him in the shell.

11 **spurn/reject,** kick 12 **general**/common good **crowned**/i.e., crowned
emperor against republican wishes 14 **bright day**/i.e., power **adder**/i.e.,
tyranny (adders were said to be deaf; Caesar is deaf in one ear) 15
craves/requires **that!**/i.e., adder, tyrant 16 **sting**/i.e., poisonous power 18
disjoins/separates 19 **Remorse**/forgiveness 20 **swayed**/influenced him
21 **common proof**/general knowledge (Brutus uses some specious
reasoning here) 22 **lowliness**/humility (used here to mean *false* humility)
24 **round**/rung (also meant to sound like *crown*) 26 **base degrees**/i.e.,
lower orders, the people 28 **lest...prevent**/i.e., he must be stopped before
getting that far 28-31 **And...extremities**/i.e., conclude on the basis of
Caesar's potential future not the way he is now 33 **kind**/type of tyrant

Commentary: Brutus begins his soliloquy to reason with a
conclusion: "It must be by his death." He searches next for the
motivations that will convince him to join in the assassination
attempt next morning. The conditional logic, echoed in his "would"
and "might" (lines 12-13), make Brutus a thinker much like Hamlet:
"there's the question." But Brutus comes to a more decisive
conclusion. Finding a series of "proofs" helps him decide. An ardent
believer in a republic without an emperor, Brutus is against all
tyranny. Once he has identified Caesar with an adder—strong focus
image for the actor—his case against Caesar strengthens. The other
image of the "ladder," ascending towards total power, chimes in
with the serpent image. In one soliloquy Brutus can sound an
intention that takes Hamlet practically a whole play to solve. But
Brutus lacks Hamlet's philosophical depth.

JULIUS CAESAR

Antony

*Act 3, Scene 1. Rome. Before the Capitol. Julius Caesar
has just been slain by the conspirators. Mark Antony
feigns support of their action with bloody handshakes.
But once alone, he discloses his real feelings and wrath
towards the murder.*

ANTONY

255 O pardon me, thou bleeding piece of earth,
　　　That I am meek and gentle with these butchers.°
　　　Thou art the ruins° of the noblest man
　　　That ever livèd in the tide of times.°
　　　Woe to the hand that shed this costly° blood!
260 Over thy wounds now do I prophesy—
　　　Which like dumb mouths do ope their ruby lips
　　　To beg the voice and utterance of my tongue—
　　　A curse shall light upon the limbs° of men;
　　　Domestic fury and fierce civil strife
265 Shall cumber° all the parts of Italy;
　　　Blood and destruction shall be so in use,°
　　　And dreadful objects° so familiar,
　　　That mothers shall but smile when they behold
　　　Their infants quartered with the hands of war,
270 All pity choked with custom of fell deeds;°
　　　And Caesar's spirit, ranging for revenge,
　　　With Até° by his side come hot from hell,
　　　Shall in these confines° with a monarch's voice
　　　Cry "Havoc!"° and let slip° the dogs of war,
275 That this foul deed shall smell above the earth
　　　With carrion° men, groaning for burial.

255-256 **O...butchers**/(Antony begs forgiveness for feigning approval of
Caesar's slaughter) 257 **ruins**/memorial 258 **tide of times**/history 259
costly/precious, dearly bought 263 **limbs**/i.e., life and limbs 265
cumber/trouble 266 **in use**/commonplace 267 **objects**/urges, hates 270

custom...deeds/commonplace evils 272 Até/goddess of revenge and
strife (pronounced *A'tay*) 273 confines/regions, boundaries 274 Havoc!/
no quarter (military cry of slaughter and pillage) let slip/unleash 276
carrion/rotting corpses

Commentary: Antony's soliloquy to Caesar's body is in the form of
a curse. His intention is to seek revenge on the murderers. The focus
in the speech comes from gazing on Caesar's bloody wounds ("like
dumb mouths do ope their ruby lips"). That image releases a flood
of fury from Antony. The ablest speaker and poet in the whole play
(Caesar earlier remarked on Antony's love of the arts), Antony's
speech is as much a moving prayer as it is a curse. The two motives
mingle. The soliloquy is also a rehearsal for his great funeral
oration in the next scene. The power he exhibits in that performance
begins to build for the actor in this intense monologue. Raw and
private grief is expiated here, so that the later public speech can
have more control and cunning. Just before this soliloquy, the
conspirators made a crucial mistake: they agreed to allow Antony
to address the crowd over Caesar's body.

JULIUS CAESAR

Antony

Act 3, Scene 2. The Forum in Rome. Brutus has just spoken to the crowd. Mark Antony enters with Caesar's slain body, and the effect on the mob is enormous. Antony's speech picks up from what Brutus has just said, parodying it in part.

ANTONY

Friends,° Romans, countrymen, lend me your
    ears.°
75 I come to bury Caesar, not to praise him.
The evil that men do lives after them;
The good is oft interrèd° with their bones.
So let it be with Caesar. The noble Brutus
Hath told you Caesar was ambitious.
80 If it were so, it was a grievous fault,
And grievously hath Caesar answered it.°
Here, under leave of Brutus and the rest°—
For Brutus is an honorable man,
So are they all, all honorable men—
85 Come I to speak in Caesar's funeral.
He was my friend, faithful and just to me.
But Brutus says he was ambitious,
And Brutus is an honorable man.
He hath brought many captives home to Rome,
90 Whose ransoms did the general coffers° fill.
Did this in Caesar seem ambitious?
When that the poor have cried, Caesar hath wept.
Ambition should be made of sterner stuff.
Yet Brutus says he was ambitious,
95 And Brutus is an honorable man.
You all did see that on the Lupercal°
I thrice presented him a kingly crown,

Which he did thrice refuse. Was this ambition?
Yet Brutus says he was ambitious,
100 And sure he is an honorable man.
I speak not to disprove what Brutus spoke,
But here I am to speak what I do know.
You all did love him once, not without cause.
What cause withholds you then to mourn for him?
105 O judgement, thou art fled to brutish beasts,°
And men have lost their reason!°
(He weeps)

                                        Bear with me.
My heart is in the coffin there with Caesar,
And I must pause till it come back to me.

---

74 Friends/(Antony immediately puts the mob and himself on the same
level) **lend...ears**/listen to me **77 interred**/buried **81 answered it**/paid
for it **82 rest**/other conspirators **90 general coffers**/public treasury **96
Lupercal**/the feast day celebrated in Act 1 **105 brutish beasts**/
(onomatopoeia sound that relates to "Brutus") **106 reason**/(that which
separates men from brutes)

Commentary: Antony's funeral oration over Caesar's body is a
hallmark of the powers of persuasion. Its every effect is calculated
to unify the mob and turn them against the conspirators. Earlier
Caesar said that Antony loves plays. And his speech is truly a
great actor's monologue. It is also a textbook piece of public oratory.
Every word is simple, clear and easy to understand; rhetorical
flourishes are artfully hidden. His three-part opening address
("Friends, Romans, countrymen") both hushes the crowd and binds it
together as a unified audience. The speech itself is but the first part
of three long speeches in this scene. Progressively, Antony wins the
mob to his side. While there are many conspirators, Antony focuses
on just one: Brutus. He contrasts "noble" Brutus with "ambitious"
Caesar in the same way that Cassius did (1.2) for a different effect.
Notice how Antony personalizes Caesar and his attributes in an
emotional way ("Caesar hath wept") to offset Caesar's ambitions.
He "befriends" Brutus in the speech but also erodes, through irony,
the meaning and sound of: "And Brutus is an honorable man." Note
his last phrasing (line 100) with its sarcastic "sure." The phrase
"brutish beast" is a certain implication of and play on the name of
Brutus. The final line, when Antony pauses to weep, is a classic bit

of histrionics. Each sentence of Antony's can mean its opposite. A master of the stage and the audience, his use of irony is most evident in his constant contrasts of "honorable" and "ambitious."

JULIUS CAESAR

Antony

Act 3, Scene 2. The Forum in Rome. Antony has excited the crowd at Caesar's funeral, and they demand that he read out Caesar's will. The crowd begins to turn against the conspirators. Antony steps down from the dais to speak to the crowd on its own level.

(*Enter Antony below*)
[ANTONY
165 Nay, press not so upon me. Stand far off.
ALL THE PLEBEIANS Stand back! Room! Bear back!]
ANTONY
  If you have tears, prepare to shed them now.
  You all do know this mantle.° I remember
  The first time ever Caesar put it on.
170 'Twas on a summer's evening in his tent,
  That day he overcame the Nervii.°
  Look, in this place ran Cassius' dagger through.
  See what a rent° the envious° Casca made.
  Through this the well-belovèd Brutus stabbed;
175 And as he plucked his cursèd steel away,
  Mark how the blood of Caesar followed it,
  As rushing out of doors to be resolved°
  If Brutus so unkindly knocked° or no—
  For Brutus, as you know,° was Caesar's angel.°
180 Judge, O you gods, how dearly Caesar loved him!
  This was the most unkindest° cut of all.
  For when the noble Caesar saw him stab,
  Ingratitude, more strong than traitors' arms,
  Quite vanquished him. Then burst his mighty
      heart,
185 And in his mantle muffling up° his face,
  Even at the base° of Pompey's statue,°

107

Which all the while ran blood,° great Caesar fell.

O, what a fall was there, my countrymen!

Then I, and you, and all of us fell down,

190 Whilst bloody treason flourished° over us.

O now you weep, and I perceive you feel

The dint° of pity. These are gracious drops.

Kind souls, what, weep you when you but behold

Our Caesar's vesture° wounded?° Look you here.°

195 Here is himself, marred, as you see, with traitors.

(He uncovers Caesar's body.)

168 **mantle**/cloak, i.e., Roman toga   171 **Nervii**/fierce barbaric tribe conquered by Caesar in a decisive victory for Rome   173 **rent**/cut (rhymes with "tent" above, giving the sound impression of ripping canvas) **envious**/malicious   177 **resolved**/melted away or, i.e., to answer the door   178 **unkindly knocked**/cruelly delivered a blow (note sound string of *unkindly, knocked, no*)   179 **know**/(wordplay with "no")   **angel**/favorite   181 **unkindest**/cruelest (continues wordplay above)   185 **muffling up**/i.e., suffocating him (note sound string *mighty, mantle, muffling*)   186 **base**/pedestal   **statue**/(pronounced as three syllables, *sta' ta u*)   187 **Which**... **blood**/i.e., Pompey's statue was bleeding in sympathy   190 **flourished**/arrogantly triumphed   192 **dint**/force   194 **vesture**/garment (Antony here turns against his acting prowess and wonders why the crowd is weeping over a piece of clothing)   **wounded**/(note sound string with *what, weep, when*) **Look you here**/ (Antony returns to the dais where Caesar's body lies in state)

Commentary: Antony continues his calculated funeral oration in the midst of the mob. His speech reaches a high, emotional pitch, and he uses Caesar's bloody cloak to personalize his thoughts. In acting terms, this is what Stanislavsky later meant by "effective memory": by focusing on a highly emotional detail, an event is recalled in order to make an acting moment more real. Antony notes each tear in the garment from the conspirators' knives. And the stabbing scene is lived once more by the whole crowd. The fall of Caesar and the resulting confusion is depicted in detail, as well. All of Antony's verbs are active. The whole crowd weeps. At this point, Antony, like a master stage director, turns the mob against the "traitors." The three leaders are named and indicted in his speech. Not only is Antony a great actor, he also doubles here as prosecutor with the mob as his jury. Caesar's dead body, dramatically uncovered, is used as evidence of crime. The action Antony describes is brought to vivid life by the sounds of his words.

KING JOHN

Philip the Bastard

Act 2, Scene 1. France. Before the city of Angiers. A sudden and convenient political truce quickly halts the English invasion of France. Philip Faulconbridge (the Bastard), the illegitimate son of King Richard the Lionhearted and knighted Sir Richard the Lionhearted by King John, mocks the reversal of events in this soliloquy on commodity, or the ways and means of power games.

BASTARD

Mad° world, mad kings, mad composition!°
John,° to stop Arthur's° title in the whole,
Hath willingly departed with a part;°
And France, whose armor conscience° buckled on,
565 Whom zeal and charity brought to the field
As God's own soldier, rounded in the ear°
With that same° purpose-changer, that sly devil,
That broker° that still breaks the pate° of faith,
That daily break-vow,° he that wins of all,
570 Of kings, of beggars, old men, young men, maids,—
Who° having no external thing to lose
But the word "maid," cheats the poor maid of
    that—
That smooth-faced° gentleman, tickling°
    commodity;°
Commodity, the bias° of the world,
575 The world who of itself is peisèd° well,
Made to run even upon even ground,
Till this advantage, this vile-drawing bias,°
This sway of motion, this commodity,
Makes it take head° from all indifferency,°
580 From all direction, purpose, course, intent;

109

And this same bias, this commodity,
This bawd,° this broker,° this all-changing word,
Clapped° on the outward eye of fickle France,°
Hath drawn him from his own determined aid,°
585 From a resolved and honorable war,
To a most base and vile-concluded peace.
And why rail I on this commodity?
But for because he hath not wooed me yet—
Not that I have the power to clutch my hand°
590 When his fair angels° would salute my palm,
But for my hand, as unattempted° yet,
Like a poor beggar raileth° on the rich.
Well, whiles I am a beggar I will rail,
And say there is no sin but to be rich,
595 And being rich, my virtue then shall be
To say there is no vice but beggary.
Since kings break faith° upon° commodity,
Gain, be my lord, for I will worship thee!

561 **Mad**/means variously: lunatic, wild, extravagant, wanton, madcap, unrestrained (all are in play here) **composition**/truce, agreement, compromise 562 **John**/King John of England **Arthur**/Duke of Bretagne and nephew of King John 562-563 **whole...part**/(the king of France demanded that John surrender his title to Arthur; King John reversed move by making Arthur, Duke of Britain) 564 **conscience**/right (i.e., France has been invaded by England) 566 **rounded in the ear**/whispered to 567 **same**/i.e., commodity 568 **broker**/commodity broker or panderer **pate**/head 569 **break-vow**/breaker of vows 571 **Who**/i.e., maids who lose their virginity and thus their goodness 573 **smooth-faced**/handsome **tickling**/shifting **commodity**/means variously: advantage, convenience, profit, gain, quantity of goods (all are in play here) 574 **bias**/indirection, manipulation (also a trick in the game of bowls when a piece of lead is put into the ball to make it take a different curve or course) (wordplay on "basis") 575 **peised**/weighted (see previous note) 577 **vile-drawing bias**/curved advantage 579 **take head**/run, rush **indifferency**/impartiality, chance 582 **bawd**/female procuress (sexual meaning) **broker**/male procurer (sexual meaning) (note sound string *bias, bawd, broker*) 583 **Clapped**/imposed (coitus, a sexual pun with *bawd, broker, eye, fickle*) **France**/King Philip of France 584 **determined aid**/defense action (against England) 589 **clutch my hand**/i.e., refuse a bribe 590 **angels**/demons or gold coins 591 **unattempted**/untried, untempted 592 **raileth**/crys out against 597 **break faith**/become disloyal **upon**/on account of

Commentary: The Bastard's arrival to position, as a confidant and agent of King John, has been as abrupt and amazing as the sudden truce between England and France. A child of fortune himself, Philip the Bastard observes the twisting turns ("bias") of events: convenient alliances, instant titles, hasty marriages between warring families, broken vows and changes of purpose. His soliloquy is a breathless catalog of bad faith, power plays and insider trading, all committed in the name of self-interest and gain: "commodity." Commodity, a term with multiple meanings, is the subject and focus of his speech. In the Bastard's opinion—and the play's actions prove him right—the world, its rulers and its entire framework is "mad" with ambition. All is likened to a vast bowling field, with one ball striking another for best position and points. It is also a bawdy world. It is easy, he says, to rail against this commodity, this ill-gotten gain, because he, the Bastard, has not yet tasted its profit. But once he has a piece of the action—and he will—poor beggars will suddenly seem vicious. As crafty and glee-ful as a Richard III or Iago, the Bastard will, however, prove to be a hero by the end of *King John*. He begins the action as a kind of madcap chorus and each of his transformations to greater nobility is marked in a series of further soliloquies.

KING LEAR

Edmond

Act 1, Scene 2. Britain. The Earl of Gloucester's castle.
Edmond, the bastard son of Gloucester, enters with a
letter. This is his first appearance in the play.

EDMOND

Thou, Nature, art my goddess. To thy law°
My services are bound. Wherefore° should I
Stand in the plague of custom° and permit
The curiosity of nations° to deprive me
5 For that ° I am some twelve or fourteen
    moonshines°
Lag of° a brother? Why "bastard?" Wherefore
    "base,"°
When my dimensions are as well compact,
My mind as generous, and my shape as true
As honest° madam's issue? Why brand they us
10 With "base," with "baseness, bastardy—base,
    base"—
Who in the lusty stealth° of nature take°
More composition° and fierce° quality
Than doth within a dull, stale, tirèd bed
Go to th' creating a whole tribe of fops°
15 Got° 'tween a sleep and wake?° Well then,
Legitimate Edgar, I must have your land.°
Our father's love is to the bastard Edmond
As to° th' legitimate. Fine word, "legitimate."°
Well, my legitimate, if this letter speed
20 And my invention° thrive, Edmond the base
Shall to° th' legitimate. I grow, I prosper.
Now gods, stand up° for bastards!

1 **law**/i.e., not man's law 2 **Wherefore**/why 3 **Stand...custom**/respect
hateful conventions 4 **curiosity of nations**/customs of society 5 **For**

112

that/just because **moonshines**/months 6 **Lag of**/behind **base**/baseborn
9 **honest**/chaste 11 **lusty stealth**/sexual secrecy **take**/take on, assume
12 **composition**/completeness, consistency **fierce**/vigorous 14 **fops**/fools
15 **Got**/begot 11-15 **Who...wake**/(i.e., the illegitimately born are far more
fair and fierce than fools born by legitimate means) 16 **land**/(property went
to the first born by birthright; in this case, Edgar) 17-18 **is to...as to**/equal to
both 18 **legitimate**/added meaning: logical 20 **invention**/plan 21 **to**/go
against (also appears as "top," which makes a stronger statement) 22 **stand
up**/make a stand, rise up

Commentary: Edmond's soliloquy and entrance are in direct
contrast to the busy court scene before this. Edmond, a true bastard
and villain, instantly separates himself from everyone else in the
play. There is an unnatural speed to the verse and a lack of
restraining end stops. Notice particularly lines 2-6 and 9-15. Each a
sentence! Since the intention of this speech is to give Edmond an
identity, see how he comes to life before us: "I stand," "I am," "I
grow," "I prosper." "Base" and "bastard" are contrasted with
"legitimate," a word said with a sneer, perhaps, and toyed with
four times. Edmond's intention is clearly sounded in line 16: "I must
have your land." As in any traditional melodrama, property and
birthright are issues; the villain holds a letter with false but
incriminating evidence. His rivalry with his brother Edgar is as
rabid as his verse speaking is rapid.

KING LEAR

Edgar

Act 2, Scene 3.   Britain.   Before Gloucester's castle.
Edgar, the legitimate son of Gloucester, has been
accused by his villainous bastard brother Edmond of
plotting to kill their father and seize his land.   Edgar
decides to escape and hide in disguise.

EDGAR   I heard myself proclaimed,°
    And by the happy° hollow of a tree
    Escaped the hunt. No port is free, no place
    That guard and most unusual vigilance
5 Does not attend my taking.° Whiles I may scape
    I will preserve° myself, and am bethought°
    To take the basest and most poorest shape°
    That ever penury° in contempt of man
    Brought near to beast. My face I'll grime with filth,
10 Blanket° my loins, elf° all my hairs in knots,
    And with presented° nakedness outface°
    The winds and persecutions of the sky.
    The country gives me proof° and precedent°
    Of Bedlam° beggars, who, with roaring° voices
15 Strike° in their numbed and mortifièd° arms
    Pins, wooden pricks,° nails, sprigs of rosemary,
    And with this horrible object° from low° farms,
    Poor pelting° villages, sheep-cotes° and mills
    Sometime with lunatic bans,° sometime with
        prayers
20 Enforce° their charity. "Poor Tuelygod, Poor
      Tom."°
    That's something yet.° Edgar I nothing am.

---

1 **proclaimed**/i.e., accused as an outlaw 2 **happy**/lucky happenstance 5
attend...taking/wait to capture me 6 **preserve**/keep, maintain **am
bethought**/have decided 7 **shape**/appearance 8 **penury**/poverty 10

114

Blanket/i.e., cover only with a blanket **elf**/tangle 11 **presented**/show of (theatrical term) **outface**/brave 13 **proof**/example **precedent**/sign 14 **Bedlam**/madhouse (asylum in London, St. Mary Bethlehem, that was called 'Bedlam for short) **roaring**/loud, argumentative 15 **Strike**/stick **mortified**/deadened 16 **pricks**/skewers 17 **object**/spectacle **low**/humble 18 **pelting**/paltry **sheep-cotes**/shelter for sheep 19 **bans**/curses 20 **Enforce**/urge **Poor...Tom**/actual catch phrases of the real Bedlam beggars 21 **That's...yet**/i.e., I can survive as that

Commentary: In a soliloquy to the audience, Edgar explains his plan of disguise. He actually transforms himself physically during the course of the speech (lines 8-11). And the verse is structured in such a way to mark each phase of the transformation. The long pause at the beginning of the speech suggests silent, stealthy action. This is, after all, an escape speech. Note how Edgar tries out his new voice as "Poor Tom" in line 20. So much of this speech is about taking on a new guise and a new role. Through the course of the soliloquy, Edgar's verse becomes far richer as he abandons himself to the mad Bedlam beggar, especially when he begins to explore the "proof and precedent" of the lunatic ways. From this point in the play, he begins to speak in a manner closer to Lear's Fool than to the people at court. Although the effect is quite different, Edgar shares his brother Edmond's taste for transformation and acting.

King Lear

Act 2. Scene 4. Britain. Before Gloucester's castle. Goneril and Regan, in a strategy to diminish Lear's power, have insisted that he reduce the number of his followers. In fact, they would like him to eliminate them altogether. Lear's stormy resentment breaks forth.

[GONERIL   Hear me, my lord.
260 What need you five and twenty, ten, or five,
    To follow in a house where twice so many
    Have a command to tend you?
REGAN   What need one?]
LEAR
    O, reason not° the need! Our basest beggars
    Are in the poorest thing superfluous.°
265 Allow not° nature° more than nature needs,
    Man's life is cheap as beast's. Thou art a lady.
    If only to go warm were gorgeous,°
    Why, nature needs not what thou, gorgeous,
       wear'st,
    Which scarcely keeps thee warm.° But for true
       need—
270 You heavens, give me that patience,° patience I
       need.
    You see me here, you gods, a poor old man,
    As full of grief as age, wretchèd in both.
    If it be you that stirs these daughters' hearts
    Against their father, fool me not so much
275 To° bear it tamely. Touch° me with noble anger,
    And let not women's weapons, water-drops,°
    Stain my man's cheeks. No, you unnatural hags,
    I will have such revenges on you both

That all the world shall—I will do such things—
280 What they are, yet I know not; but they shall be
The terrors of the earth. You think I'll weep.
No, I'll not weep. I have full cause of weeping,
(Storm and tempest)
But this heart shall break into a hundred thousand
    flaws°
Or ere° I'll weep.—O Fool, I shall go mad!

263 **reason not**/don't even question 264 **Are...superfluous**/i.e., have more
than they need in the merest trifle 265 **Allow not**/if you don't allow
nature/i.e., human nature 267 **gorgeous**/becoming, flattering 269
Which...warm/i.e., gorgeous, fine clothes do not keep you warm 270
patience/endurance 274-275 **fool...To**/do not make me such a fool as to
Touch/taint, infect 276 **water-drops**/tears 283 **flaws**/fragments and
passionate outbursts 284 **Or ere**/before

Commentary: As Lear demonstrates throughout the first two acts,
any threat to his majesty meets with a storm of protest. This speech
is no different. But the crack of the initial thunderous line, "O,
reason not the need!", is followed by calm verse lines in fairly
regular rhythm as Lear reasons his position. Then the verse turns to
curses as he directs his anger and revenge against his daughters. He
first passes through a stage of rumbling grief (lines 269-277), and
then into a rage (lines 277-284) so sharp that "storm and tempest"
accompany him in concert. This is Lear's most dramatic monologue
before fleeing into the storm and madness. It is interesting to note
the steps he takes towards insanity: reason, to need, to patience, to
grief, to anger, to just short of tears, to revenge, to cursing, to
storming, and finally to madness. The pattern is carefully plotted
and laid out for the actor. Notice how the crackling line "The
terrors of the earth" is prepared for by a build that begins at line
277.

KING LEAR

King Lear

Act 3, Scene 2. On the heath in the middle of a storm. Lear enters with his Fool. Both have been battered by the full violence of the tempest. Lear surrenders to the storm's power.

LEAR

    Blow, winds, and crack° your cheeks! Rage! Blow!
    You cataracts° and hurricanoes,° spout
    Till you have drenched our steeples, drowned the
       cocks!°
    You sulph'rous and thought-executing° fires,°
5 Vaunt-couriers° of oak-cleaving thunderbolts,
    Singe my white head; and thou all-shaking
       thunder,
    Strike flat the thick rotundity° o'th' world,
    Crack nature's molds,° all germens° spill at once
    That makes° ingrateful man.

[FOOL

10 O nuncle, court holy water in a dry house is better
    than this rain-water out o' door. Good nuncle, in,
    ask thy daughters blessing. Here's a night pities
    neither wise men nor fools.]

LEAR

    Rumble thy bellyful;° spit, fire; spout, rain!
15 Nor rain, wind, thunder, fire are my daughters.
    I tax° not you, you elements, with unkindness.
    I never gave you kingdom, called you children,
    You owe me no subscription.° Then let fall
    Your horrible pleasure.° Here I stand your slave,
20 A poor, infirm, weak and despised old man,
    But yet I call you servile ministers,°
    That will with two pernicious° daughters join

Your high-engendered battles° 'gainst a head
So old and white as this. O, ho, 'tis foul!°

1 **crack**/explode, rupture in virginity (the second meaning sets off a series of sexual allusions scattered throughout the speech) 2 **cataracts**/great typhoon of wind and water **hurricanoes**/hurricane, waterspout 3 **cocks**/weathercocks (sexual meaning) 4 **thought-executing**/like a flashing thought **fires**/lightning 5 **Vaunt-couriers**/heralds 7 **rotundity**/swollen globe, pregnancy 8 **molds**/forms (sexual meaning with *cracks*, i.e., deflower) **germens**/seeds, semen 9 **makes**/begets 14 **bellyful**/stomach or womb 16 **tax**/accuse 18 **subscription**/allegiance 19 **pleasure**/will or sexual pleasure 21 **ministers**/agents, spirits 22 **pernicious**/wicked 23 **high...battles**/armies formed in heaven 24 **foul**/horrible or obscene

Commentary: Lear's monologue has all the properties of the storm itself: wind, thunder, lightning, rain and convulsion. The speech is a harangue, thick with onomatopoeic sounds that mimic the storm. The verse is full of incantory demands and death wishes: "Singe my white head;" "Crack nature's molds." The consonants in the speech ("spit, fire; spout, rain!") are particularly resonant because the actor must be heard above the tempest of offstage clatter. Like a tympanist, the actor has to artfully orchestrate his booming sounds. While the first half of the speech catches Lear at the height of his rage, by the second part of the speech the battering seems to have diminished him to "A poor, infirm, weak and despised old man." The "But" at line 21 shows, though, that there is still some fire left. Notice, too, that the speech is full of sexual images that lend it further potency.

KING LEAR

Fool

Act 3, Scene 2. During the storm. Lear is led offstage by Kent to the shelter of a hovel. The Fool remains behind to speak this soliloquy.

FOOL This is a brave° night° to cool° a courtesan. I'll
80   speak a prophecy ere I go:
        When priests are more in word than matter;°
        When brewers mar their malt with water;°
        When nobles are their tailors' tutors,
        No heretics burned, but wenches' suitors,°
85   Then shall the realm of Albion°
        Come to great confusion.

        When every case in law is right;
        No squire in debt nor no poor knight;
        When slanders do not live in tongues,
90   Nor cutpurses come not to throngs;°
        When usurers tell their gold i'th' field,°
        And bawds and whores do churches build,
        Then comes the time, who lives to see't,
        That going shall be used with feet.°
95 This prophecy Merlin° shall make; for I live before
    his time.

79 **brave**/fine, handsome **night**/(perhaps a pun on "knight", i.e., *fair knight*) **to cool**/i.e., to cool the sexual heat 81 **more...matter**/preach better than they practice 82 **mar...water**/dilute their beer 84 **No...suitors**/ (pun on "cool a courtesan" and "tailors") 85 **Albion**/Britain 90 **Nor... throngs**/(pickpockets who cut purse strings in crowds) 91 **tell...field**/ count their gold in the open 94 **going...feet**/feet will be used for walking 95 **Merlin**/King Arthur's wizard who actually lived centuries later than Lear

Commentary: The Fool's rhyming soliloquy is directly to the audience. It is part sense and part nonsense. The character is totally oblivious of the storm as he speaks. But it is the license of fools to break or interrupt the illusion of action in order to deliver a moral on what we've seen. The Fool's intention is to highlight the onstage confusion with general observations about confusion itself. The whole speech is a catalog of petty and criminal vanities probably then prevalent in Shakespeare's England. The break between lines 86 and 87 suggests that the whole nature of the prophecies change. They are more general than specific. Each is unattainable and goes against the very nature of their subjects. What is prophesized by the Fool in eighth century B.C. will again be said by the wizard Merlin in sixth century A.D. Folly lives forever. Both prophecies are written as single long sentences.

LOVE'S LABOR'S LOST

Don Armado

Act 1, Scene 2. Navarre. The King's park. Don Armado, a comic and fantastical Spanish knight, confesses that he loves the country wench Jaquenetta. Pangs of love force him to speak this prose soliloquy.

ARMADO

165 I do affect° the very ground—which is base°—
where her shoe—which is baser—guided by her
foot—which is basest—doth tread. I shall be
forsworn°—which is a great argument of
falsehood—if I love. And how can that be true
170 love which is falsely attempted? Love is a
familiar;° love is a devil. There is no evil angel but
love. Yet was Samson so tempted, and he had an
excellent strength. Yet was Solomon so seduced,
and he had a very good wit.° Cupid's butt-shaft° is
175 too hard for Hercules' club, and therefore too much
odds for a Spaniard's rapier.° The first and second
cause° will not serve my turn: the passado° he
respects not, the duello° he regards not. His
disgrace is to be called boy,° but his glory is to
180 subdue men. Adieu, valor; rust, rapier; be still,
drum:° for your manager° is in love; yea, he
loveth. Assist me, some extemporal° god of rhyme,
for I am sure I shall turn° sonnet. Devise wit, write
pen, for I am for° whole volumes, in folio.°

---

165 **affect**/love, aim at **base**/low and lowborn or illegitimate (*base, baser, basest* suggest a string of proofs used to argue a point; here they are reduced to nonsense and "lower" the character) 168 **forsworn**/abandoned, repulsed 171 **familiar**/intimate friend or demon 174 **wit**/wisdom **butt-shaft**/arrow tip 176 **rapier**/sword 176-77 **first...cause**/i.e., reasons that justify a duel (with love) 177 **passado**/thrust (fencing term) 178 **duello**/ rules, code of fencing 179 **boy**/i.e., Cupid 181 **drum**/war drum **manager**/ commander 182 **extemporal**/extemporaneous, sudden 183 **turn**/

compose or change into 184 for/in the character of folio/i.e., a large book
(also wordplay on *foil*, defeated or a sword, and *fool*)

Commentary: Armado's farcical-rhetorical speeches stand in
contrast to the more elegiac, romantic speeches of Berowne. Words
lose their intended sense in Armado's monologues and are ridicu-
lously transmuted into new meanings. Note his fractured use of
"base." His whole speech is intended as an elaborate fencing
exercise. To love is to duel, and one imagines that the actor will
physically represent this. The opening of the speech is a series of
steps forwards. Then he steps backwards at love, and forwards
again at love's enemies. Passado and parry mark the passage of his
speech. Notice that once Armado is touched, or hit, by love (lines
172-173) he dissolves into words; first a "sonnet" then "whole
volumes" in "folio." The last word is a nice play on both foil
(sword) and fool (which Armado is). Armado is also a bleeding
poet, or so he imagines.

LOVE'S LABOR'S LOST

Berowne

Act 3, Scene 1. Navarre. The King's park. Berowne, who has forsworn his pact to avoid all women in favor of contemplation and academic study, falls madly in love with the bewitching Rosaline. He has just given the clown Costard a letter to deliver to her, declaring his passion.

BEROWNE
And I, forsooth, in love—I, that have been love's
    whip,
175 A very beadle° to a humorous° sigh,
A critic, nay, a night-watch constable,
A domineering pedant o'er the boy,°
Than whom no mortal so magnificent.
This wimpled,° whining, purblind,° wayward boy,
180 This Signor Junior,° giant dwarf, Dan° Cupid,
Regent of love-rhymes, lord of folded arms,°
Th'anointed sovereign of sighs and groans,
Liege of all loiterers and malcontents,
Dread prince of plackets,° king of codpieces,°
185 Sole imperator° and great general
Of trotting paritors°—O my little heart!
And I to be a corporal of his field,°
And wear his colors like a tumbler's hoop!°
What? I love, I sue, I seek a wife?—
190 A woman, that is like a German clock,°
Still a-repairing, ever out of frame,°
And never going aright, being a watch,
But being watched that it may still go right.
Nay, to be perjured,° which is worst of all,
195 And among three° to love the worst of all,
A whitely° wanton with a velvet brow,

With two pitch-balls stuck in her face for eyes—
Ay, and, by heaven, one that will do the deed°
Though Argus° were her eunuch and her guard.
200 And I to sigh for her, to watch for her,
To pray for her—go to, it is a plague
That Cupid will impose for my neglect
Of his almighty dreadful little might.
Well, I will love, write, sigh, pray, sue, groan:
205 Some men must love my lady, and some Joan.°

175 **beadle**/parish constable who could whip petty offenders **humorous**/
melancholy 177 **boy**/i.e., Cupid 179 **wimpled**/blindfolded **purblind**/
totally blind 180 **Signor Junior**/i.e., Mister Little **Dan**/variant of "Don"
(Latin: *dominus* or Master) 181 **folded arms**/i.e., sign of melancholy love
184 **plackets**/petticoat or slit in petticoat (sexual sense) **codpieces**/a
pouch in front of men's breeches (sexual sense) 185 **imperator**/absolute
ruler 186 **paritors**/officers of the Ecclesiastical Courts who issued
summonses for sexual offenses 187 **corporal...field**/a field officer to a
general 188 **tumbler's hoop**/multicolored ring used by acrobats to jump
through 190 **German clock**/elaborately constructed clock 191 **frame**/
order 194 **perjured**/to be guilty of corruption 195 **among three**/i.e., the
three ladies who wait on the princess: Rosaline, Maria and Katherine 196
whitely/pale 198 **do the deed**/i.e., have sexual intercourse 199 **Argus**/
monster with a hundred eyes 205 **Joan**/a common wench compared to a
lady

Commentary: Berowne's romantic soliloquy begins with an
unusually long twelve-syllable line. The pause in the middle of the
line breaks it into two parts. Berowne is totally overwhelmed by
his reversal of feelings: a man in service to a "boy" Cupid. After
having been a "whip" and scourge of love, Berowne finds himself
now enlisted in love's ranks as a "corporal." The whole series of
lines up to line 188 are marvelous descriptions of Cupid. His
incredulity switches to Rosaline at line 189, highlighted by a
brilliant description of her in lines 196-197. Notice the sound string
of "which," "worst," "whitely wanton," and "with." The actor must
sound the depths of Berowne's passion as well as his wonder that he
has fallen so deep.

LOVE'S LABOR'S LOST

Berowne

Act 4, Scene 3. Navarre. The King's park. The lovesick Berowne enters, composing verses to Rosaline. He has already sent a letter to her by way of Costard the clown. His mood is melancholy.

BEROWNE

The king, he is hunting the deer. I am coursing°
myself. They have pitched a toil,° I am toiling in a
pitch°—pitch that defiles. Defile—a foul word.
Well, set thee down, sorrow; for so they say the
5   fool said, and so say I, and I the fool. Well proved,
wit! By the Lord, this love is as mad as Ajax,° it
kills sheep, it kills me, I a sheep—well proved
again o' my side. I will not love. If I do, hang me;
i'faith, I will not. O, but her eye! By this light, but
10   for her eye I would not love her. Yes, for her two
eyes. Well, I do nothing in the world but lie, and
lie in my throat.° By heaven, I do love, and it hath
taught me to rhyme and to be melancholy, and
here *(showing a paper)* is part of my rhyme, and
15   here *(touching his breast)* my melancholy. Well,
she hath one o' my sonnets already. The clown
bore it, the fool° sent it, and the lady hath it. Sweet
clown, sweeter fool, sweetest lady. By the world, I
would not care a pin if the other three were in.
20   Here comes one with a paper. God give him grace
to groan.
(He stands aside. The King entereth with a paper.)

---

1 **coursing**/pursuing   2 **pitched a toil**/set a trap   2-3 **toiling...pitch**/i.e., struggling in the dark (also a reference to Rosaline's eyes)   6 **Ajax**/Greek warrior who went mad and slaughtered a herd of sheep, thinking they were the enemy   11-12 **lie...throat**/i.e., a very deep lie   17 **fool**/i.e., himself

Commentary: Berowne's soliloquy is all in prose, which he manages to make sound like verse. We catch him in the midst of creation. His word associations become the subject of the speech itself. The words he chooses to dwell upon—"toil," "pitch," "defile"—underscore his melancholy. Yet his wordplay also sounds like that of a clown. And, indeed, Berowne identifies himself as a "fool" in line 15, giving himself license to speak the way he does. Notice how he dwells on Rosaline's eyes (lines 8-10). That alone provides the actor with a special motivation.

MACBETH

Macbeth

Act 1, Scene 7. Inverness. The inner courtyard of Macbeth's castle at night. Macbeth and Lady Macbeth have set in motion their plan to kill King Duncan of Scotland and seize the crown from his heirs Malcolm and Donalbain. Macbeth stops to brood on the plan.

MACBETH

If it were done° when 'tis done, then 'twere well
It were done quickly. If th'assassination
Could trammel up° the consequence,° and catch
With his surcease° success: that but this blow
5   Might be the be-all and the end-all, here,
But here upon this bank and shoal° of time,
We'd jump° the life to come. But in these cases
We still° have judgement here, that we but teach
Bloody instructions which, being taught, return
10 To plague th'inventor. This even-handed justice
Commends° th'ingredience° of our poisoned
    chalice
To our own lips. He's° here in double trust:
First, as I am his kinsman and his subject,
Strong both against the deed; then, as his host,
15 Who should against his murderer shut the door,
Not bear the knife myself. Besides, this Duncan
Hath borne his faculties° so meek, hath been
So clear° in his great office, that his virtues
Will plead like angels, trumpet-tongued against
20 The deep damnation of his taking-off,°
And pity, like a naked new-born babe,
Striding° the blast,° or heaven's cherubin, horsed
Upon the sightless couriers° of the air,
Shall blow the horrid deed in every eye

25 That tears° shall drown the wind. I have no spur
    To prick the sides of my intent, but only
    Vaulting ambition which o'erleaps° itself
    And falls on th'other.°

1 **done**/finished, over and done with 3 **trammel up**/catch up in a net
consequence/royal succession 4 **surcease**/cessation, i.e., Duncan's
death 6 **bank and shoal**/shore and shallow 7 **jump**/risk 8 **still**/always,
continue to 11 **Commends**/conveys **ingredience**/ingredients, contents
12 **He's**/Duncan is 17 **faculties**/powers, virtues 18 **clear**/spotless 20
taking-off/murder 22 **Striding**/bestriding **blast**/noise, din 23 **sightless
couriers**/winds 25 **tears**/rain 27 **o'erleaps**/overreaches 28 **other**/other
side (followed by a half-line pause)

Commentary: Macbeth's soliloquy, like so many of the others he
delivers, is not about self-doubt but about the compelling fear that
his crime will be discovered. He wishes the killing act were over
and "done" with and that he were already in power. Notice how he
dwells on "done" in lines 1-2. Macbeth has all too clear a sense of
the moral injustice of his approaching crime (lines 10-25). By taking
the "poisoned chalice" of injustice to his own lips, he knows he will
be committing moral suicide. Yet his "vaulting ambition" is too
strong an urge. The resonance of monosyllabic words like "done,"
"blow" and "fall" characterize the steady beats in the verse. They
also sound Macbeth's steady, downward spiral into crime and "deep
damnation." It is fitting that the speech ends with "falls." Note,
too, the presence of witnesses in the speech: the heavenly angels
who will announce the deed. Having no right on his side to condone
the murder of the pure Duncan, Macbeth only has his bloody
intention to urge him forward.

MACBETH

Macbeth

Act 2, Scene 1. Inverness. The inner courtyard of Macbeth's castle at night. Lady Macbeth has urged Macbeth not to think of failure, but to screw his "courage to the sticking place." Now Macbeth must act on that motivation and goes to stab Duncan in his sleep.

MACBETH *(to the Servant)*
    [Go bid thy mistress, when my drink is ready,
    She strike upon the bell. Get thee to bed. *Exit*
    Servant]
    Is this a dagger which I see before me,
    The handle toward my hand? Come, let me clutch
       thee.
35   I have thee not, and yet I see thee still.
    Art thou not, fatal° vision, sensible°
    To feeling as to sight? Or art thou but
    A dagger of the mind, a false creation
    Proceeding from the heat-oppressèd° brain?
40   I see thee yet, in form as palpable°
    As this which now I draw.
    Thou marshall'st° me the way that I was going,
    And such an instrument I was to use.
    Mine eyes are made the fools o'th' other senses,
45   Or else worth all the rest. I see thee still,
    And on thy blade and dudgeon° gouts° of blood,
    Which was not so before. There's no such thing.
    It is the bloody business which informs°
    Thus to mine eyes. Now o'er the one half-world
50   Nature seems dead, and wicked dreams abuse°
    The curtained sleep. Witchcraft celebrates
    Pale Hecate's° offerings, and withered murder,
    Alarumed by his sentinel the wolf,

Whose howl's his watch, thus with his stealthy
    pace,
55 With Tarquin's° ravishing strides, towards his
    design°
Moves like a ghost. Thou sure and firm-set earth,
Hear not my steps which way they walk, for fear
Thy very stones prate° of my whereabout,
And take the present horror from the time,
60 Which now suits° with it. Whiles I threat,° he
    lives.
Words to the heat of deeds too cold breath gives.
(A bell rings)
I go, and it is done. The bell invites me.
Hear it not, Duncan; for it is a knell°
That summons thee to heaven, or to hell.

36 **fatal**/deadly **sensible**/sensitive 39 **heat-oppressèd**/fevered 40
palpable/tangible, visible 42 **marshall'st**/guides 46 **dudgeon**/handle
gouts/drops 48 **informs**/gives shape 50 **abuse**/deceive 52 **Hecate**/
underworld goddess who dwelled at two crossroads; her approach was
signaled by howling dogs 55 **Tarquin**/Roman tyrant who raped Lucrece
design/intention 58 **prate**/speak 60 **suits**/agrees **threat**/threaten 63
knell/death toll

Commentary: Macbeth's soliloquy is in the form of an apostrophe
to the bloody dagger he both imagines seeing and the one he
actually unsheathes from his side. The monologue is deeply
psychological, anxious and fevered. And since we, the audience, do
not actually witness the crime, Macbeth's speech images and
captures it in all its horror. It is a kind of rehearsal of both the act
itself and all the guilty visions that Macbeth will later experience
once it is over and done with. The half-line at line 41 is completed
by the act of drawing the actual knife. The hypnotic quality of the
verse, with its ghostly images and slow motion, suggests that
Macbeth is *other directed* in his slow, steady advance. Only his
words, "threats," hold him back. But then the bell signals him on.
The tangibility of knife, footsteps across the "firm-set earth," time
and the sound of the bell defeats all the imaginative and moral
horrors that ought to halt Macbeth's progress. The verse is full of
directed motion, and the actor must act on the impulse of that
movement and the beckoning crime.

MACBETH

Porter

Act 2, Scene 3. Inverness. The gates of Macbeth's castle at night. As a black comic counterpoint to Macbeth's murder of King Duncan inside the castle, the drunken clowning of the Porter relieves some of the tension of that scene. It is interrupted by loud knocking that competes with his speech.

    (Enter a Porter. Knocking within)
PORTER
    Here's a knocking indeed! If a man were porter of
    hell-gate he should have old° turning the key.
    (Knock within)
    Knock, knock, knock. Who's there, i'th' name of
    Beelzebub?° Here's a farmer that hanged himself
5   on th'expectation of plenty.° Come in time!° Have
    napkins° enough about you; here you'll sweat°
    for't.
    (Knock within)
    Knock, knock. Who's there, in th'other devil's
    name?° Faith, here's an equivocator° that could
10 swear in both the scales° against either scale, who
    committed treason enough for God's sake, yet
    could not equivocate to heaven. O, come in,
    equivocator.
    (Knock within)
    Knock, knock, knock. Who's there? 'Faith, here's
15 an English tailor come hither for stealing out of a
    French hose.° Come in, tailor. Here you may roast
    your goose.°
    (Knock within)
    Knock, knock. Never at quiet. What are you?—
    But this place is too cold for hell. I'll devil-porter it

20   no further. I had thought to have let in some of all
      professions° that go the primrose way° to th'ever-
      lasting bonfire.°
      (Knock within)
      Anon, anon!
      (He opens the gate)
      I pray you remember the porter.
      (Enter Macduff and Lennox)

2 **should have old**/i.e., would have plenty of   4 **Beelzebub**/the Devil   4-5
Here's...plenty/i.e., the farmer hoards his crops in the expectation of
selling at a profit but surplus undoes him   **Come in time!**/i.e., opportunity
knocks   6 **napkins**/handkerchiefs   **sweat**/i.e., in hell's fire   8-9 **other...
name**/(cannot remember the name of the other devil to swear by)   9
equivocator/i.e., one who swears to something while mentally denying it
10 **scales**/scales of justice   16 **French hose**/tight-fitting stockings   17
goose/tailor's iron and prostitute (double meaning)   21 **professions**/i.e.,
those skilled in knowledge (*house of profession*, house of prostitution)
primrose way/way of pleasure   22 **bonfire**/hell's fire

Commentary: The Porter's drunken monologue is a small cameo
soliloquy that functions as noisy farce to the confusion and dis-
turbance that is about to fill the castle with the entrance of Macduff
and Lennox. The Porter's stupor, in which he imagines that he is
gate keeper of hell, is both an antidote to and ironic comment on
Macbeth's fiendish act of murder. His gallows humor contains
references to hanging, treason, equivocation, stealing, cooked goose,
the Devil and the everlasting fires of hell. Like Macbeth, the
Porter's brain and reason is fevered and tainted. But with drink and
not murder. He signals the hell that has broken loose inside. His
own repetition of the word "knock," together with the actual sound,
heightens the intensity of the speech.

MACBETH

Macbeth

Act 5. Scene 5. Dunsinane. Macbeth's castle during the seige by forces of Malcolm and Macduff. Macbeth is full of fright until he hears "a cry of women within." Seyton reports that Lady Macbeth has died. The news stuns Macbeth and stops him in his tracks.

[SEYTON

    The Queen, my lord, is dead.]

MACBETH

              She should° have died hereafter.°

  There would have been a time for such a word.

  Tomorrow,° and tomorrow, and tomorrow

20 Creeps in this petty pace from day to day

  To the last syllable of recorded time,

  And all our yesterdays have lighted fools

  The way to dusty death. Out, out, brief candle.°

  Life's but a walking shadow, a poor player

25 That struts and frets° his hour upon the stage,

  And then is heard no more. It is a tale

  Told by an idiot, full of sound and fury,

  Signifying nothing.

---

17 should/would certainly **hereafter**/i.e., sometime in the future **19 Tomorrow**/(some editions lengthen the word further with the hyphenated spelling *(To-morrow)* **23 brief candle**/i.e., life **25 frets**/plays, angers or rots (multiple meanings)

Commentary: Macbeth's soliloquy is bracketed at start and finish by two long half-line pauses. Between these silences, Macbeth delivers a slow, pondering monologue that is, in part, about the fortunes and ravages of time. He covers the full constellation of the image: "hereafter," "tomorrow," "day to day," "yesterdays," "hour." Words and phrases like "creeps," "petty pace," "last syllable," "dusty death," "Out, out," "walking shadow," "heard no more" and "nothing" retard the verse lines and echo the utter futility and fatality of time and death. The tick-tock rhythm of the monologue's most commanding line ("Tomorrow and tomorrow and tomorrow") sets the pace for the whole delivery. Each active image, like that of the "poor player" strutting and fretting upon the stage, is undercut and stopped in each of these six carefully modulated sentences. The actor will have to decide for himself how much grief or indifference is contained in Macbeth's feelings at this point. Just before this soliloquy, at the sound of the cries, Macbeth said: "I have supp'd full with horrors;/Direness, familiar to my slaughterous thoughts,/Cannot once start me." He is hardened.

THE MERCHANT OF VENICE

Shylock

Act 1, Scene 3. Venice. A public place. The merchant Antonio has agreed to lend his friend Bassanio three thousand ducats. But in order to secure the money himself, Antonio borrows it from the usurer Shylock. No friend to Antonio, Shylock attaches some diabolical conditions to the bond for the loan.

SHYLOCK

> Three thousand ducats. 'Tis a good round sum.
> Three months from twelve—then let me see the
>   rate.

[**ANTONIO**

> Well, Shylock, shall we be beholden° to you?]

SHYLOCK

105 Signor Antonio, many a time and oft
> In the Rialto° you have rated° me
> About my moneys and my usances.°
> Still° have I borne it with a patient shrug,
> For suff'rance° is the badge° of all our tribe.
110 You call me misbeliever,° cut-throat dog,
> And spit upon my Jewish gaberdine,°
> And all for use of that° which is mine own.
> Well then, it now appears you need my help.
> Go to,° then. You come to me, and you say
115 "Shylock, we would have moneys"—you say so,
> You, that did void your rheum° upon my beard,
> And foot me° as you spurn° a stranger cur°
> Over your threshold. Moneys is your suit.°
> What should I say to you? Should I not say
120 "Hath a dog money? Is it possible
> A cur can lend three thousand ducats?" Or
> Shall I bend low, and in a bondman's key,°

136

With bated breath and whisp'ring humbleness
Say this: "Fair sir, you spat on me on Wednesday
    last;
125 You spurned me such a day; another time
You called me dog; and for these courtesies
I'll lend you thus much moneys?"
[ANTONIO
I am as like to call thee so again,
To spit on thee again, to spurn thee too.
130 If thou will lend this money, lend it not
As to thy friends; for when did friendship take
A breed for barren metal or his friend?
But lend it rather to thine enemy,
Who if he break, thou mayst with better face
Exact the penalty.]
SHYLOCK
135   Why, look you, how you storm!
I would be friends with you, and have your love,
Forget the shames that you have stained me with,
Supply your present wants, and take no doit°
Of usance for my moneys; and you'll not hear me.
140 This is kind° I offer.
[BASSANIO   This were kindness.]
SHYLOCK   The kindness will I show.
Go with me to a notary, seal me there
Your single bond,° and, in a merry sport,°
145 If you repay me not on such a day,
In such a place, such sum or sums as are
Expressed in the condition, let the forfeit°
Be nominated for° an equal pound
Of your fair flesh to be cut off and taken
150 In what parts of your body pleaseth me.

104 **beholden**/obligated 106 **Rialto**/exchange market of Venice **rated**/
berated, scolded 107 **usances**/money loaned at high interest 108 **Still**/
always 109 **suff'rance**/endurance **badge**/mark 110 **misbeliever**/i.e., not
a believer in Christ 111 **gaberdine**/long, loose upper garment of coarse

material 112 **use of that**/i.e., use of that money 114 **Go to**/(used to express derision) 116 **void your rheum**/i.e., spit (says this twice) 117 **foot me**/kick me **spurn**/kick **cur**/dog 118 **suit**/petition 122 **key**/tune 138 **doit**/coin of no value 140 **kind**/favor 144 **single bond**/just one assurance against the loan **a merry sport**/a kind of joke 147 **forfeit**/loss against assurance 148 **nominated for**/stipulated as

Commentary: Shylock's speeches rely on a heavy use of vowels, which slows the actor's delivery, but makes the words of the speeches more distinct. The cadence can also be altered. It allows the actor to add some inflection to the words, characterizing Shylock through accent and manner of speech. He begins the speech with a calculation ("let me see the rate."), also allowing himself time to realize this may be an opportunity for revenge on Antonio. At line 105 Shylock immediately launches into a slow building tirade against Antonio. The offenses to Shylock have been what could only be called anti-Semitic disdain. Indeed, the actor must see Antonio as a hated adversary because the evidence Shylock cites are marks of persecution: accusations of usury, misbelieving, curses, spitting, kicking. He mentions the spitting and kicking incident three times. None of this Antonio denies, but rather enforces (lines 128-134). From this point, Shylock builds up a lust for vengeance which will ultimately be his downfall.

THE MERCHANT OF VENICE

Lancelot Gobbo

Act 2, Scene 1. Venice. A street. The clown Lancelot Gobbo is seen in flight from his master, Shylock. He stops to deliver this soliloquy to the audience.

LANCELOT

Certainly my conscience will serve° me to run
from this Jew my master. The fiend is at mine
elbow and tempts me, saying to me "Gobbo,
Lancelot Gobbo, good Lancelot," or "good Gobbo,"
5 or "good Lancelot Gobbo—use your legs, take the
start, run away." My conscience says "No, take
heed, honest Lancelot, take heed, honest Gobbo,"
or, as aforesaid, "honest Lancelot Gobbo—do not
run, scorn running with thy heels." Well, the most
10 courageous fiend bids me pack. "*Via!*" says the
fiend; "Away!" says the fiend. "For the heavens,°
rouse up a brave mind," says the fiend, "and run."
Well, my conscience hanging about the neck of my
heart says very wisely to me, "My honest friend
15 Lancelot"— being an honest man's son, or rather
an honest woman's son, for indeed my father did
something smack, something grow to; he had a
kind of taste°—well, my conscience says, "Lancelot,
budge not," "Budge!" says the fiend; "Budge not,"
20 says my conscience. "Conscience," say I, "you
counsel well," "Fiend," say I, "you counsel well."
To be ruled by my conscience I should stay with the
Jew my master who, God bless the mark, is a kind
of devil; and to run away from the Jew I should be
25 ruled by the fiend who, saving your reverence, is
the devil himself. Certainly the Jew is the very
devil incarnation; and in my conscience, my

conscience is but a kind of hard conscience to offer
to counsel me to stay with the Jew. The fiend gives
30   the more friendly counsel. I will run, fiend. My
heels are at your commandment. I will run.

1 **serve**/encourage   11 **For the heavens**/i.e., for heaven's sake   18
taste/i.e., for lechery

Commentary: Lancelot Gobbo is caught, literally, on the run.
And his prose speech has the tempo of running in place. He is also
full of the devil, becoming the medium for a dialogue between his
good and bad fiends. His speech is full of more nonsense than
matter. But the actor who puts energy into this speech often does it
best. Lancelot is a minor clown and not a superior wit. This is really
one of his few sustained moments in the play.

THE MERRY WIVES OF WINDSOR

Master Ford

Act 2, Scene 1. Windsor, The Garter Inn. Jack Ford, disguised as one Master Brook, sounds out Falstaff on his plan to seduce Mistress Ford and Mistress Page. As soon as the bragging Falstaff leaves, Ford drops the disguise and flies into a jealous rage.

FORD

What a damned epicurean° rascal is this! My heart
is ready to crack with impatience. Who says this is
improvident° jealousy? My wife hath sent° to him,
280 the hour is fixed, the match is made. Would any
man have thought this? See the hell of having a
false woman! My bed shall be abused,° my coffers°
ransacked, my reputation gnawn° at, and I shall not
only receive this villainous wrong, but stand
285 under° the adoption of abominable terms,° and by
him that does me this wrong. Terms! Names!
"Amaimon"° sounds well, "Lucifer"° well,
"Barbason"° well; yet they are devils' additions, the
names of fiends. But "cuckold," "wittol!"
290 "Cuckold"—the devil himself hath not such a
name. Page is an ass, a secure° ass. He will trust his
wife, he will not be jealous. I will rather trust a
Fleming° with my butter, Parson Hugh the
Welshman with my cheese, an Irishman with my
295 aqua-vitae° bottle, or a thief to walk my ambling
gelding,° than my wife with herself. Then she
plots, then she ruminates, then she devises; and
what they think in their hearts they may effect,°
they will break their hearts but they will effect. God
300 be praised for my jealousy! Eleven o'clock the
hour. I will prevent this, detect my wife, be

revenged on Falstaff, and laugh at Page. I will
about it. Better three hours too soon than a minute
too late. God's my life: cuckold, cuckold, cuckold!

277 **epicurean**/libertine   279 **improvident**/rash **sent**/invited   282
abused/i.e., with the sin of adultery **coffers**/money chests 283 **gnawn**/
chewed   284-285 **stand under**/submit 285 **abominable terms**/called
horrible names   287-288 **Amaimon/Lucifer/Barbason**/names of devils
291 **secure**/confident 293 **Fleming**/one from Flanders (Belgium) 295
aqua-vitae/brandy, spirits 296 **gelding**/horse 298 **effect**/make happen

Commentary: Jack Ford is too frequently overlooked as one of
Shakespeare's great comic characters. He has several soliloquies
like this throughout the play, and he spends much of the time by
himself looking for plots, but never actually seeing them, especially
when they are right under his nose. This monologue is all in prose
and is so full of rage and exclamations that Ford seems ready to
burst. All of the jealous humors in the play are poured into Ford. By
contrast, Master George Page, the other prosperous Windsor citizen,
is serene when he hears of Falstaff's seduction plot. Ford and Page
are at opposite ends of the comic spectrum. When it comes to anger,
Ford can kick and curse with the best of them. His speech is full of
slurs on different nationalities. But his main obsession is with
cuckoldry. The mere thought of it sends him around the stage
muttering the hated word like an exorcism.

142

A MIDSUMMER NIGHT'S DREAM

Oberon

Act 2, Scene 1.   The wood near Athens at night.
Oberon, King of the fairies, and his Queen, Titania, are
quarreling over possession of "a little changeling boy"
stolen from an Indian king.   The Queen will not sur-
render the child to Oberon and so he plots this revenge
on her after she leaves the stage.

OBERON

Well, go thy way. Thou shalt not from° this grove
Till I torment thee for this injury.—
My gentle Puck, come hither. Thou rememb'rest
Since° once I saw upon a promontory
150 And heard a mermaid on a dolphin's back
Uttering such dulcet and harmonious breath°
That the rude° sea grew civil° at her song
And certain stars shot madly from their spheres
To hear the sea-maid's music?

[ROBIN   I remember.]

OBERON

155 That very time I saw, but thou couldst not,
Flying between the cold moon and the earth
Cupid,° all armed. A certain aim he took
At a fair vestal° thornèd by the west,
And loosed his love-shaft° smartly from his bow
160 As it should pierce a hundred thousand hearts.
But I might° see young Cupid's fiery shaft
Quenched in the chaste beams of the wat'ry moon,°
And the imperial vot'ress passèd on,
In maiden meditation, fancy-free.°
165 Yet marked I where the bolt of Cupid fell.
It fell upon a little western flower—

Before, milk-white; now, purple with love's
   wound—
And maidens call it love-in-idleness.°
Fetch me that flower; the herb° I showed thee once.
170 The juice of it on sleeping eyelids laid
Will make or° man or woman madly dote
Upon the next live creature that it sees.
Fetch me this herb, and be thou here again
Ere the leviathan° can swim a league.
[ROBIN
175 I'll put a girdle round about the earth
In forty minutes. *(Exit)*]
OBERON   Having once this juice
I'll watch Titania when she is asleep,
And drop the liquor of it in her eyes.
The next thing then she waking looks upon—
180 Be it on lion, bear, or wolf, or bull,
On meddling monkey, or on busy° ape—
She shall pursue it with the soul of love.
And ere° I take this charm from off her sight—
As I can take it with another herb—
185 I'll make her render up° her page° to me.
But who comes here? I am invisible,°
And I will overhear their conference.
(Enter Demetrius, Helena following him.)

146 **from**/leave 149 **Since**/when 151 **breath**/voice, song 152 **rude**/rough
civil/well-mannered (note the antithesis between "rude" and "civil") 157
Cupid/blind son of Venus, agent of Love 158 **vestal**/virgin 159 **love-
shaft**/arrow 161 **But I might**/But that I could 162 **moon**/(refers to Diana,
the virgin goddess of chastity) 164 **fancy-free**/free of love's powers 168
love-in-idleness/i.e., the pansy 169 **herb**/(the *h* is pronounced) 171
or/either 174 **leviathan**/sea monster, whale 181 **busy**/bustling 183 **ere**/
before 185 **render up**/surrender **page**/i.e., the changeling boy that is the
subject of the quarrel between Oberon and Titania 186 **invisible**/(Spoken
for the sake of the audience to signal that a stage convention is in effect,
and that the character cannot be seen by mortals.)

Commentary: Oberon's verse is full of strong, spell-casting
sibilants: "the rude sea grew civil at her song/And certain stars

shot madly from their spheres/To hear the sea-maid's music." It
gives his speech a rich vocal effect. Oberon's anger towards Titania
is the key motivation that sets in motion all of the mischief in *A
Midsummer Night's Dream*. When he says of Titania that he will
"torment thee for this injury," the actor must realize that Oberon is
in a rage for revenge. He is a proud and injured ruler, denied what
he feels is rightfully his. Note, however, how each of his rough
and warlike images is softened by sweeter and more tempered ones:
"But I might see young Cupid's fiery shaft/Quenched in the chaste
beams of the wat'ry moon." The real malevolence in the play is
passed on to Puck. He is the agent of revenge. Oberon, like a stage
director, steps aside to watch the results of Puck's tricks. Less
tormented by his feelings of revenge, Oberon later switches to more
sentimental goals as he becomes enchanted by the plight of the
young lovers lost in the wood.

A MIDSUMMER NIGHT'S DREAM

Puck

Act 3, Scene 2.   The wood near Athens at night.   Puck has administered Oberon's magic, inducing Titania to fall in love with Bottom, who has been transformed into an ass.   He reports the episode to Oberon.

PUCK

My mistress with a monster is in love.
Near to her close° and consecrated bower
While she was in her dull and sleeping hour
A crew of patches,° rude mechanicals°
10   That work for bread upon Athenian stalls,°
Were met together to rehearse a play
Intended for great Theseus' nuptial day.°
The shallowest thickskin° of that barren° sort,
Who Pyramus presented,° in their sport
15   Forsook° his scene° and entered in a brake,°
When I did him at this advantage take.
An ass's nole° I fixèd on his head.
Anon° his Thisbe° must be answerèd,
And forth my mimic° comes.   When they° him spy—
20   As wild geese that the creeping fowler° eye,
Or russet-pated choughs,° many in sort,
Rising and cawing at the gun's report,
Sever themselves and madly sweep the sky—
So, at his sight, away his fellows fly;
25   And at our stamp° here o'er and o'er one falls.
He "Murder" cries, and help from Athens calls.
Their sense thus weak, lost with their fears thus strong,
Made senseless things begin to do them wrong.
For briers and thorns at their apparel snatch;

146

30 Some sleeves, some hats—from yielders all things
    catch.
I led them on in this distracted° fear,
And left sweet Pyramus translated° there;
When in that moment, so it came to pass,
Titania waked and straightway loved an ass.

7 close/hidden 9 patches/fools rude mechanicals/uneducated
workingmen 10 stalls/shops, booths 12 Theseus' nuptial day/(the action
of the play centers around the marriage of Theseus, Duke of Athens, to
Hippolyta, Queen of Amazons) 13 thickskin/blockhead, i.e., Bottom
barren/empty headed, stupid 14 Who Pyramus presented/who acted
Pyramus 15 Forsook/left scene/i.e., the space in which he was playing
brake/thicket of bushes 17 nole/head 18 Anon/immediately Thisbe/i.e.,
other actor playing role in scene 19 mimic/actor they/i.e., the other
mechanicals 20 fowler/bird-catcher 21 chough/bird of crow family 25
stamp/authority 31 distracted/mad 32 translated/transformed

Commentary: Puck's verse is full of rhyming couplets, which add
entertainment to his report and help to vividly dramatize action.
His first line, the only single line ending with a full stop,
summarizes the triumph of his mission. Note how the speech is full
of verbal pursuit and confusion; the verbs are alive with activity.
We can understand why Puck is often played with high energy. As
Oberon's agent provocateur, Puck has been charged to do harm and
mischief. He is not a benign character, even though his tricks have
comic consequences. His role is to manipulate and terrorize. Notice
the mayhem in lines 19-30. The actor who can capture this side of
the character can add substance to an otherwise lightweight role.
Puck's speech also captures the theme of illusion and reality—
"sense" and "senseless"—which dominates the play. Note, also,
the severe disdain that Puck has for Bottom and the other
mechanicals: "The shallowest thickskin of that barren sort." Like
Oberon, Puck favors the use of sibilants to strike his malicious
purpose.

A MIDSUMMER NIGHT'S DREAM

Bottom

Act 4, Scene 1. The wood near Athens at dawn. Nick Bottom, the weaver, awakes after a mad night of romance as an ass. He has been restored to his rude, physical self. Still in a drowsy state, he muses on his "dream," after calling for his friends.

BOTTOM

When my cue comes, call me, and I will answer.
My next is "most fair Pyramus." Heigh-ho!° Peter
200 Quince? Flute the bellows-mender? Snout the
tinker? Starveling? God's my life!° Stolen hence,°
and left me asleep?—I have had a most rare°
vision. I have had a dream past the wit° of man to
say what dream it was. Man is but an ass if he go
205 about° t'expound this dream. Methought I was—
there is no man can tell what. Methought I was,
and methought I had—but man is but a patched°
fool if he will offer to say what methought I had.
The eye of man hath not heard, the ear of man
210 hath not seen, man's hand is not able to taste, his
tongue to conceive, nor his heart to report what my
dream was. I will get Peter Quince° to write a ballad
of this dream. It shall be called "Bottom's Dream,"
because it hath no bottom,° and I will sing it in the
215 latter end of a play, before the Duke. Peradventure,° to make it the more gracious, I shall sing it at
her° death.

199 **Heigh-ho!**/(both a call and a yawn) 201 **God's my life!**/an oath **Stolen hence**/sneaked off 202 **rare**/strange, splendid 203 **wit**/understanding 204-205 **go about**/endeavor 207 **patched**/i.e., dressed in the patchwork motley of the court jester (Note that Bottom goes on, in the next line, to deliver the kind of nonsense wisdom usually spoken by a Fool.) 212 **Peter Quince**/i.e., the mechanical in charge of writing and producing

the play for the nuptials   214 **no bottom**/cannot be fathomed or understood   215-216 **Peradventure**/perhaps   217 **her**/Thisbe's

Commentary: Bottom awakes at the same point he fell asleep in Act 3, and he blusters with the same shouts and commands as before. He is a loudmouth who suddenly stops, at line 202, to reflect on his "most rare vision." Then a new eloquence enters his speech. Astonishment causes him to fumble and slow down (lines 205-208). Confusion of the senses complicates his sage pronouncements (lines 209-212). Lyric sentiment closes the rest of the speech. Notice that this prose soliloquy is rich in rounded and elongated vowel sounds. They help to slow down the speech and actor, keeping both within the confines of Bottom's drowsiness. By the end of the speech, Bottom begins to get back into the role of Pyramus, which he'll play at the Duke's nuptials. He uses the romantic motivation of the "dream" to add to his Pyramus character.

A MIDSUMMER NIGHT'S DREAM

Theseus

Act 5, Scene 1. Athens. Palace of Theseus the Duke.
After hearing reports of the young lovers' adventures
in the wood during the night, Theseus delivers this
sage reflection in the form of a set speech.

[HIPPOLYTA
    'Tis strange, my Theseus, that these lovers speak
      of.]
THESEUS
    More strange than true. I never may believe
    These antique° fables, nor these fairy toys.°
    Lovers and madmen have such seething° brains,
5   Such shaping fantasies,° that apprehend°
    More than cool reason ever comprehends.°
    The lunatic, the lover, and the poet
    Are of imagination all compact.°
    One sees more devils than vast hell can hold:
10 That is the madman. The lover, all as frantic,
    Sees Helen's beauty in a brow of Egypt.°
    The poet's eye, in a fine frenzy rolling,
    Doth glance from heaven to earth, from earth to
      heaven,
    And as imagination bodies forth°
15 The forms of things unknown, the poet's pen
    Turns them to shapes, and gives to airy nothing
    A local habitation and a name.
    Such tricks hath strong imagination
    That if it would but apprehend some joy
20 It comprehends some bringer° of that joy;
    Or in the night, imagining some fear,
    How easy is a bush supposed a bear!

3 antique/old-fashioned (also a wordplay on *antic:* grotesque and foolish)
fairy toys/trifles or games about fairies 4 seething/feverish 5 shaping
fantasies/fertile imaginations apprehend/imagine 6 comprehends/
understands 8 compact/composed 11 brow of Egypt/face of a gypsy 14
bodies forth/gives form to 20 bringer/source

Commentary: Duke Theseus and his betrothed, Hippolyta, are
the only lovers in the play untouched by a night of romantic lunacy.
Both are older and more experienced at romance. Each, no doubt,
has previously passed through the follies of love and has arrived
at a more detached plane. Notice that Theseus' monologue is full of
the rational point of view. He looks at love from a distance and his
speech is a kind of examination of a proposition. He twice pits
"apprehend" (to imagine) against "comprehend" (to understand).
The actor should know that Theseus is used by Shakespeare to offer
a stern rationale to all the dreamy confusion. Each of his phrases is
metrically balanced. His primary motivation is to say, "do not let
your eyes deceive you; do not let your imagination run away."
Theseus is a sermonizer like Jaques in *As You Like It.* And
pronouncement is the object of a set speech; although we should not
necessarily believe the speaker. In the mortal world, Theseus is
Oberon's double and opposite.

MUCH ADO ABOUT NOTHING

Benedick

Act 2, Scene 1. Messina. Leonato's house. A plot is underway to make the quarreling Beatrice and Benedick fall in love. Don Pedro sounds out Benedick on the subject of Beatrice. The future lovers had danced together at a masked ball where Beatrice openly ridiculed the disguised Benedick.

[DON PEDRO The lady Beatrice hath a quarrel to you. The gentleman that danced with her told her she is much wronged by you.]

BENEDICK

O, she misused me past the endurance of a block.
225 An oak° but with one green leaf on it would have answered her. My very visor° began to assume life and scold with her. She told me—not thinking I had been myself—that I was the Prince's jester, that I was duller than a great thaw, huddling jest upon
230 jest with such impossible conveyance° upon me that I stood like a man at a mark,° with a whole army shooting at me. She speaks poniards,° and every word stabs. If her breath were as terrible as her terminations,° there were no living near her,
235 she would infect to the North Star. I would not marry her though she were endowed with all that Adam had left him before he transgressed.° She would have made Hercules have turned spit,° yea, and have cleft his club to make the fire, too. Come,
240 talk not of her. You shall find her the infernal Ate° in good apparel. I would to God some scholar would conjure her,° for certainly, while she is here a man may live as quiet in hell as in a sanctuary, and people sin upon purpose because they would

245 go thither, so indeed all disquiet, horror, and
  perturbation° follows her.

225 oak/i.e., something mighty 226 visor/mask 230 impossible con-
veyance/incredible dexterity 231 mark/target 232 poniards/daggers,
darts 234 terminations/words 237 transgressed/sinned 238 turned
spit/turned on a roasting spit 240 Ate/goddess of discord (pronounced
A'tay) 242 conjure her/exorcise the devil from her 246 perturbation/
anxiety

Commentary: A confident wit like Benedick is quick to feel
criticism and ridicule. He hates being a target. Beatrice's reference
to him as a "jester" is too much; it is even painful. Don Pedro's
probing allows Benedick an opportunity to open up and vent his
anger. As he fumes he gives Beatrice a noxious aura (lines 233-235).
We know that his protests are the signs of man who has met his
equal and is falling in love. Part of Benedick's quandary is that he
has been, for so long, a solitary fortress against Cupid's arrows. So it
makes all the more sense that he should acutely feel the fact that
Beatrice has penetrated his defenses. He speaks like a soldier
under attack by "the infernal Ate in good apparel." The comedy of
the speech is in the fact that Benedick so grossly overreacts to so
small a slight. It's fun to watch him squirm at the end of her verbal
poinard.

MUCH ADO ABOUT NOTHING

Benedick

Act 2, Scene 3. Messina. Leonato's house. Beginning to feel pangs of love for Beatrice, the soldier Benedick tries to deflect his feelings onto Claudio's affair with Hero.

BENEDICK

I do much wonder that one man, seeing how much
another man is a fool when he dedicates his
behaviors to love, will, after he hath laughed at
10 such shallow follies in others, become the
argument° of his own scorn by falling in love. And
such a man is Claudio. I have known when there
was no music with him but the drum and the fife,
and now had he rather hear the tabor° and the pipe.
15 I have known when he would have walked ten
mile afoot to see a good armor,° and now will he lie
ten nights awake carving° the fashion of a new
doublet. He was wont to speak plain and to the
purpose, like an honest man and a soldier, and
20 now is he turned orthography.° His words are a
very fantastical banquet, just so many strange
dishes. May I be so converted, and see with these
eyes? I cannot tell. I think not. I will not be sworn
but love may transform me to an oyster, but I'll
25 take my oath on it, till he have made an oyster of
me he shall never make me such a fool. One
woman is fair, yet I am well. Another is wise, yet I
am well. Another virtuous, yet I am well. But till
all graces be in one woman, one woman shall not
30 come in my grace. Rich she shall be, that's certain.
Wise, or I'll none.° Virtuous, or I'll never
cheapen° her. Fair, or I'll never look on her. Mild,

154

or come not near me. Noble, or not I for an angel.
Of good discourse, an excellent musician, and her
35 hair shall be of what color it please God. Ha! The
Prince and Monsieur Love.° I will hide me in the
arbor.
(He hides)

11 **argument**/subject of 14 **tabor**/little drum 16 **armor**/suit of armor 17
carving/planning 20 **orthography**/pedantic speaking 31 **I'll none**/I'll
have none of her 32 **cheapen**/bargain for 36 **Monsieur Love**/Claudio

Commentary: Benedick's romantic prose soliloquy is his final
protest before actually surrendering to love. The speech is a
soldier's final redoubt, his last lines of defense. The fact that he
goes on at such length to protest should tell us something. The very
privacy of the soliloquy illustrates how cut off Benedick is from
himself and reality. Isolation is a key factor with this character.
He always seems outside a group, maintaining a separate stance.
The image of an oyster (line 25) is a perfect way to describe
Benedick to himself and others. But his hard shell will soon crack
when he overhears what Don Pedro and Claudio say in the orchard.

OTHELLO

Othello

Act 1, Scene 3. Venice. Council chamber. Othello appears before the Duke and Senators to answer Brabantio's charges that he has abducted Brabantio's daughter, Desdemona, against her will. Othello tells the story of falling in love with Desdemona as his defense.

[A SENATOR But Othello, speak.
    Did you by indirect and forcèd courses
    Subdue and poison this young maid's affections,
    Or came it by request and such fair question
    As soul to soul affordeth?]
OTHELLO   I do beseech you,
115 Send for the lady to the Sagittary,
    And let her speak of me before her father.
    If you do find me foul° in her report,
    The trust, the office I do hold of you
    Not only take away, but let your sentence
120 Even fall upon my life.
[DUKE *(to officers)*   Fetch Desdemona hither.]
OTHELLO
    Ensign, conduct them. You best know the place.
    (Exit Iago with two or three officers)
    And till she come, as truly as to heaven
    I do confess the vices of my blood,°
    So justly° to your grave ears I'll present
125 How I did thrive in this fair lady's love,
    And she in mine.
[DUKE   Say it, Othello.]
OTHELLO
    Her father loved me, oft invited me,
    Still° questioned me the story of my life
    From year to year, the battles, sieges, fortunes

130 That I have passed.
 I ran it through even from my boyish days
 To th' very moment that he bade me tell it,
 Wherein I spoke of most disastrous chances,
 Of moving accidents° by flood and field,
135 Of hair-breadth scapes° i'th' imminent deadly°
     breach,
 Of being taken by the insolent foe
 And sold to slavery, of my redemption thence,
 And portance° in my traveller's history,
 Wherein of antres° vast and deserts idle,°
140 Rough quarries, rocks, and hills whose heads touch
     heaven,
 It was my hint° to speak. Such was my process,
 And of the cannibals that each other eat,
 The Anthropophagi,° and men whose heads
 Do grow beneath their shoulders. These things to
     hear
145 Would Desdemona seriously incline,
 But still the house affairs would draw her thence,
 Which ever as she could with haste dispatch
 She'd come again, and with a greedy ear
 Devour up my discourse; which I observing,
150 Took once a pliant° hour, and found good means
 To draw from her a prayer of earnest heart
 That I would all my pilgrimage dilate,°
 Whereof by parcels° she had something heard,
 But not intentively.° I did consent,
155 And often did beguile her of her tears
 When I did speak of some distressful stroke
 That my youth suffered. My story being done,
 She gave me for my pains a world of kisses.
 She swore in faith 'twas strange, 'twas passing
     strange,
160 'Twas pitiful, 'twas wondrous pitiful.
 She wished she had not heard it, yet she wished

That heaven had made her such a man. She
    thankèd me,
And bade me, if I had a friend that loved her,
I should but teach him how to tell my story,
165 And that would woo her. Upon this hint I spake.
She loved me for the dangers I had passed,
And I loved her that she did pity them.
This only is the witchcraft I have used.
(Enter Desdemona, Iago, and attendants)
Here comes the lady. Let her witness it.

117 foul/sinful 123 vices...blood/human failings 124 justly/truthfully 128
Still/continually 134 moving accidents/exciting events 135 scapes/
escapes imminent deadly/life-threatening 138 portance/behavior 139
antres/caves idle/empty 141 hint/cue 143 Anthropophagi/man-eating
tribe 150 pliant/favorable 152 dilate/tell at length 153 by parcels/in bits
and pieces 154 intentively/continuously

Commentary: Othello begins his monologue as a defense speech:
he starts by calling for the chief witness, Desdemona. Then he
instantly defuses Brabantio's rage with, "Her father loved me."
Throughout Act 1 Othello is more quiet, sage and self-assured than
anyone else on stage. And so he naturally commands attention when
he gets the hushed opportunity to tell his side of the story. His tale
is full of heroic and romantic exploits told in a manner that is
simple and unadorned; except for exotic and carefully placed details
like "cannibals" and "Anthropophagi." Oddly enough, there is no
mention of any pain or injury. When he introduces Desdemona at
line 145, the exposition changes from battles fought to hearts won.
Now the speech turns private and personal, pointing to Othello's
prowess at conquering his listeners. Notice his stress on lulling
adverbs (lines 159-160): "passing strange" and "wondrous pitiful."
The final stage of the speech also prepares the way for
Desdemona's dramatic entrance (line 170). Othello is a very self-
conscious speech maker, histrionic in an understated way. And there
is a strong indication that Desdemona fell in love with him the way
an audience falls in love with a favorite actor. Othello himself
seems conscious of this fact. One indication of his future flaw may be
in his assertion of Desdemona: "She loved me for the dangers I had
passed,/And I loved her that she did pity them." Desdemona's
love is a cause of wonder and pity to Othello. And, we might
wonder, can his love for her not be easily corrupted?

OTHELLO

Iago

Act 1, Scene 3. Venice. Near the council chamber. Iago slyly agrees to help the foolish Roderigo win Desdemona from Othello. Roderigo has promised to pay Iago handsomely for his aid. This bit of criminal commerce gives Iago the cue to launch into his first soliloquy.

IAGO

375 Thus do I ever° make my fool my purse—
For I mine own gained knowledge° should profane
If I would time expend with such a snipe°
But for my sport, and profit. I hate the Moor,
And it is thought abroad° that 'twixt my sheets
380 He has done my office.° I know not if't be true,
But I, for mere suspicion in that kind,
Will do as if for surety.° He holds° me well:
The better shall my purpose work on him.
Cassio's a proper man.—Let me see now:
385 To get° his place, and to plume up my will°
In double knavery—How? How? Let's see—
After some time, to abuse Othello's ears
That he is too familiar with his wife;
He hath a person and a smooth dispose°
390 To be suspected, framed° to make women false.
The Moor is of a free and open nature,
That thinks men honest that but seem to be so,
And will as tenderly° be led by th' nose
As asses are.
395 I ha't!° It is ingendered!° Hell and night
Must bring this monstrous birth to the world's
    light.

159

375 **ever**/eternally 376 **gained knowledge**/experience of the world 377 **snipe**/dumb bird 379 **it...abroad**/there is gossip (no one else in the play mentions this fact) 379-380 **twixt...office**/cuckolded Iago 382 **surety**/certainty **holds**/esteems 385 **get**/gain or beget **plume up my will**/advance my cause; feather my nest 389 **dispose**/disposition 390 **framed**/designed 393 **tenderly**/readily 395 I **ha't**/I have it (also close to "I hate") **ingendered**/engineered or beget with child

Commentary: Iago's sudden change of attitude towards Roderigo —from friend to fool—gives the audience an immediate indication of Iago's duplicity. He is master of quick and sudden transformations, all carried out in front of us. All of the main motivations of his corruption are on display: greed, lust, hate, envy, adulterous thoughts, and a twisted view of human nature. "I hate the Moor," is a line that stands out in relief from all the rest. Note the radical shifts in thought process throughout the speech. One reason that a clear motivation has never been found for Iago's actions is that they all exist together in the same tangled web. There is, however, Iago's odd assertion that Othello has slept with his wife, Emilia. But Iago thinks that everyone has slept with her. We can actually see a plan taking shape in his mind (lines 384-390). Iago is good at thinking aloud in public. All parts of different revenge plans converge into one line of action. The long pause at line 394 is followed by his triumphant ejaculation at line 395. The scheme is literally conceived and given birth to in the final two lines. Throughout, the verse is laden with sexual images, usually of a monstrous kind.

OTHELLO

Iago

Act 2, Scene 1. A seaport in Cyprus at night. Iago has just fabricated a tale to Roderigo about intimacy between Desdemona and Michael Cassio. He urges Roderigo to draw Cassio into a fight as a sure means of winning Desdemona. When Roderigo leaves, Iago launches into another soliloquy.

IAGO

That Cassio loves her, I do well believe it.
That she loves him, 'tis apt and of great credit.°
The Moor—howbe't that I endure him not°—
Is of a constant, loving, noble nature,
290 And I dare think he'll prove to Desdemona
A most dear° husband. Now I do love her too,
Not out of absolute lust—though peradventure°
I stand accountant° for as great a sin—
But partly led to diet° my revenge,
295 For that I do suspect the lusty Moor
Hath leapt into my seat,° the thought whereof
Doth, like a poisonous mineral,° gnaw my inwards;
And nothing can or shall content my soul
Till I am evened° with him, wife for wife—
300 Or failing so, yet that I put the Moor
At least into a jealousy so strong
That judgement cannot cure. Which thing to do;
If this poor trash of Venice whom I trace
For his quick hunting stand the putting on,°
305 I'll have our Michael Cassio on the hip,°
Abuse° him to the Moor in the rank garb°—
For I fear Cassio with my nightcap,° too—
Make the Moor thank me, love me, and reward me
For making him egregiously° an ass,

310 And practising° upon his peace and quiet
     Even to madness. 'Tis here, but yet confused.°
     Knavery's plain face is never seen till used.

287 **apt...credit**/plausible and credible 288 **howbe't...not**/although I
cannot endure him 291 **dear**/precious, loving 292 **peradventure**/perhaps,
by accident 293 **accountant**/accountable 294 **diet**/feed 296 **leapt...seat**/
usurped Iago's place in Emilia's bed 297 **mineral**/drug made from mineral
299 **evened**/have evened the score 303-304 **trash...on**/i.e., dog that I am
hounding on (Roderigo) can withstand the urging 305 **hip**/in a wrestling
position to be thrown down (also a sexual allusion) 306 **Abuse**/slander
rank garb/foulest fashion 307 **nightcap**/i.e., wife 309 **egregiously**/in the
most shameful manner 310 **practising**/playing or plotting 311 **'Tis
here...confused**/i.e., the plot is almost formed but not quite

Commentary: Iago's commitment as a villain is based on a firm
belief in each and every lie he fabricates. He *believes* that Cassio
and Desdemona are in love just as he *believes* that Othello has
cuckolded him. His malevolence must have these motivations in
order for him to act. And lust adds an edge to the whole enterprise.
Whenever Iago is hatching more schemes, his sexual appetite
increases. Notice the physical sensations in the soliloquy at lines
295-297 and 305-306. They add heat to Iago's fertile imagination.
The speech builds to the word "madness" (line 311), at which point
we can detect Iago backing away, a bit "confused." Suddenly there
is a human touch and sense of fraility here amidst all the wild
plotting. A characterization of Iago always suffers when only one
dimension is played at the expense of the other.

OTHELLO

Iago

Act 2, Scene 3. Cyprus. The Citadel. Iago has gotten Cassio drunk, pushing him into a quarrel with Roderigo. Othello stops the fight and punishes Cassio with demotion. Iago springs a trap whereby he says he will help Cassio regain Othello's favor through Desdemona.

[IAGO I protest, in the sincerity of love and honest
      kindness.
CASSIO
330 I think it freely, and betimes in the morning I will
      beseech the virtuous Desdemona to undertake for
      me. I am desperate of my fortunes if they check me
      here.
IAGO
      You are in the right. Good night, lieutenant. I
      must to the watch.
CASSIO
335 Good night, honest Iago.   *(Exit)*]
IAGO
      And what's he then that says I play the villain,
      When this advice is free I give, and honest,
      Probal to° thinking, and indeed the course
      To win the Moor again? For 'tis most easy
340 Th'inclining° Desdemona to subdue°
      In any honest suit. She's framed as fruitful°
      As the free elements;° and then for her
      To win the Moor, were't to renounce his baptism,
      All seals and symbols of redeemèd sin,
345 His soul is so enfettered° to her love
      That she may make, unmake, do what she list,°
      Even as her appetite shall play the god
      With his weak function.° How am I then a villain,

To counsel Cassio to this parallel course
350 Directly to his good? Divinity of hell!°
When devils will the blackest sins put on,
They do suggest at first with heavenly shows,°
As I do now; for whiles this honest fool
Plies Desdemona to repair his fortune,
355 And she for him pleads strongly to the Moor,
I'll pour this pestilence into his ear:
That she repeals him for her body's lust,°
And by how much she strives to do him good
She shall undo her credit° with the Moor.
360 So will I turn her virtue into pitch,°
And out of her own goodness make the net
That shall enmesh them all.

338 **Probal to**/provable by 340 **inclining**/favorable, pliant **subdue**/win
over 341 **fruitful**/generous or fertile 342 **free elements**/nature 345
enfettered/enchained 346 **list**/will 347-348 **Even...function**/i.e., Desdemona has sexual power over Othello 350 **Divinity of hell!**/an oath 352
shows/appearances 357 **That...lust**/That she restores him in order to have
him for herself 359 **credit**/reputation 360 **pitch**/foul black tar

Commentary: All of Iago's soliloquies have been to the audience.
"Outside" the play he is a villain. "Inside" he is a sympathetic
listener. Yet this speech seems to address the audience more
forcefully, as though it were a character. Iago needs someone to
boast to about the workings of his villainy. He tends to use language
that is tinged with sexual malice. It is not just enough for him to
ensnare Othello, Desdemona and Cassio in circumstantial plots, he
wants to *corrupt* them as well. And the verse is full of licentious
wording: "free," "easy," "subdue," "fruitful," "enfettered," "weak
function," etc. In order for Iago to continue his provocative course, he
must imagine crimes being done: "When devils will the blackest
sins put on,/They do suggest at first with heavenly shows,/As I do
now." His soliloquies always serve as a kind of rehearsal where
the next step is played out in advance. "pour this pestilence into
[Othello's] ear," is the next act to play.

OTHELLO

Othello

*Act 3, Scene 3. Cyprus. The garden of the Citadel. Iago
has begun to poison Othello's thoughts against Desdemona and Cassio with wicked interpretations of what
Othello observes of the two together. Jealousy begins to
take its course as Othello delivers his first sustained
soliloquy.*

OTHELLO

This fellow's of exceeding honesty,
And knows all qualities° with a learned spirit
Of human dealings. If I do prove her haggard,°
260 Though that her jesses° were dear heart-strings
I'd whistle her off and let her down the wind
To prey at fortune.° Haply for I am black,
And have not those soft parts° of conversation
That chamberers° have; or for I am declined
265 Into the vale of years—yet that's not much—
She's gone. I am abused, and my relief
Must be to loathe her. O curse of marriage,
That we can call these delicate creatures ours
And not their appetites!° I had rather be a toad
270 And live upon the vapor of a dungeon
Than keep a corner° in the thing I love
For others' uses. Yet 'tis the plague of great ones;
Prerogatived° are they less than the base.
'Tis destiny unshunnable,° like death.
275 Even then this forkèd plague° is fated to us
When we do quicken.°

258 **qualities**/ranks of persons 259 **haggard**/wild, untrained (falconry
term) 260 **jesses**/tethers (falconry) 261-262 **let...fortune**/dismiss her and
set her free (falconry) 263 **soft parts**/easy lines 264 **chamberers**/
courtiers who frequent ladies' chambers 269 **appetites**/desires 271
corner/horn, i.e., cuckold 273 **Prerogatived**/privileged 274

unshunnable/unavoidable   275 **forked plague**/cuckoldry   276
quicken/live and age

Commentary: This interior monologue is full of questions and
doubts. The actor must decide why Othello is so quickly taken in by
Iago. Being black (line 262) is one problem, being older (line 264-
265) is another. But notice how totally Othello surrenders: "She's
gone. I am abused, and my relief/Must be to loathe her." Perhaps
the reason for the reversal lies in Othello's continuing doubts about
Desdemona's love and an even greater fear of cuckoldry. From the
point where Desdemona is "gone," Othello's language turns rancid:
"curse," "toad," "dungeon," and "plague." From this moment until
the end of the play, passion, jealousy and rage will be Othello's
main themes. So this speech is a crucial start for all that follows.
Notice the way Othello refers to himself as one of the "great ones."
He sets himself on a plane higher than the "base." Pride, of course,
is probably his greatest flaw. From this point in the action, Othello
becomes the most monologous character in the play. His jealousy
isolates him.

OTHELLO

Othello

Act 5, Scene 2. Cyprus. Desdemona's darkened bed chamber. Othello enters with a candle and is resolved to kill Desdemona for her supposed crime, adultery. This quiet and tense scene is in striking contrast to a loud, brawling scene that just took place in the streets outside.

    (Enter Othello with a light. He draws back a
    curtain, revealing Desdemona asleep in her bed)
OTHELLO
  It is the cause,° it is the cause, my soul.
  Let me not name it to you, you chaste stars.
  It is the cause. Yet I'll not shed her blood,
  Nor scar that whiter skin of hers than snow,
5 And smooth as monumental alabaster.°
  Yet she must die, else she'll betray more men.
  Put out the light, and then put out the light.
  If I quench thee, thou flaming minister,°
  I can again thy former light restore
10 Should I repent me;° but once put out thy° light,
  Thou cunning'st° pattern of excelling° nature,
  I know not where is that Promethean heat°
  That can thy light relume. When I have plucked
    thy rose°
  I cannot give it vital° growth again.
15 It needs must wither. I'll smell thee on the tree.
  (He kisses her)
  O balmy breath, that dost almost persuade°
  Justice to break her sword! One more, one more.
  Be thus when thou art dead, and I will kill thee
  And love thee after. One more, and that's the last.
  (He kisses her again)

20 So sweet was ne'er so fatal. I must weep,
    But they are cruel° tears. This sorrow's heavenly,
    It strikes where it doth love.° She wakes.

1 **cause**/various meanings: offense, motive for action, business at hand
(i.e., murder), a situation or grounds for honor which justify a duel 5
alabaster/delicate white stone carved into ornamental objects 8 **flaming
minister**/i.e., candle flame 10 **repent me**/change my mind **thy**/
Desdemona 11 **cunning'st**/ingeniously wrought **excelling**/surpassing 12
Promethean heat/divine fire that infuses life 13 **rose**/life's bloom 14
vital/living 16 **persuade**/convince 21 **cruel**/avenging 21-22 **This...love**/
i.e., I must be cruel in order to be kind

Commentary: Othello's best and most moving soliloquies are
saved for the final act of the play. Here he performs the double
role of anguished, jealous lover and avenging angel. The speech
alternates between two antithetical motives: to kill and to save.
Each of Othello's advances is retarded by a qualifier; a "yet" or
"but." His resolved and dirge-like, "It is the cause," is undercut by
"Yet I'll not shed her blood." Notice that whenever Othello
actually *looks* at Desdemona, and then kisses her, his killing
motive is blocked. He puts out the light in order to kill her in the
darkness. Apart from all the philosophical justifications contained
in the speech, there remains the carrying out of a physical act. The
deep and resonant vowel sounds throughout the verse, especially
the rounded ones ("One more, one more."), add to the retardation of
action and heighten the tension in the speech. Together with the
sibilants, a strange musicality results. All of this snaps in the last
line, "She wakes." We then realize that the speech has been like a
dream. A fury of action follows next.

OTHELLO

Othello

Act 5, Scene 2. Cyprus. Desdemona's bed chamber.
Iago has just stabbed his wife Emilia and flees from the
bed chamber after his villainy against Othello has been
discovered. Othello seizes a weapon in sudden panic.

OTHELLO   Behold, I have a weapon;
  A better° never did itself sustain°
  Upon a soldier's thigh. I have seen the day
  That, with this little arm and this good sword,
270 I have made my way through more impediments°
  Than twenty times your stop.° But O, vain boast!
  Who can control his fate? 'Tis not so now.
  Be not afraid, though you do see me weaponed.
  Here is my journey's end, here is my butt°
275 And very sea-mark of my utmost sail.°
  Do you go back dismayed? 'Tis a lost fear.
  Man but a rush° against Othello's breast
  And he retires. Where should Othello go?
  (To Desdemona) Now, how dost thou look now? O
    ill-starred wench,
280 Pale° as thy smock! When we shall meet at count°
  This look of thine will hurl my soul from heaven,
  And fiends will snatch at it.°
  (He touches her)
                Cold, cold, my girl,
  Even like thy chastity. O cursèd, cursèd slave!
  Whip me, ye devils,
285 From the possession of° this heavenly sight.
  Blow me about in winds, roast me in sulphur,
  Wash me in steep-down gulfs of liquid fire!
  O Desdemon! Dead Desdemon! Dead! O! O!

267 **better**/better one **sustain**/hold its place 270 **impediments**/obstacles
271 **stop**/check, barrier 274 **butt**/stopping point 275 **sea mark**...**sail**/sign
of my farthest journey 277 **Man**...**rush**/attack with but a reed 280
Pale/white **count**/i.e., Day of Reckoning 281-282 **This**...**it**/your innocence
will be the cause of my eternal damnation in hell 285 **From**...**of**/from being
possessed by

Commentary: Othello's warrior instinct causes him to
immediately seize a weapon and defend his position. Notice how
the jagged quality of the verse—short statements and questions—
captures Othello's feeling of entrapment. Immediately the tone
changes (line 272) to remorse and then surrender (line 278). The
objective reality of the dead Desdemona reduces Othello to intense
weeping that interrupts his speech at line 284. The speech closes
with words that enhance his sobbing. The irregularity of the verse
reinforces Othello's deeply distracted state.

OTHELLO

Othello

Act 5, Scene 2. Cyprus. Desdemona's bed chamber.
After killing Desdemona and then learning of her
innocence and Iago's villainy, Othello decides to
commit suicide in the full view of assembled witnesses.

OTHELLO
Soft° you, a word or two before you go.
I have done the state some service, and they
   know't.
No more of that. I pray you, in your letters,
350 When you shall these unlucky deeds relate,
Speak of me as I am. Nothing extenuate,°
Nor set down aught° in malice. Then must you
   speak
Of one that loved not wisely but too well,
Of one not easily jealous but, being wrought,°
355 Perplexed° in the extreme; of one whose hand,
Like the base Indian,° threw a pearl away
Richer than all his tribe; of one whose subdued°
   eyes,
Albeit unusèd to the melting° mood,
Drops tears as fast as the Arabian trees
360 Their medicinable gum.° Set you down this,
And say besides that in Aleppo° once,
Where a malignant and a turbaned Turk
Beat a Venetian and traduced° the state,
I took by th' throat the circumcisèd dog
365 And smote him thus.
   (He stabs himself)
[LODOVICO O bloody period!
GRAZIANO All that is spoke is marred.]

347 **Soft**/stay   351 **extenuate**/relax, modify   352 **aught**/anything   354 **wrought**/worked upon and deeply stirred   355 **Perplexed**/bewildered, excited   356 **base Indian**/ignorant infidel   357 **subdued**/overcome (with tears)   358 **melting**/grieving   360 **medicinable gum**/healing substance   361 **Aleppo**/city in what is now northern Syria   363 **traduced**/slandered

Commentary: Othello's final monologue is delivered in the form of a funeral epitaph. The stature he had in Act 1 returns to him in this final moment.   An alternation of simple words with complicated ones (i.e., "perplexed" and "medicinable"), and the use of exotic phrases ("in Aleppo once...") restore Othello's greatness. He is further humanized as he extols his virtues and his failings. The speech is also, on a more practical level, a commander's final report to his superiors. In miniature, it is like Othello's Act 1 defense speech to the Venetian council. It is terse, factual, and to the point. The stabbing at the end, abruptly done in one swift move, is a final mark of punctuation. This is Othello's biggest moment on stage. The verse has a steady, regular rhythm that displays little emotion. The suicide comes almost as a surprise.

RICHARD II

John of Gaunt

Act 2, Scene 1. London. The residence of the Bishop of Ely. The aged Duke of Lancaster, John of Gaunt, lies ill and near his death. He speaks to the Duke of York about the rash actions of the King immediately before Richard II enters.

JOHN OF GAUNT
 Methinks I am a prophet new-inspired,°
 And thus, expiring, do foretell of him.°
 His rash, fierce blaze of riot° cannot last,
 For violent fires soon burn out themselves.
35 Small showers last long, but sudden storms are
   short.
 He tires betimes° that spurs too fast betimes.
 With eager feeding food doth choke the feeder.
 Light vanity, insatiate cormorant,°
 Consuming means,° soon preys upon itself.
40 This royal throne of kings, this sceptred° isle,
 This earth of majesty, this seat of Mars,
 This other Eden, demi-paradise,°
 This fortress° built by nature for herself
 Against infection° and the hand of war,
45 This happy breed of men, this little world,°
 This precious stone set in the silver sea,
 Which serves it in the office° of a wall,
 Or as a moat defensive to a house
 Against the envy of less happier lands;
50 This blessèd plot, this earth, this realm, this
   England,
 This nurse, this teeming womb of royal kings,
 Feared by their breed° and famous by their birth,
 Renownèd for their deeds as far from home

For Christian service° and true chivalry
55 As is the sepulchre, in stubborn Jewry,
Of the world's ransom, blessèd Mary's son;
This land of such dear° souls, this dear dear land,
Dear for her reputation through the world,
Is now leased out—I die pronouncing it—
60 Like to a tenement° or pelting° farm.
England, bound in with the triumphant sea,
Whose rocky shore beats back the envious siege
Of wat'ry Neptune, is now bound in with shame,
With inky blots° and rotten parchment bonds.°
65 That England that was wont to conquer others
Hath made a shameful conquest of itself.
Ah, would the scandal vanish with my life,
How happy then were my ensuing death!

31 **new-inspired**/(pun on "expired") 32 **him**/i.e., Richard II 33 **riot**/
profligacy 36 **betimes**/early 38 **cormorant**/gluttony 39 **means**/appetite
40 **sceptred**/sovereign 42 **demi-paradise**/little Eden 43 **fortress**/i.e.,
natural island 44 **infection**/contamination 45 **little world**/world unto
itself 47 **office**/function 52 **breed**/i.e., hereditary race of valiant warriors
54 **Christian service**/i.e., refers to the Crusades 57 **dear**/precious 60
tenement/leased land **pelting**/paltry 64 **blots**/stains **parchment
bonds**/official documents (usurping land ownership)

Commentary: John of Gaunt's monologue, with its rich images of
England and its appeal for the preservation of the kingdom against
the abuse of King Richard, is one of Shakespeare's most quoted
patriotic anthems; especially lines 40-60, one complete sentence.
The actor can best rest at the semicolons. But the final two lines of
irony in that part of the speech (lines 59-60) undercut the finer
pronouncements, and make them seem like clichés. Gaunt's speech is
more bitter than uplifting when taken in context. Like a seer, "a
prophet new-inspired," Gaunt sees a flow of destruction that will, in
fact, ensue in civil war. A fortress without, England is corrupted
from within. It is important to note that Gaunt is personifying
Richard as much as England. Gaunt also alludes, however
obliquely, to Richard's most fatal flaw: the seizing of the nobles'
lands. That will be Richard's downfall, along with his aloof pride.
Note the Old Testament fierceness displayed throughout the verse.
The speech is constructed as a fire and brimstone sermon.

RICHARD II

King Richard

Act 3, Scene 2. The coast of Wales. Richard II has just returned from quelling a rebellion in Ireland. Stepping once again onto English soil and happy to be home, Richard delivers this monologue in the form of an apostrophe to the earth.

(Flourish. Enter King Richard, the Duke of Aumerle, the Bishop of Carlisle, and soldiers, with drum and colors.)

KING RICHARD

Harlechly Castle call they this at hand?

[AUMERLE

Yea, my lord. How brooks your grace the air
After your late tossing on the breaking seas?]

KING RICHARD

Needs must I like it well. I weep for joy
5   To stand upon my kingdom once again.
(He touches the ground)
Dear earth, I do salute° thee with my hand,
Though rebels wound thee with their horses'
    hoofs.
As a long-parted mother with° her child
Plays fondly with her tears, and smiles in meeting.
10 So, weeping, smiling, greet I thee my earth,
And do thee favors with my royal hands.°
Feed not thy sovereign's foe, my gentle earth,
Nor with thy sweets comfort his ravenous sense;°
But let thy spiders that suck up thy venom
15 And heavy-gaited toads° lie in their way,
Doing annoyance to the treacherous feet
Which with usurping steps do trample thee.
Yield stinging nettles to mine enemies,

And when they from thy bosom pluck a flower
20 Guard it, I pray thee, with a lurking adder,
Whose double tongue may with a mortal° touch
Throw° death upon thy sovereign's enemies.—°
Mock not my senseless conjuration,° lords.
This earth shall have a feeling, and these stones
25 Prove armèd soldiers, ere her native° king
Shall falter under foul rebellion's arms.

6 **salute**/greet 8 **with**/i.e., from 11 **do...hands**/(indicates that he is
caressing the earth) 13 **Nor...sense**/do not gratify his voracious appetite
with your bounty 15 **toads**/i.e., plagues (Richard is casting a spell here and
in the following lines) 21 **mortal**/deadly 22 **Throw**/inflict —/(pause that
indicates that Richard becomes aware that others are watching) 23
senseless conjuration/strange spells 25 **native**/legitimate, hereditary

Commentary: Richard II, in the words of Walter Pater, is
Shakespeare's most "sweet-tongued" king. He rivals Hamlet in the
ability to deliver extended soliloquies that are rich in poetic
content and images. As his verse illustrates, he is more at home as a
poet than as a ruler. With his forces facing a threat of more civil
rebellion at home, Richard stops to address the earth as if it were
his dearest friend. The speech is highly rhetorical and descriptive,
echoing John of Gaunt's paean to England in Act 2, Scene 1 (See
above). His instincts are maternal. Note the ease with which
Richard is brought to tears. The actor should be aware that at this
point Richard begins his passage into a state of high emotions that
will last until his death in Act 5. The speech is marked with
references to "wound" and "feeling." Richard's repeated use of the
possessive "my" is but one indication of his isolation and self-
centeredness. He also indulges in some witchcraft in lines 14-22.

RICHARD II

King Richard

Act 3, Scene 2. The coast of Wales. The Duke of Aumerle cautions the King about Henry Bolingbroke's treachery and growing power. King Richard responds with customary haughtiness that centers on his hereditary power as monarch.

[AUMERLE
    He means, my lord, that we are too remiss,
30   Whilst Bolingbroke, through our security,
    Grows strong and great in substance and in friends.]
KING RICHARD
    Discomfortable° cousin, know'st thou not
    That when the searching eye of heaven is hid
    Behind the globe° that lights the lower world,°
35   Then thieves and robbers range abroad unseen
    In murders and in outrage bloody here;
    But when from under this terrestrial ball
    He fires the proud tops of the eastern pines,
    And darts his light through every guilty hole,
40   Then murders, treasons, and detested sins,
    The cloak of night being plucked from off their
       backs,
    Stand bare and naked, trembling at themselves?
    So when this thief, this traitor, Bolingbroke,
    Who all this while hath revelled in the night
45   Whilst we were wand'ring with the Antipodes,°
    Shall see us rising in our throne, the east,
    His treasons will sit blushing in his face,
    Not able to endure the sight of day,
    But, self-affrighted, tremble at his sin.
50   Not all the water in the rough rude sea
    Can wash the balm from an anointed king.

The breath of worldly men cannot depose
The deputy elected by the Lord.
For every man that Bolingbroke hath pressed°
55   To lift shrewd° steel against our golden crown,
God for his Richard hath in heavenly pay
A glorious angel. Then if angels fight,
Weak men must fall; for heaven still° guards the
  right.°

32 **Discomfortable**/uneasy 34 **globe**/earth **lower world**/Antipodes,
lower half of the world (a sample of Richard's inflation of a simple response)
45 **Antipodes**/people on the other side of the earth 54 **pressed**/enlisted
55 **shrewd**/sharp 58 **still**/always **right**/lawful right of kingship

Commentary: Richard's monologues are always characterized by
a rich and complex use of imagery that underscores the natural
rights of a divinely ordained ruler. His verse is studded with poetic
artifice that bypasses simple words and phrases. "Night" becomes
"when the searching eye of heaven is hid/Behind the globe that
lights the lower world...." Instead of "daybreak," he says "when
from under this terrestrial ball/He fires the proud tops of the
eastern pines,/And darts his light...." Like a mythical Jove,
Richard wields torrents of words as though they were celestial
weapons. But his verbal strengths do not equate with his lack of
armed might. Instead of addressing the real and tangible threat of
Bolingbroke, Richard allegorizes a response, putting his faith in
some "glorious angel" of vengeance. His language is always miles
above the given circumstances of his reality. Yet he believes in
what he says.

RICHARD II

King Richard

Act 3, Scene 2. The coast of Wales. King Richard has just received "tidings of calamity" from Sir Stephen Scroop. A general rebellion is underway against the King. Even his most loyal nobles have either turned sides or have been killed by the rebels. Richard reflects on the impending doom.

[AUMERLE
    Where is the Duke my father, with his power?]
KING RICHARD
140 No matter° where. Of comfort no man speak.
    Let's talk of graves, of worms and epitaphs,
    Make dust° our paper, and with rainy° eyes
    Write sorrow on the bosom of the earth.
    Let's choose executors° and talk of wills—
145 And yet not so, for what can we bequeath
    Save our deposèd bodies to the ground?°
    Our lands, our lives, and all are Bolingbroke's;
    And nothing can we call our own but death,
    And that small model° of the barren earth
150 Which serves as paste° and cover° to our bones.
    (Sitting) For God's sake, let us sit upon the ground,
    And tell sad stories of the death of kings—
    How some have been deposed, some slain in war,
    Some haunted by the ghosts° they have deposed,
155 Some poisoned by their wives, some sleeping
        killed,
    All murdered. For within the hollow° crown
    That rounds° the mortal temples of a king
    Keeps Death his court; and there the antic° sits,
    Scoffing his state and grinning at his pomp,
160 Allowing him a breath, a little scene,

To monarchize,° be feared, and kill with looks,
Infusing him with self and vain conceit,
As if this flesh which walls about our life°
Were brass impregnable; and humored° thus,
165 Comes at the last, and with a little pin
Bores through his castle wall; and farewell, king.
Cover your heads, and mock not flesh and blood
With solemn reverence. Throw away respect,
Tradition, form, and ceremonious duty,
170 For you have but mistook me all this while.
I live with bread, like you; feel want,
Taste grief, need friends. Subjected° thus,
How can you say to me I am a king?

140 **No matter**/it doesn't matter 142 **dust**/earth **rainy**/moist, crying 144 **executors**/powers of attorney for an estate 146 **ground**/grave 149 **model**/mold 150 **paste**/crust **cover**/i.e., coffin 154 **ghosts**/i.e., ghosts of kings 156 **hollow**/empty, transitory 157 **rounds**/encircles 158 **antic**/clown, court fool 161 **monarchize**/play the king 163 **flesh...life**/i.e., body 164 **humored**/cheered 172 **Subjected**/made a subject, lowered

Commentary: After having used inflated and mythical language to describe his lawful rights as king in the other monologues in this scene (see above), Richard now turns to images that use exquisite miniatures to signal his downfall (lines 165-166). He even "sits" upon the ground, all that is left of his "kingdom." The speech is a lamentation. Its subject is loss. A king transforms into a commoner. The verse is marked by the motion of descent and collapse. Note how simple and common his speech becomes in lines 168-173. The actor should have guessed by now that Richard is given to extended moments of pathos and self-dramatization. He does not even think to fight back. Elsewhere he is described as "woe's slave." And grief is certainly the intention he enjoys playing the best. He excells as the ruler of his emotions and the dramatist of his undoing. Notice, too, how Richard draws into his orbit *all* of the kings who have fallen before him. Along with playing his grief he likes to cast it with a good company as well.

RICHARD II

King Richard

Act 4, Scene 1. London. The Parliament in Westminster Hall. King Richard is brought before Parliament to surrender the symbols of kingship to the usurper Henry Bolingbroke (later King Henry IV). But Richard refuses to yield without having the last words.

(Enter Richard and the Duke of York, with attendants bearing the crown and sceptre)

RICHARD

    Alack, why am I sent for to a king
    Before I have shook off the regal thoughts
    Wherewith I reigned? I hardly yet have learned
165 To insinuate,° flatter, bow, and bend° my knee.
    Give sorrow leave awhile to tutor me
    To this submission. Yet I well remember
    The favors° of these men. Were they not mine?
    Did they not sometime cry "All hail!" to me?
170 So Judas° did to Christ. But He in twelve
    Found truth in all but one; I, in twelve thousand,
      none.
    God save the King! Will no man say "Amen?"
    Am I both priest and clerk?° Well then, Amen.
    God save the King, although I be not he.
175 And yet Amen, if heaven do think him me.
    To do what service am I sent for hither?

[YORK

    To do that office° of thine own good will
    Which tired majesty did make thee offer:
    The resignation of thy state and crown
180 To Henry Bolingbroke.]

RICHARD *(to an attendant)*

    Give me the crown. *(To Bolingbroke)* Here, cousin,
      seize the crown.

Here, cousin. On this side my hand, on that side
  thine.
Now is this golden crown like a deep well
That owes° two buckets filling one another,
185 The emptier ever dancing in the air,
The other down, unseen, and full of water.
That bucket down and full of tears am I,
Drinking my griefs, whilst you mount up on high.
[BOLINGBROKE
I thought you had been willing to resign.]
RICHARD
190 My crown I am, but still my griefs are mine.
You may my glories and my state depose,
But not my griefs; still am I king of those.
[BOLINGBROKE
Part of your cares you give me with your crown.]
RICHARD
Your cares° set up do not pluck my cares° down.
195 My care is loss of care by old care done;
Your care is gain of care by new care won.
The cares I give I have, though given away;
They 'tend° the crown, yet still with me they stay.
[BOLINGBROKE
Are you contented to resign the crown?]
RICHARD
200 Ay, no; no, ay; for I must nothing be;
Therefore no, no, for I resign to thee.
Now mark me how I will undo° myself.
I give this heavy weight from off my head,
(Bolingbroke accepts the crown)
And this unwieldy sceptre from my hand,
(Bolingbroke accepts the sceptre)
205 The pride of kingly sway from out my heart.
With mine own tears I wash away my balm,°
With mine own hands I give away my crown,
With mine own tongue deny my sacred state,

With mine own breath release all duteous oaths.
210 All pomp and majesty I do forswear.
My manors, rents, revenues° I forgo.
My acts, decrees, and statutes I deny.
God pardon all oaths that are broke to me.
God keep all vows unbroke are° made to thee.
215 Make me, that nothing have, with nothing grieved,
And thou with all pleased, that hast all achieved.
Long mayst thou live in Richard's seat to sit,
And soon lie Richard in an earthy pit.
"God save King Henry," unkinged Richard says,
220 "And send him many years of sunshine days."
What more remains?

165 **insinuate**/wheedle favor **bend**/kneel 168 **favors**/charms and
appearances 170 **Judas**/Christ's betrayer 173 **clerk**/scholar 177 **office**/
official duty 184 **owes**/owns 194 **cares**/responsibilities **cares**/sorrows 198
'tend/attend on 202 **undo**/strip or kill 206 **balm**/coronation anointment
211 **revenues**/incomes (accent always on second syllable) 214 **are**/that are

Commentary: Few scenes in Shakespeare's history plays
challenge the actor more than the dramatic deposition of King
Richard II to the status of commoner. It includes a string of lengthy
monologues, one divided here and in the following speech into two
parts. On its own, the scene is a play in itself, best described as a
"woeful pageant." Richard's performance is a superb piece of acting.
His verse has a suppleness that is commanding and mesmerizing,
rich with conceits, contrasts and opposition. When Richard
confronts Bolingbroke he outplays and upstages him. Although
powerless now, Richard uses his command of grief, sentiment and
language to great advantage. The centerpiece of this part of the
scene is when Richard un-kings himself (lines 193-232). He reverses
the whole investiture process in a manner that would almost parody
it were it not done so solemnly. So many moods are touched on in
these moments that they require careful scoring by the performer.
Note how Richard, with such devices as wordplay and rhyming
couplets, begins to transform into a court fool with phrasing that
verges on nonsense. His use of simple words is unmatched.

RICHARD III

Richard of Gloucester

Act 1, Scene 2. London. A street. Richard has just interrupted the funeral procession of Henry VI. Over the corpse of one of his victims, Richard first bears the curses of Lady Anne—whose husband (Prince Edward) and father he has also had murdered—and then begins to woo and win her. He manages to convince Lady Anne that his villainy was done for her love. He offers her his ring.

RICHARD OF GLOUCESTER

215 Was ever woman in this humor° wooed?
Was ever woman in this humor won?
I'll have her,°but I will not keep her long.
What, I that killed her husband and his father,
To take her° in her heart's extremest hate,
220 With curses in her mouth, tears in her eyes,
The bleeding witness of my hatred by,
Having God, her conscience, and these bars against
me,
And I no friends° to back my suit withal
But the plain devil and dissembling looks—
225 And yet to win her, all the world to nothing? Ha!
Hath she forgot already that brave prince,
Edward her lord, whom I some three months since
Stabbed in my angry mood at Tewkesbury?°
A sweeter and a lovelier gentleman,
230 Framed in the prodigality° of nature,
Young, valiant, wise, and, no doubt, right royal,
The spacious world cannot again afford—°
And will she yet abase° her eyes on me,
That cropped° the golden prime° of this sweet
prince

235 And made her widow to a woeful bed?
     On me, whose all not equals Edward's moiety?°
     On me, that halts° and am misshapen thus?
     My dukedom to a beggarly *denier*,°
     I do mistake my person all this while.
240 Upon my life she finds, although I cannot,
     Myself to be a marv'lous proper° man.
     I'll be at charges for° a looking-glass
     And entertain° a score or two of tailors
     To study fashions to adorn my body.
245 Since I am crept in favor with myself,
     I will maintain it with some little cost.
     But first I'll turn yon fellow° in° his grave,
     And then return lamenting to my love.
     Shine out, fair sun, till I have bought a glass,
250 That I may see my shadow as I pass.

215 **humor**/mood 217 **have her**/possess her carnally 219 **take her**/to
copulate with her 223 **no friends** /(an indication of how alone Richard is)
228 **Tewkesbury**/scene of an important Yorkist victory 230 **prodigality**/
lavishness 232 **afford**/supply 233 **abase**/lower 234 **cropped**/cut off
prime/springtime, i.e., life 236 **Edward's moiety**/half of Edward 237
halts/trips 238 **denier**/French coin of no value 241 **marv'lous proper**/
wonderfully handsome 242 **be...for**/buy 243 **entertain**/engage 247 **yon
fellow**/i.e., Henry VI **in**/into

Commentary: Richard begins his speech with two incredulous
questions. He is as surprised as anyone that his bold play-acting at
penance has won Lady Anne to his sympathy. The actor would be
wise to look at this previous scene in order to see the extraordinary
reversal that Richard makes in this soliloquy. All characters are
playthings to Richard. Lady Anne will later become his Queen.
There is absolute delight in the way Richard speaks of his
dissemblance (lines 218-225). He savors each part of his trick. Yet
he also cannot believe that one so ugly in shape and purpose as he
could appear so handsome to a woman in such a state. Glee and
surprise turn to vanity as he calls for a looking glass and tailors, "To
study fashions to adorn my body." Shakespeare likes to present
Richard with the utmost of challenges so that we can watch him
perform and then hear him comment afterwards. Each of such scenes
is followed by a soliloquy. Duplicity and sudden reversal of mood

and strategy are built into his character with the darting quality of
the verse. The repetitions of lines 215-216 and 236-237 show   how
Richard loves to gloat over one of his tricks.

ROMEO AND JULIET

Chorus

Prologue. The Chorus begins the action on an empty stage, setting the scene and argument for the audience.

CHORUS

    Two households, both alike in dignity°
      In fair Verona, where we lay our scene,
    From ancient° grudge break to new mutiny,°
      Where civil blood° makes civil hands° unclean.
5   From forth the fatal loins° of these two foes
      A pair of star-crossed° lovers take their life,°
    Whose misadventured° piteous overthrows°
      Doth with their death bury their parents' strife.
    The fearful passage° of their death-marked° love
10 And the continuance of their parents' rage—
    Which, but their children's end, naught° could
      remove—
      Is now the two-hours' traffic° of our stage;
    The which if you with patient ears attend,
    What here shall miss, our° toil shall strive to
      mend.

---

1 **dignity**/rank 3 **ancient**/so old no one seems to know its source **mutiny**/violence, quarreling 4 **civil blood**/passion of civil strife **civil hands**/citizens' hands 5 **loins**/parentage 6 **star-crossed**/fated to disaster, doomed **take their life**/commit suicide 7 **misadventured**/ unfortunate **overthrows**/defeats (by death) 9 **passage**/course **death-marked**/doomed 11 **naught**/nothing 12 **traffic**/business 14 **our**/i.e., the players

Commentary: The Chorus speaks a sonnet (14 lines of alternating end rhymes) in both this instance and later between Acts 1 and 2. He/She sets the terms of the play: Montagues and Capulets, dignified houses, have an old blood feud that has recently broken out in new arguments. The scene is Verona. What the Chorus *never* tells us is the original cause of the feud. But what he/she does tell us is that Romeo and Juliet ("star-crossed" by fortune) will suffer as a result of consequences. They themselves are not tragic, but are victims caught up in circumstances that are. The chorus also refers to the play's length—two hours; one of the few references to a playing time in Shakespeare. The verse here is quite regular and elegant, forecasting much of the tone of the verse in the play ahead. "Break" and "bury" are two words whose prominent stresses disrupt the steady pattern. Both words signal the rupture which is the subject of the Chorus' speech.

ROMEO AND JULIET

Mercutio

Act 1, Scene 4. Verona. The street in front of the Capulet's house at night. Romeo, Mercutio, Benvolio and a group of maskers are on their way to the Capulet's ball. Mercutio launches into this bright, fantastical speech to draw Romeo out of his dreamy gloom.

MERCUTIO

O, then I see Queen Mab° hath been with you.°
She is the fairies' midwife,° and she comes
55 In shape no bigger than an agate stone°
On the forefinger of an alderman,°
Drawn with a team of little atomi°
Athwart men's noses as they lie asleep.
Her wagon spokes made of long spinners'° legs;
60 The cover,° of the wings of grasshoppers;
Her traces,° of the moonshine's wat'ry beams;
Her collars, of the smallest spider web;
Her whip, of cricket's bone, the lash of film;°
Her wagoner, a small grey-coated gnat
65 Not half so big as a round little worm
Pricked from the lazy finger of a maid.°
Her chariot is an empty hazelnut
Made by the joiner squirrel° or old grub,°
Time out o' mind the fairies' coachmakers.
70 And in this state° she gallops night by night
Through lovers' brains, and then they dream of
    love;
O'er courtiers' knees, that dream on° curtsies
    straight;°
O'er ladies' lips, who straight on kisses dream,
Which oft the angry Mab with blisters plagues°

75 Because their breaths with sweetmeats tainted are.°
    Sometime she gallops o'er a lawyer's lip,
    And then dreams he of smelling out a suit;°
    And sometime comes she with a tithe-pigs° tail
    Tickling a parson's nose as a lies asleep;
80 Then dreams he of another benefice.°
    Sometime she driveth o'er a soldier's neck,
    And then dreams he of cutting foreign throats,
    Of breaches, ambuscados,° Spanish blades,°
    Of healths° five fathom deep; and then anon
85 Drums in his ear, at which he starts and wakes,
    And being thus frighted, swears a prayer or two,°
    And sleeps again. This is that very Mab
    That plaits the manes of horses in the night,
    And bakes the elf-locks in foul sluttish hairs,°
90 Which once untangled much misfortune bodes.
    This is the hag,° when maids lie on their backs,
    That presses them and learns them first to bear,
    Making them women of good carriage.°
    This is she—
[ROMEO   Peace, peace, Mercutio, peace!
95 Thou talk'st of nothing.]
MERCUTIO   True. I talk of dreams,
    Which are the children of an idle brain,
    Begot of nothing but vain fantasy,°
    Which is as thin of substance as the air,
    And more inconstant than the wind, who woos
    Even now the frozen bosom of the north,
    And, being angered, puffs away from thence,
    Turning his face to the dew-dropping south.

53 **Queen Mab**/fairy queen (Celtic) **been with you**/slept with you
(bawdy) 54 **midwife**/i.e., delivers men's fantasies like births 55 **agate
stone**/common ring gemstone 56 **alderman**/local magistrate 57 **atomi**/
tiny, speck-like creatures 59 **spinners'**/spiders' 60 **cover**/canopy 61
traces/harnesses 63 **film**/gossamer 66 **Pricked...maid**/i.e., lazy maids
were said to have worms breeding in their fingers (besides being grotesque,
the image is also bawdy with "pricked") 68 **squirrel/grub**/both work on the

wood of the nut by gnawing and boring 70 **state**/stately grandeur 72 **on**/of **curtsies straight**/bows 74 **blisters plague**/i.e., sign of venereal disease 75 **Because...are**/(sexual allusion) 77 **smelling out a suit**/discovering a petition that will lead to a fee 78 **tithe-pig**/part of a parson's yearly dues 80 **benefice**/income 83 **ambuscados**/ambushes **blades**/Toledo swords 84 **healths**/toasts 86 **swears...two**/to ward off evil 89 **bakes...hairs**/matts the hairs of foul sluts 91 **hag**/witch or evil spirit (produces pain of childbirth) 93 **carriage**/bearing (pun on "bear") 97 **fantasy**/fancy

Commentary: A showy set speech—"a vain fantasy"—that is full of dazzling images and jewel-like miniatures, Mercutio's soliloquy bears little relation to the action. It is speech-making for its own sake. It is meant to be an entertaining divertissement that captures the carnival atmosphere of the scene. This is not a monologue to rush through. Delicacy is woven into each image and artfulness of delivery lurks behind each phrase. Note the heavy use of sibilants in the verse: "O'er courtiers' knees, that dream on curtsies straight;/O'er ladies' lips, who straight on kisses dream." The "s" sounds prevent the actor from rushing past the details. This is a speech where all the exquisite details must be imagined and heard. Mercutio is presenting a pageant-like fantasia. He mixes child-like dreams, bawdy sexuality and a darker grotesque element (see lines 83-89) that gradually transform the speech into a nightmare. In a way, the whole Queen Mab speech resembles the movement of the play from innocence to the macabre. The actor must remember that Mercutio is an agile character physically. So a speech like this naturally lends itself to all manner of performance.

ROMEO AND JULIET

Romeo

*Act 2, Scene 2. Verona. The Capulet's garden at night.
Romeo enters the garden stealthily, instantly aware of
any sign of movement or sound. He has left his friends
to go in search of Juliet who he met at the masked ball.
Suddenly she appears on her balcony.*

(Exeunt Benvolio and Mercutio)
ROMEO *(coming forward)*

He jests at scars that never felt a wound.°
But soft,° what light through yonder window
    breaks?
It is the east, and Juliet is the sun.
Arise, fair sun, and kill the envious moon,
5 Who is already sick and pale with grief
That thou, her maid,° art far more fair than she.
Be not her maid, since she is envious.
Her vestal° livery is but sick and green,°
And none but fools do wear it; cast it off.
(Enter Juliet aloft)
10 It is my lady!° O, it is my love!
O that she knew she were!°
She speaks,° yet she says nothing. What of that?
Her eye discourses;° I will answer it.
I am too bold.° 'Tis not to me she speaks.
15 Two° of the fairest stars in all the heaven,
Having some business, do entreat her eyes
To twinkle in their spheres° till they return.
What if her eyes were there, they in her head?—
The brightness of her cheek would shame those
    stars
20 As daylight doth a lamp; her eye in heaven
Would through the airy region stream° so bright

That birds would sing and think it were not night.
See° how she leans her cheek upon her hand!
O, that I were a glove upon that hand,
25 That I might touch that cheek!
[JULIET   Ay me.]
ROMEO *(aside)*   She speaks.°
O, speak again, bright angel; for thou art
As glorious to this night, being o'er my head,°
As is a wingèd° messenger of heaven
Unto the white upturnèd wond'ring eyes°
30 Of mortals that fall back to gaze on him
When he bestrides° the lazy-passing° clouds
And sails upon the bosom of the air.

1 **He...wound**/i.e., Mercutio mocks love's scars because he has never felt love's wounds 2 **But soft**/Hush! (Romeo suddenly sees Juliet on her balcony) 6 **her maid**/i.e., maid to the goddess of moon, Diana 8 **vestal**/virginal **green**/anemia or "greensickness"; also may mean *jealous* 10 **my lady**/fully recognizes Juliet 10-11 **It...were**/(both lines are short and make uses of added pauses between exclamations as Romeo dwells on Juliet) 12 **speaks**/lips move (out of his hearing) 13 **discourses**/speaks 14 **I...bold**/(Romeo retreats from his advance) 15 **Two**/i.e., her eyes 17 **spheres**/orbits 21 **stream**/shine 23 **See**/(notes an action) 23 **She speaks**/(notes another action with a start) 27 **being...head**/placed above me 28 **wingèd**/(pronounced as two syllables) 29 **white...eyes**/i.e., wide-eyed amazement ("upturnèd" is pronounced as three syllables) 31 **bestrides**/straddles **passing**/(various editions use "pacing" or "puffing"; "passing" has a more certain sound value in the context of other sibilant words in sentence)

Commentary: Romeo's soliloquy is in the form of a courtier's address. He pays homage to Juliet's beauty, virginity, solitude, and distance. He likens her beauty to the celestial spheres. It is all the appropriate rhetoric of romance and projects the belief in woman as unattainable beauty. Romeo is in love with love at this stage. The verse is further elevated by the fact that Romeo delivers his words *upwards* to Juliet's position on the balcony or upper stage. Note, too, that the speech is also being addressed to the heavens. The convention is established that Juliet does not yet hear him, allowing Romeo to make his declaration as big and open as possible. Romeo seems to "sketch" Juliet with his words; he dwells on her features to make a word portrait. All of the references in the verse to "light," "sun," "star," "daylight," "lamp," and "bright" add chiaroscuro lighting touches to the dark shadows of the night. The soliloquy presents Juliet as an ideal picture even though she has said but only a sigh. The verse is marked by sibilants which keep the speaking under control.

ROMEO AND JULIET

Romeo

Act 5, Scene 3. Verona. A churchyard at night. The
Capulet family crypt. Romeo has forced his way into
the crypt in a frantic search for Juliet. He encounters
Paris and kills him before recognizing him.

[PARIS
    O, I am slain! If thou be merciful,
    Open the tomb, lay me with Juliet.]
ROMEO
    [In faith, I will.   *(Paris dies)*]
                           Let me peruse° this face.
75 Mercutio's kinsman, noble County° Paris!
    What said my man when my betossèd soul°
    Did not attend° him as we rode? I think
    He told me Paris should have married Juliet.
    Said he not so? Or did I dream it so?
80 Or am I mad, hearing him talk of Juliet,
    To think it was so? O, give me thy hand,°
    One writ with me in sour misfortune's book.
    I'll bury thee in a triumphant grave.
    (He opens the tomb, revealing Juliet)
    A grave—O no, a lantern,° slaughtered youth,
85 For here lies Juliet, and her beauty makes
    This vault a feasting presence° full of light.
    (He bears the body of Paris to the tomb)
    Death,° lie thou there, by a dead man interred.°
    How oft, when men are at the point of death,
    Have they been merry,° which their keepers° call
90 A lightning° before death! O, how may I
    Call this° a lightning? O my love, my wife!
    Death, that hath sucked the honey° of thy breath,
    Hath had no power° yet upon thy beauty.

Thou art not conquered. Beauty's ensign° yet
95 Is crimson in thy lips and in thy cheeks,
And death's pale flag is not advancèd there.
Tybalt, liest thou there in thy bloody sheet?
O, what more favor° can I do to thee
Than with that hand that cut thy youth in twain
100 To sunder his° that was thine enemy?
Forgive me, cousin.° Ah, dear Juliet,
Why art thou yet so fair? Shall I believe
That unsubstantial° death is amorous,
And that the lean abhorrèd monster keeps
105 Thee here in dark to be his paramour?°
For fear of that I still will stay with thee,
And never from this pallet° of dim night
Depart again. Here,° here will I remain
With worms that are thy chambermaids. O, here
110 Will I set up° my everlasting rest,°
And shake the yoke of inauspicious stars°
From this world-wearied flesh. Eyes, look your last.
Arms, take your last embrace, and lips, O you
The doors of breath, seal with a righteous kiss
115 A dateless° bargain to engrossing° death.
(He kisses Juliet, then pours poison into the cup)
Come, bitter conduct,° come unsavory° guide,
Thou desperate pilot, now at once run on
The dashing rocks thy seasick weary bark!°
Here's to my love.
(He drinks the poison)

                              O true° apothecary,
120 Thy drugs are quick!° Thus with a kiss I die.
(He kisses Juliet, falls, and dies.)

74 **peruse**/look at 75 **County**/count 76 **betossèd soul**/distracted mind
77 **attend**/listen to 81 **give me thy hand**/(indicates that he lifts Paris'
lifeless body) 84 **lantern**/palace of light (because of Juliet's sudden
presence) 86 **feasting presence**/banqueting chamber 87 **Death**/i.e.,
Paris **interred**/buried 89 **merry**/elated **keeper**/jailers 90 **lightning**/
recognition or sudden elation 91 **this**/i.e., the tomb of Juliet 92 **honey**/

196

sweetness 93 **power**/i.e., transforming, decaying sign 94 **ensign**/mark, sign 98 **favor**/good turn (Here Romeo apologizes to Tybalt for killing him.) 100 **sunder his**/kill himself (Romeo) 101 **cousin**/friend 103 **unsubstantial**/ bodiless 105 **paramour**/mistress, lover 107 **pallet**/hard bed (Some editions substitute the word "palace;" yet "pallet" adds to the image of a lover's bed that Romeo has been developing. It also seems clear that Romeo is lying next to Juliet at this point.) 108 **Here**/i.e., on the pallet of stone 110 **set up**/stake, settle **everlasting rest**/eternal death 111 **shake...stars**/relieve myself of the doom 115 **dateless**/endless **engrossing**/overwhelming 116 **conduct**/escort (i.e., the poison that will usher him to death) **unsavory**/foul-tasting 118 **bark**/vessel, body (i.e., Romeo) 119 **true**/right-speaking 120 **quick**/speedy, sharp

Commentary: Although the soliloquy is a somber discourse with death, Romeo performs it by talking to three separate bodies (Paris, Tybalt and Juliet). Romeo believes he may have entered a "dream." As soon as he discovers Juliet (line 84) the image of light that he used in the Act 1 balcony speech returns. This scene is the direct antithesis of that one. The pause in the midst of line 84 allows the shock and recognition to register. Now Romeo knows that he, too, is marked for death. At line 88 his speech suddenly turns almost tranquil and romantic. The irony is that Juliet is not dead, but asleep from a potion taken to feign death, which is why her face still has its lustre (lines 92-96). In a sense, Romeo performs the rites for his own funeral, ending the speech with a macabre toast and drinking of poison. Note the calm and resignation that settles into the verse. In lines 109-115 he steps outside himself to watch his actions. There are even lighthearted moments of laughter (line 89) at death's cruel triple joke, soon to be added to with Romeo's suicide. He seems to find courage to commit his deadly act by playing the event as a love scene with Juliet. The building climax in lines 116-118 pushes Romeo into his final gesture before the second kiss. Death and the consummation of a marriage are all contained in this single coup de grace.

THE TAMING OF THE SHREW

Petruchio

Act 4, Scene 1. Petruchio's country house outside Padua. Petruchio has just returned home with his new wife Kate, a tempermental shrew. He has set in motion a plan to break Kate of her willful habits and turn her into a proper wife. Here he discloses the progress of his plan.

[GRUMIO Where is he?
CURTIS In her chamber,
　　Making a sermon of continency to her,
170 And rails, and swears, and rates, that she, poor soul,
　　Knows not which way to stand, to look, to speak,
　　And sits as one new risen from a dream.
　　Away, away, for he is coming hither. *Exeunt*]
　　(*Enter Petruchio*)
PETRUCHIO
　　Thus have I politicly° begun my reign,
175 And 'tis my hope to end successfully.
　　My falcon° now is sharp° and passing empty,°
　　And till she stoop° she must not be full-gorged,
　　For then she never looks upon her lure.°
　　Another way I have to man my haggard,°
180 To make her come and know her keeper's call—
　　That is, to watch her as we watch these kites°
　　That bate and beat, and will not be obedient.
　　She ate no meat today, nor none shall eat.
　　Last night she slept not, nor tonight she shall not.
185 As with the meat, some undeservèd° fault
　　I'll find about the making of the bed,
　　And here I'll fling the pillow, there the bolster,
　　This way the coverlet, another way the sheets,
　　Ay, and amid this hurly° I intend°

190 That all is done in reverent care of her,
     And in conclusion she shall watch° all night,
     And if she chance to nod I'll rail and brawl
     And with the clamor keep her still awake.
     This is a way to kill a wife with kindness,
195 And thus I'll curb her mad and headstrong
         humor.°
     He that knows better how to tame a shrew,
     Now let him speak. 'Tis charity to show.°

174 **politicly**/cleverly, artfully 176 **falcon**/i.e., Kate **sharp**/hungry passing **empty**/missing prey 177 **stoop**/trained to attack the lure 177-178 **And...lure**/i.e., until she learns to submit to authority she will never follow commands 179 **haggard**/wild, untrained bird 181 **kites**/birds of prey 185 **undeservèd**/trifle 189 **hurly**/confusion, hurlyburly I **intend**/I'll pretend 191 **watch**/stay awake and alert 195 **humor**/mood 197 **to show**/i.e., to share methods with one another

Commentary: Petruchio's expository soliloquy uses the training language of falconry. Indeed, Kate is like a wild bird of prey, attacking whatever she lights upon. Like all such trainers who have a way with wild things, Petruchio enjoys sharing his trade secrets with the audience. He lays out a step by step process. He is mean in order to be kind. All of this is part of the ultimate taming motive: "killing kindness." Involved in it is a high degree of torment and deprivation not unlike brainwashing. To Petruchio, Kate is, after all, a kind of animal. There is little in the speech to indicate she is human. Notice how the verse is set in motion by images of flight, first of the falcon and then of the bedclothes. The third part of the soliloquy is given over to brawling sounds.

THE TEMPEST

Ariel

Act 3, Scene 3. Prospero's island. A banquet has magically appeared. Ariel, Prospero's spirit agent, is lowered onto the stage dressed as a winged harpy. He is invisible and speaks here to Alonso, Antonio and Sebastian to remind them of their crimes against Prospero and to frighten them into repentence.

[ALONSO *(rising)*   I will stand to and feed,
50   Although my last—no matter, since I feel
     The best is past. Brother, my lord the Duke,
     Stand to, and do as we.]
     (Alonso, Sebastian, and Antonio approach the
     table. Thunder and lightning. Ariel descends like a
     harpy,° claps his wings upon the table, and, with a
     quaint device, the banquet vanishes.)
ARIEL
     You are three men of sin, whom destiny°—
     That hath to instrument° this lower world
55   And what is in't—the never-surfeited° sea
     Hath caused to belch up° you, and on this island
     Where man doth not inhabit, you 'mongst men
     Being most unfit to live. I have made you mad,
     And even with suchlike valor° men hang and
        drown
60   Their proper° selves.
     (Alonso, Sebastian, and Antonio draw)
                 You fools! I and my fellows°
     Are ministers of fate. The elements
     Of whom your swords are tempered may as well
     Wound the loud winds, or with bemocked-at° stabs
     Kill the still-closing° waters, as diminish

65 One dowl° that's in my plume. My fellow
      ministers
   Are like° invulnerable. If° you could hurt,
   Your swords are now too massy° for your strengths
   And will not be uplifted.
   (*Alonso, Sebastian, and Antonio stand amazed*)
                                        But remember,
   For that's my business to you, that you three
70 From Milan did supplant good Prospero;
   Exposed unto the sea, which hath requit° it,
   Him and his innocent child; for which foul deed,
   The powers, delaying not forgetting, have
   Incensed the seas and shores, yea, all the creatures,
75 Against your peace. Thee of thy son, Alonso,
   They have bereft,° and do pronounce by me
   Ling'ring perdition°—worse than any death
   Can be at once°—shall step by step attend
   You and your ways; whose wraths to guard you
      from—
80 Which here in this most desolate isle else falls
   Upon your heads—is nothing but heart's sorrow
   And a clear° life ensuing.
   (*He ascends and vanishes in thunder.*)

SD **harpy**/i.e., like one of the ancient Furies 53 **destiny**/fate 54 **to instrument**/as its agent 55 **surfeited**/full from feeding 56 **belch up**/throw up 59 **valor**/a strength brought on by madness 60 **proper**/own **fellows**/(indicates he has other spirits on stage with him) 63 **bemocked-at**/laughable, ludicrous 64 **still-closing**/repeatedly healed when stabbed 65 **dowl**/feather (he is wearing the wings of a harpy) 66 **like**/also **If**/even if 67 **massy**/bulky, heavy 71 **requit it**/paid for the injustice 76 **bereft**/robbed 77 **Ling'ring perdition**/prolonged destruction 78 **once**/one time 82 **clear**/innocent

Commentary: Ariel's speech is not nearly as convincing as it would be were it heard and seen with all its theatrical tricks. Notice how he makes the banquet vanish. Like Puck in *A Midsummer Night's Dream,* Ariel is a trickster who takes his commands from a stage director, Prospero. His job is to play different roles: here he is Vengeance characterized by his menacing epithets ("I have made you mad"). Note how his verse sounds like it is resonant with echoes. Its tones are all accusatory and judgmental. There is neither doubt nor compassion in anything he says. The speech is a series of pounding declarative sentences without any variations. It is divided into three sections and gradually focuses on Alonso. The rhetorical devices are those of an impersonal and angered god: "Thee of thy son, Alonso,/They have bereft, and do pronounce by me/Ling'ring perdition...." He punctuates all this with a clap of thunder. The high theatricality of the scene is matched by the bigness and complexity of the speech.

THE TEMPEST

Prospero

Act 4, Scene 1. Prospero's island. Before Prospero's cell. Prospero has just made a fanciful masque appear and disappear for the delight of Miranda and Ferdinand. Then he becomes agitated by the thought of Caliban. To regain composure, he gives this speech.

[FERDINAND *(to Miranda)*
　　This is strange. Your father's in some passion
　　That works him strongly.
MIRANDA　　　　　　　　　　　　Never till this day
145 Saw I him touched with anger so distempered.]
PROSPERO
　　You do look, my son, in a movèd sort,°
　　As if you were dismayed. Be cheerful, sir.
　　Our revels° now are ended. These our actors,
　　As I foretold you, were all spirits, and
150 Are melted into air, into thin air;
　　And like the baseless fabric° of this vision,
　　The cloud-capped towers, the gorgeous palaces,
　　The solemn temples, the great globe itself,
　　Yea, all which it inherit,° shall dissolve;
155 And, like this insubstantial° pageant° faded,
　　Leave not a rack° behind. We are such stuff°
　　As dreams are made on,° and our little life
　　Is rounded° with a sleep.° Sir, I am vexed.
　　Bear with my weakness. My old brain is troubled.
160 Be not disturbed with° my infirmity.
　　If you be pleased, retire into my cell,
　　And there repose. A turn or two I'll walk
　　To still my beating mind.
[FERDINAND *and* MIRANDA　　We wish your peace.
　　Exeunt Ferdinand and Miranda.]

146 **movèd** **sort**/agitated state   148 **revels**/festive entertainments   151 **baseless fabric**/insubstantial foundation   154 **it inherit**/occupy it   155 **insubstantial**/without material substance   **pageant**/show   156 **rack**/wisp of cloud   **stuff**/material   157 **on**/of   158 **rounded**/ended, completed   **sleep**/death (followed by a pause)   160 **with**/by

Commentary: Prospero delivers one of Shakespeare's great set speeches. It comes as a momentary interruption in the action and its function seems to be one of restoring calm to tensions. It is a speech rich in heightened visions: "cloud-capped towers, the gorgeous palaces,/The solemn temples, the great globe itself." But these the god-like magician/poet can make disappear, "dissolve" and "faded." At the heart of Prospero's monologue is a resonant antithesis: the creative *and* vanishing powers of the imagination. The theatre itself and the play are the metaphors for this contrast of the substantial and insubstantial. For the actor, the speech brings into focus the player's power *and* failure. The performance lives only to die immediately afterwards. Life itself is a vain,"baseless" conceit, an act of supernatural conjuring: "We are such stuff/As dreams are made on, and our little life/Is rounded with a sleep." Although the ideas are beautiful they are also unsettling. Prospero himself is "vexed," "troubled" and "disturbed" by the thought. Each line ends with discomfort or death. Ultimately, the speech is for the sake of the audience. The whole art of the stage is but a microcosm of the greater reality that life is but a dream: all will melt into air, "into thin air."

THE TEMPEST

Prospero

Act 5, Scene 1. Prospero's island. Before Prospero's cell. Fighting to exert "nobler reason" over the "fury" of his revenge against his usurping brother Alonso, Prospero decides to surrender his magical powers and seek restitution in forgiveness. This is his last piece of conjuring before burying his magical staff and book of spells.

(Prospero draws a circle with his staff)

PROSPERO

Ye elves of hills, brooks, standing° lakes and
    groves,
And ye that on the sands with printless foot
35 Do chase the ebbing Neptune,° and do fly° him
When he comes back; you demi-puppets° that
By moonshine do the green sour ringlets° make
Whereof the ewe not bites: and you whose pastime
Is to make midnight° mushrooms, that rejoice
40 To hear the solemn curfew;° by whose aid,
Weak masters° though ye be, I have bedimmed°
The noontide sun, called forth the mutinous
    winds,
And 'twixt the green sea and the azured vault°
Set roaring war—to the dread rattling thunder
45 Have I given fire, and rifted° Jove's stout oak°
With his own bolt;° the strong-based promontory°
Have I made shake, and by the spurs° plucked up
The pine and cedar; graves at my command
Have waked their sleepers, oped, and let 'em forth
50 By my so potent art. But this rough° magic
I here abjure.° And when I have required°
Some heavenly music—which even now I do—

To work mine end° upon their senses° that
This airy charm is for, I'll break my staff,°
55 Bury it certain fathoms in the earth,
And deeper than did ever plummet sound
I'll drown my book.°
(Solemn music. Here enters first Ariel, invisible;
then Alonso, with a frantic gesture, attended by
Gonzalo; Sebastian and Antonio, in like manner,
attended by Adrian and Francisco. They all enter
the circle which Prospero had made, and there
stand charmed; which Prospero observing, speaks)
(To Alonso) A solemn air,° and° the best comforter
To an unsettled fancy,° cure thy brains,
Now useless, boiled within thy skull.
60 *(To Sebastian and Antonio)*   There stand,°
For you are spell-stopped.—
Holy Gonzalo, honorable man,
Mine eyes, ev'n sociable to the show of thine,
Fall fellowly drops.° *(Aside)* The charm dissolves
     apace,°
65 And as the morning steals upon the night,
Melting the darkness, so their rising senses
Begin to chase the ignorant fumes° that mantle
Their clearer reason.—O good Gonzalo,°
My true preserver, and a loyal sir
70 To him thou follow'st, I will pay thy graces°
Home both in word and deed.—Most cruelly
Didst thou, Alonso, use me and my daughter.
Thy brother° was a furtherer in the act.—
Thou art pinched for't now, Sebastian.
(To Antonio)   Flesh and blood,
75 You, brother mine, that entertained ambition,
Expelled remorse° and nature,° whom, with
     Sebastian—
Whose inward pinches therefore are most
     strong,—

Would here have killed your king, I do forgive
thee,
Unnatural though thou art. *(Aside)* Their
understanding.°
80 Begins to swell, and the approaching tide
Will shortly fill the reasonable shores°
That now lie foul and muddy. Not one of them
That yet looks on me, or would know me.—Ariel,
Fetch me the hat and rapier in my cell.
85 I will discase° me, and myself present
As I was sometime Milan.° Quickly, spirit!
Thou shalt ere° long be free.

33 standing/still 35 Neptune/god of the sea fly/flee 36 demi-puppets/
fairies 37 green sour ringlets/"fairy rings" or circle of rank grass
(Prospero is drawing his circle on the ground at this point.) 39 midnight/
appearing overnight 40 curfew/i.e., the dawn when magic ceased 41
Weak masters/incapable of magic by themselves bedimmed/eclipsed
43 azured vault/the sky 45 rifted/split oak/Jove's sacred tree 46
bolt/thunderbolt promontory/land 47 spurs/roots 50 rough/violent 51
abjure/renounce required/asked for 53 end/purpose their senses/the
minds of Alonso, Sebastian and others 54 staff/sign of power to cast magic
57 book/i.e., book of spells 58 air/tune and/which is 59 unsettled
fancy/distracted mind 60 stand/remain (An order for the other actors to
stop.) 64 fellowly drops/tears of sympathy (A sign that Prospero is
returning to his humanity.) apace/quickly 67 ignorant fumes/dreamy
haze 68 Gonzalo/(The only lord in the group who had been faithful to
Prospero, and, like him, a philosopher.) 70 pay thy graces/repay your
kindness 73 brother/Sebastian 76 remorse/pity nature/natural frater-
nal feelings 79 their understanding/i.e., of their crimes 81 reasonable
shores/i.e., their powers of reason 85 discase/uncase, disrobe 86
sometime Milan/i.e., formerly as Duke of Milan 87 ere/before

Commentary: Prospero begins this taxing soliloquy by first
addressing the spirits he commands. He starts slowly with his
incantation and then gradually builds to greater proportions: from
"elves" and "demi-puppets" to "mutinous winds" and "roaring war."
There is tremendous growth between lines 33 and 50. A break occurs
at that point. Then the verse begins a downward turn with "bury,"
"fathoms," "deeper," "plummet" and "drown." "Solemn music"
overtakes the speech and a "curing" spell replaces the rage. A
healing forgiveness becomes the subject of the monologue as Prospero
takes on the natural characteristics of being a human once more: "I
will discase me, and myself present/As I was sometime Milan."

Like a king reversing his coronation, Prospero goes from immortal to mortal. He literally returns to the point years before when he was the rightful Duke of Milan. Ariel is no longer his spirit, but just a page. Prospero has stepped from the circle of magic back into the circle of life. The trick for the actor is to make pronounced each stage of this transition.

TITUS ANDRONICUS

Aaron the Moor

Act 2, Scene 1. Rome. Before the palace. Aaron, a black Moor, enters to deliver this soliloquy. It is his first appearance in the play, and he makes his presence felt.

AARON
    Now climbeth Tamora Olympus'° top,
    Safe out of fortune's shot,° and sits aloft,
    Secure of° thunder's crack or lightning flash,
    Advanced above pale envy's° threat'ning reach.
5   As when the golden sun salutes the morn
    And, having gilt the ocean with his beams,
    Gallops° the zodiac° in his glistering coach
    And overlooks the highest-peering hills,
    So Tamora.°
10 Upon her wit° doth earthly honor wait,
    And virtue° stoops and trembles at her frown.
    Then, Aaron, arm thy heart and fit thy thoughts
    To mount° aloft with thy imperial mistress,
    And mount her pitch° whom thou in triumph
       long
15 Hast prisoner held fettered in amorous chains,
    And faster bound to Aaron's charming° eyes
    Than is Prometheus tied to Caucasus.°
    Away with slavish weeds° and servile thoughts!
    I will be bright, and shine in pearl and gold
20 To wait upon this new-made empress.
    To wait, said I?—to wanton° with this queen,
    This goddess, this Semiramis,° this nymph,
    This siren that will charm Rome's Saturnine°
    And see his shipwreck and his commonweal's.

---

1 **Olympus'**/Mount Olympus, home of the gods 2 **shot**/range of its shot 3 **of**/from 4 **envy's**/hate's 7 **Gallops**/gallops through **zodiac**/i.e., the

heavens 9 **So Tamora**/(a long pause comes after this) 10 **wit**/power of imagination or invention 11 **virtue**/goodness 13 **mount**/ascend (also bawdy reference to "intercourse" made even more clear in next lines) 14 **mount her pitch**/rise to the highest point of flight (a term from falconry) 16 **charming**/spellbinding 17 **Prometheus tied to Caucasus**/the fire god who was tied to the mountains of Caucasus because he gave fire to man 18 **weeds**/raggish apparel 21 **wanton**/to sport amorously 22 **Semiramis**/Assyrian queen noted for her lust and beauty 23 **Saturnine**/Saturnius, the young Roman emperor

Commentary: Aaron is an early sketch for all of Shakespeare's later theatrical villains (Richard III, Iago, Edmund, etc.). His soliloquy is a richly rhetorical homage to the Empress Tamora, the revengeful Queen of the Goths and later Roman Empress. In this speech the ambitious Aaron quite literally hitches his wagon to Tamora's star. He will become her lover and carry out all her vengeful atrocities on the family of Titus Andronicus. Aaron is described as having a "fiend-like face." He is also a gleeful villain who commits crimes with gloating laughter. His verse is confident and triumphant. Whenever he is on stage, the otherwise dour events suddenly come alive and sparkle because of the relish he displays. Notice, for instance, the way he corrupts Olympian conceits with bawdy ones: "Then, Aaron, arm thy heart and fit thy thoughts/To mount aloft with thy imperial mistress,/And mount her pitch whom thou in triumph long/Hast prisoner held fettered in amorous chains...." No other character in this early tragedy has Aaron's devious facility. He can both manipulate and entertain in the same breath.

TROILUS AND CRESSIDA

Prologue

Prologue. The stage. The Prologue enters armed. His soliloquy is full of exposition.

PROLOGUE

In Troy there lies the scene. From isles of Greece
The princes orgulous,° their high blood° chafed,
Have to the port of Athens sent their ships,
Fraught° with the ministers° and instruments°
5 Of cruel war. Sixty and nine, that wore
Their crownets regal, from th'Athenian bay
Put forth toward Phrygia,° and their vow is made
To ransack Troy, within whose strong immures°
The ravished Helen, Menelaus' queen,
10 With wanton Paris sleeps—and that's the quarrel.
To Tenedos° they come,
And the deep-drawing barques° do there disgorge
Their warlike freightage; now on Dardan° plains
The fresh and yet unbruisèd Greeks do pitch
15 Their brave° pavilions. Priam's six-gated city—
Dardan and Timbria, Helias, Chetas, Troien,
And Antenorides°—with massy staples
And corresponsive and full-filling bolts°
Spar up° the sons of Troy.
20 Now expectation, tickling skittish° spirits
On one and other side, Trojan and Greek,
Sets all on hazard. And hither am I come,
A Prologue armed—but not in confidence
Of author's pen or actor's voice, but suited°
25 In like conditions as our argument—
To tell you, fair beholders, that our play
Leaps o'er the vaunt° and firstlings of those broils,°
Beginning in the middle, starting thence away
To what may be digested in a play.

30   Like or find fault; do as your pleasures are;
      Now, good or bad, 'tis but the chance of war.

2 **orgulous**/proud **high blood**/noble lineage 4 **Fraught**/loaded down
ministers/i.e., soldiers **instruments**/weapons 7 **Phrygia**/western Asia
Minor 8 **immures**/walls 11 **Tenedos**/port of Troy 12 **deep-drawing
barques**/boats sitting low in the water from their heavy burdens 13
Dardan/Trojan 15 **brave**/splendid 16-17 **Dardan...Antenorides**/names
for the gates of Troy 18-19 **massy...bolts**/i.e., heavy sockets into which fit
heavy bolts 19 **Spar-up**/lock up 20 **skittish**/nervous 24 **suited**/dressed,
costumed (The actor who played the Prologue would then have played
other role(s) in the play itself.) 27 **vaunt**/beginning **broils**/fights

Commentary: The Prologue's soliloquy is full of Homeric splendor
and epithets (i.e., "The princes orgulous, their high blood chafed").
He sets the scene at Troy and provides the background for the
quarrel between the Greeks and Trojans: the theft of Helen,
Menelaus' wife, by Paris, son of King Priam. Like the Prologue to
Henry V, the Prologue's function is to add the larger dimension to
the event that the stage is too small to capture: all of the Greek
princes, their ships and troops, the size of Troy itself, the back and
forth sparring of the warriors. He also moves us past the opening
years of the battle to set us down *in medias res*, in the midst of the
event that the play's action dramatizes. There is an ironic splendor
in the speech that is quickly revealed once the play starts. The war
is at a standstill. Nothing has happened for some time. The
Prologue suggests we will witness action, but what we get is
nonaction. Another irony is that Troilus and Cressida, who are not
even mentioned here, will replace Menelaus, Helen and Paris as the
relationship of primary focus. The speech is in three parts (lines 1-
10; 11-19; 20-31).

TROILUS AND CRESSIDA

Ulysses

Act 1, Scene 3. Outside the gates of Troy in the Greek camp. Before Agamemnon's tent. The war is at a stalemate. The Greek champion, Achilles, refuses to fight. A council meets to try and resolve the issue. Ulysses, the wisest and wiliest of the Greeks, offers this observation.

ULYSSES

75 Troy, yet upon his basis, had been down
    And the great Hector's° sword had lacked a master
    But for these instances:°
    The specialty of rule° hath been neglected.
    And look how many Grecian tents do stand
80 Hollow° upon this plain: so many hollow
        factions.°
    When that the general is not like the hive
    To whom the foragers shall all repair,
    What honey is expected?° Degree being vizarded,
    Th'unworthiest shows as fairly in the masque°
85 The heavens themselves, the planets, and this
        center°
    Observe degree,° priority, and place,
    Infixture,° course, proportion,° season, form,
    Office and custom, in all line of order.
    And therefore is the glorious planet Sol
90 In noble eminence enthroned and sphered
    Amidst the other, whose med'cinable° eye
    Corrects the ill aspects° of planets evil
    And posts,° like the commandment of a king,
    Sans° check, to good and bad. But when the planets
95 In evil mixture° to disorder wander,
    What plagues and what portents,° what mutiny?
    What raging of the sea, shaking of earth?

Commotion in the winds, frights, changes, horrors
Divert and crack, rend and deracinate°
100 The unity and married calm of states
Quite from their fixture.° O when degree is shaked,
Which is the ladder to all high designs,
The enterprise° is sick. How could communities,
Degrees° in schools, and brotherhoods in cities,
105 Peaceful commerce from dividable shores,
The primogenity° and due of birth,
Prerogative of age, crowns, sceptres, laurels,°
But by degree stand in authentic place?°
Take but degree away, untune that string,
110 And hark what discord follows. Each thing meets
In mere oppugnancy.° The bounded waters
Should lift their bosoms° higher than the shores
And make a sop° of all this solid globe;
Strength should be lord of imbecility,°
115 And the rude son should strike his father dead.
Force should be right—or rather, right and wrong,
Between whose endless jar° justice resides,
Should lose their names,° and so should justice
    too.
Then everything includes itself in power,°
120 Power into will, will into appetite;
And appetite, an universal wolf,°
So doubly seconded with will and power,
Must make perforce° an universal prey,
And last eat up himself. Great Agamemnon,
125 This chaos, when degree is suffocate,°
Follows° the choking.
And this neglection of degree it is
That by a pace goes backward in a purpose°
It hath to climb. The general's disdained
130 By him° one step below; he, by the next;
That next, by him beneath. So every step,
Exampled° by the first pace that is sick

Of his superior, grows to an envious fever
Of pale and bloodless emulation.°
135 And 'tis this fever that keeps Troy on foot,°
Not her own sinews.° To end a tale of length:°
Troy in our weakness lives, not in her strength.

76 Hector/Troy's champion 77 **instances**/reasons 78 **specialty of rule**/
chain of authority 80 **Hollow**/empty of resolve (Ulysses is obliquely
referring to Achilles' tent.) **factions**/individual and disunified segments
81-83 **When...expected**/i.e., when no one is producing what products can
be expected 83-84 **Degree...masque**/When authority is masked along
with everyone else even the lowliest looks as good as the highest 85 **center**/
earth 86 **degree**/means variously hierarchy, order, chain of authority 87
Infixture/position **proportion**/relationship 91 **med'cinable**/healing 92
ill aspects/astrological effects 93 **posts**/speeds 94 **Sans**/without (French)
95 **evil mixture**/unlucky conjunction 96 **portents**/omens 99 **deracinate**/
uproot, weed out 101 **fixture**/fixed position 103 **enterprise**/i.e., any
undertaking 104 **Degrees**/academic ranks 106 **primogenity**/i.e., right of
oldest son to succeed father 107 **laurels**/distinctions 108 **authentic
place**/acknowledged authority 111 **oppugnancy**/total opposition 112
bosoms/surface, waves 113 **sop**/i.e., like bread steeped in liquid (note
sound string with "shores," "solid," "strength," "should") 114 **imbecility**/
stupidity 117 **jar**/discord 118 **names**/identity 119 **includes...power**/i.e.,
all becomes power 121 **wolf**/i.e., predator 123 **perforce**/of necessity 125
suffocate/suffocated 126 **Follows**/i.e., what follows it is (note the pause at
the end of the line) 127-128 **it is...purpose**/reverses its forward purpose
130 **him**/i.e., one lower in rank (Ulysses is beginning to refer more directly
to Achilles.) 132 **Exampled**/given precedence 134 **pale...emulation**/
rivalry (pallor was associated with envy; a white complexion and chills were
part of the signs of envy) 135 **on foot**/standing, immobile 136 **sinews**/
muscles **tale of length**/long story

Commentary: Ulysses' speech on degree, or order, is an elaborate
discourse couched in terms of one extended simile: the current state
of the Greeks is likened to the order of the universe. Unless
strength, chain of command and priorities prevail, the whole campaign will end in wasted chaos. Ulysses' verse, as a means of backing up his theme, is full of order and balance. "Take but degree
away, untune that string,/And hark what discord follows." Antitheses are played off one another: "Strength should be lord of
imbecility." Notice how Ulysses goes down the list from the highest to the lowest: from the "heavens," to the "earth," to "communities," to "group" and "individual" concerns. The speech is based on
the Elizabethan notion of the great chain of being, the rich line of
priority from the cosmic to the earthly. It is all laid out like a
series of steps on a ladder. Although he has not mentioned it yet,

the end of the speech begins to ferret out the problem in the Greek camp under Agamemnon's command: Achilles. He has thrown the whole Greek effort off balance and made it "sick." For the actor, this speech is closer to a lecture. Its discourse must be clearly set out and neatly projected. Ulysses himself knows that he is telling a "tale of length." Keeping such a long story interesting is a real challenge.

TROILUS AND CRESSIDA

Ulysses

Act 1, Scene 3. The Greek camp outside Troy. Before Agamemnon's camp. The war is at a stalemate. The Greek champion, Achilles, refuses to fight. Ulysses, the wisest and wiliest of the Greeks, uncovers the cause of the problem.

ULYSSES

The great Achilles, whom opinion° crowns
The sinew° and the forehand of our host,°
Having his ear full of his airy° fame
145 Grows dainty of° his worth, and in his tent
Lies mocking our designs.° With him Patroclus°
Upon a lazy bed the livelong day
Breaks° scurrile° jests
And, with ridiculous and awkward action°
150 Which, slanderer, he "imitation"° calls,
He pageants° us. Sometime, great Agamemnon,
Thy topless deputation° he puts on,°
And like a strutting player, whose conceit°
Lies in his hamstring° and doth think it rich
155 To hear the wooden dialogue° and sound
'Twixt his stretched footing and the scaffoldage,°
Such to-be-pitied and o'er-wrested seeming°
He acts thy greatness in. And when he speaks
'Tis like a chime a-mending,° with terms
    unsquared°
160 Which from the tongue of roaring Typhon°
    dropped
Would seem hyperboles.° At this fusty° stuff
The large Achilles on his pressed bed lolling
From his deep chest laughs out a loud applause,
Cries "Excellent! 'Tis Agamemnon just.°

165 Now play me Nestor,° hem and stroke thy beard,
    As he being dressed to° some oration."
    That's done as near as the extremest ends
    Of parallels,° as like as Vulcan and his wife.
    Yet god Achilles still cries, "Excellent!
170 'Tis Nestor right. Now play him me,° Patroclus,
    Arming to answer in a night alarm."
    And then forsooth the faint defects of age
    Must be the scene of mirth:° to cough and spit,
    And with a palsy, fumbling on his gorget,°
175 Shake in and out the rivet. And at this sport
    Sir Valor° dies, cries, "O enough, Patroclus!
    Or give me ribs of steel. I shall split all
    In pleasure of my spleen."° And in this fashion
    All our° abilities, gifts, natures, shapes,
180 Severals and generals° of grace exact,
    Achievements, plots, orders, preventions,
    Excitements to the field or speech for truce,
    Success or loss, what is or is not, serves
    As stuff for these two to make paradoxes.°

142 **opinion**/reputation 143 **sinew**/source of strength **host**/body, i.e., army
144 **airy**/lofty, elevated 145 **dainty of**/fastidious about 146 **designs**/plans
Patroclus/Achilles' catamite, a boy in his mid- or late-teens 148 **Breaks**/
cracks (crude jokes) **scurrile**/scurrilous, obscene (Intentionally sounds
like "puerile" in order to make Achilles seem a rude schoolboy.) (There is a
long pause at the half line.) 149 **action**/gestures, i.e., acting 150
"**imitation**"/i.e., the true goal of the actor was an imitation of life (c.f.,
Aristotle's *Poetics*); but that is different from Achilles' and Patroclus'
burlesque acting 151 **pageants**/mimics (lowest form of acting) 152 **topless
deputation**/unlimited office **puts on**/performs (the same as the modern
"put on") 153 **conceit**/imagination 154 **Lies...hamstring**/i.e., lies in his
foot or walk 155 **wooden dialogue**/i.e., sounds his feet make on the
floorboards of the stage 156 **scaffoldage**/theatrical stage 157 **o'er-
wrested seeming**/strained in the histrionics of his performance 159
chime a-mending/broken chime undergoing repairs **terms
unsquared**/inappropriate words or dialogue 160 **Typhon**/hundred-
headed monster who lived beneath Mt. Etna the volcano 161 **hyperboles**/
exaggerations **fusty**/second-rate, bombastic 164 **just**/precisely (some
editions use the word "right") 165 **Nestor**/King of Pylos, present with the
Greeks at Troy, noted for his wisdom and eloquence 166 **dressed
to**/preparing to address 167-168 **That's...parallels**/i.e., that was as far
away from the real thing as 170 **me**/for me 173 **scene of mirth**/subject of
low comedy 174 **gorget**/throat armor 176 **Sir Valor**/i.e., Achilles 178

spleen/(believed to be the seat of hilarity) 179 **our**/i.e., the Greek notables 180 **Severals and generals**/specific and general qualities 184 **paradoxes**/absurdities

Commentary: After a monologue that spoke eloquently but generally about the loss of order and "degree" (lines 75-138 above), Ulysses here addresses the more specific problem of the lazy, inactive Achilles. His language abruptly changes from the balanced verse of the earlier speech to the mocking, colloquial and theatrical conceits he now uses to deflate Achilles. By embarrassing the Greeks, through the person of their greatest hero, Ulysses hopes to turn inaction into action. Each line contains words that touch on the mockery, parody and histrionics of Achilles and Patroclus, gross signs of Greek weakness. The theatre of low burlesque is used to symbolize vulgarity and disorder. And Ulysses goes further by using the metaphor of acting to infuriate the Greek generals with vivid references to the derisive displays of Achilles and Patroclus. This is precisely Ulysses' intention. But he takes the metaphor further by turning the entertainment of the two warriors into something lurid and perverse. Ulysses knows that the upright Greeks will not tolerate sarcasm. With a speech like this, our view of the "heroic" Achilles is undermined forever.

TROILUS AND CRESSIDA

Thersites

Act 2, Scene 3. The Greek camp outside of Troy. Before the tent of Achilles. The bitter Thersites delivers this denunciation of Achilles and the very idea of Greek heroism.

THERSITES

How now, Thersites? What, lost in the labyrinth of
thy fury? Shall the elephant Ajax carry it° thus?
He beats me and I rail at him. O worthy
satisfaction! Would it were otherwise: that I could
5   beat him whilst he railed at me. 'Sfoot,° I'll learn
to conjure and raise devils but I'll see some issue°
of my spiteful execrations.° Then there's Achilles:
a rare engineer.° If Troy be not taken till these two
undermine it, the walls will stand till they fall of
10 themselves. O thou great thunder-darter of
Olympus, forget that thou art Jove, the king of gods;
and Mercury, lose all the serpentine craft of thy
caduceus,° if ye take not that little, little, less than
little wit from them that they have—which short
15 armed ignorance itself knows is so abundant—
scarce it will not in circumvention deliver a fly
from a spider without drawing their massy irons
and cutting the web. After this, the vengeance on
the whole camp—or rather, the Neapolitan bone
20 ache,° for that methinks is the curse dependent on
those that war for a placket.° I have said my
prayers, and devil Envy say "Amen."—What ho!
My lord Achilles!

2 **carry it**/achieve it 5 **'Sfoot**/God's foot (an oath) 6 **issue**/outcome 7 **execrations**/curses 8 **engineer**/i.e., plotter 13 **caduceus**/Mercury's wand topped by twinned serpents 19-20 **Neapolitan bone-ache**/syphillis 21 **placket**/opening in a petticoat (here used obscenely)

Commentary: Thersites has several damning soliloquies in the play that rival this one in their fierce intensity. He is described in the play as a "Deform'd and scurrilous Grecian;" "scurvy, railing knave, a very filthy rogue." The trick in playing the character is to make all of his unattractive qualities clear, while also maintaining the inherent philosophical and comic possibilities of the role. Thersites carries a most fearsome wit and is ready to insult anyone, just like all the other "licensed-to-kill" Shakespearian clowns. The opening questions in the monologue give you Thersites' method: he is automatically set off railing at the slightest instance. That is pretty much all he does throughout the play. A character who is worlds away from someone like Ulysses, Thersites' commentaries on the Greek "heroes" are but one more means of demystifying them in words. Probably more than anyone, Thersites underscores the unheroic atmosphere of *Troilus and Cressida.* But Thersites plays only one note: cynicism.

TROILUS AND CRESSIDA

Ulysses

Act 3, Scene 3. The Greek camp outside the walls of Troy. The Greek generals have shunned Achilles, their great warrior who will not fight. Ulysses, who instigated the shunning, here tells Achilles that a hero cannot rest upon past deeds, and that only perseverance can keep honor bright.

ULYSSES   Time hath, my lord,
140   A wallet° at his back, wherein he puts
      Alms for oblivion,° a great-sized monster°
      Of ingratitudes. Those scraps are good deeds past,
      Which are devoured as fast as they are made,
      Forgot as soon as done. Perseverance,° dear my
          lord,
145   Keeps honor bright.° To have done is to hang
      Quite out of fashion, like a rusty mail°
      In monumental mock'ry.° Take the instant° way,
      For honor travels in a strait so narrow,
      Where one but goes abreast.° Keep then the path,
150   For emulation hath a thousand sons
      That one by one pursue: if you give way,
      Or hedge aside from the direct forthright,°
      Like to an entered tide they all rush by
      And leave you hindmost;
155   Or, like a gallant horse fall'n in first rank,
      Lie there for pavement to the abject rear,°
      O'errun and trampled on. Then what they do in
          present,
      Though less than yours in past, must o'ertop yours.
      For Time is like a fashionable host,
160   That slightly shakes his parting guest by th' hand
      And, with his arms outstretched as he would fly,°

Grasps in the comer. Welcome ever smiles,
And Farewell goes out sighing. O let not virtue
    seek
Remuneration for the thing it was;
165 For beauty, wit,°
High birth, vigor of bone,° desert in service,
Love, friendship, charity, are subjects all
To envious and calumniating time.
One touch of nature makes the whole world kin°—
170 That all with one consent praise new-born gauds,°
Though they are made and molded of things past,
And give to dust that is a little gilt°
More laud than gilt o'er-dusted.°
The present eye praises the present object.
175 Then marvel not, thou great and complete° man,
That all the Greeks begin to worship Ajax,
Since things in motion sooner catch the eye
Than what not stirs. The cry° went once on thee,
And still it might, and yet it may again,
180 If thou wouldst not entomb thyself alive
And case° they reputation in thy tent,
Whose glorious deeds but in these fields of late
Made emulous missions 'mongst the gods°
    themselves,
And drove great Mars to faction.°

140 **wallet**/knapsack 141 **oblivion**/forgetfulness (of good deeds)
monster/i.e., Time 144 **Perseverance**/(accented on second syllable) 145
bright/shining 146 **mail**/suit of armor 147 **monumental mock'ry**/i.e., a
mocking monument to past actions **instant**/immediate 149 **abreast**/
single file 152 **forthright**/path 156 **abject rear**/miserable rear ranks of a
charge 161 **his...fly**/(example of Ulysses use of personification, probably
indicated with an action) 165 **wit**/(The half line suggests a pause and
slowing down of speech by Ulysses, driving home his single words.) 166
vigor of bone/physical strength 169 **One...kin**/i.e., all men share in one
natural inclination 170 **gauds**/trifles, amusements 172 **And...gilt**/i.e., dirt
that is mixed with some gold dust 173 **More...o'er-dusted**/i.e., more of a
dusting of praise than the gold content deserves 175 **complete**/perfect
178 **cry**/praise, applause 181 **case**/encase (as in a coffin) 185 **Made...
gods**/caused the gods to take sides (on the battlefields between Greek and
Trojan) 184 **to faction**/to take sides

Commentary: Ulysses' chastening monologue comes alive as Time (lines 159-163) and other abstract qualities are richly personified. Although his function in the play is to manipulate, Ulysses continually marvels us with his surprising and rich use of language. He manages to be didactic and entertaining at the same time. And he seems to frame each speech for a specific listener; never using the same strategy twice. Playing on Achilles' vanity and pride, Ulysses' intention is to tell Achilles that time has passed him by in favor of Ajax (lines 175-178). His backhand compliments to Achilles are part of a pattern: Achilles is seen as receding into the past, into the "dust." Ajax, "in motion," has passed him by. Everything Ulysses says in glory of Achilles is in the past tense. All his "complete" qualities are subject to Time's calumny.

TROILUS AND CRESSIDA

Troilus

*Act 5, Scene 2. The Greek camp before the tent of
Calchas. Troilus, together with Ulysses, seeks out
Cressida and observes her making love to Diomedes.
She has even given her new lover the token which
Troilus himself gave to her and swore her to keep.
Troilus reflects on the deception.*

TROILUS
140 This, she? No, this is Diomed's Cressida.
    If beauty have a soul, this is not she.
    If souls guide vows, if vows be sanctimonies,°
    If sanctimony be the gods' delight,
    If there be rule in unity itself,°
145 This is not she. O madness of discourse,°
    That cause sets up° with and against thyself!
    Bifold° authority, where reason can revolt
    Without perdition,° and loss assume all reason
    Without revolt! This is and is not Cressid.
150 Within my soul there doth conduce° a fight
    Of this strange nature, that a thing inseparate
    Divides more wider than the sky and earth,
    And yet the spacious breadth of this division
    Admits no orifex° for a point as subtle°
155 As Ariachne's broken woof° to enter.
    Instance,° O instance, strong as Pluto's gates:
    Cressid is mine, tied with the bonds of heaven.
    Instance, O instance, strong as heaven itself:
    The bonds of heaven are slipped, dissolved, and
        loosed,
160 And with another knot, five-finger-tied,°
    The fractions of her faith, orts° of her love,
    The fragments, scraps, the bits and greasy relics

Of her o'er-eaten° faith, are bound to Diomed.
[ULYSSES
May worthy Troilus e'en be half attached
165 With that which here his passion doth express?]
TROILUS
Ay, Greek, and that shall be divulgèd well
In characters° as red as Mars his heart
Inflamed with Venus. Never did young man
    fancy°
With so eternal and so fixed a soul.
170 Hark, Greek: as much as I do Cressid love,
So much by weight° hate I her Diomed.
That sleeve° is mine that he'll bear in his helm.°
Were it a casque° composed by Vulcan's° skill,
My sword should bite it. Not° the dreadful spout°
175 Which shipmen do the hurricano call,
Constringed in mass° by the almighty sun,
Shall dizzy with more clamor Neptune's ear
In his descent, than shall my prompted° sword
Falling on Diomed.

142 **sanctimonies**/sacred things 144 **rule...itself**/i.e., if a person is one and not two people 145 **discourse**/reasoning 146 **cause sets up**/dispute (of reason) sets up a debate 147 **Bifold**/double, two fold 148 **perdition**/ loss 150 **conduce**/bring about 154 **orifex**/opening, aperture **subtle**/fine, thin 155 **Ariachne's...woof**/i.e., a strand of broken spider's web 156 **Instance**/evidence, proof 160 **five-finger-tied**/i.e., knotted by the entwined fingers of Cressida and Diomed rather than the "bonds of heaven" 161 **orts**/bits, scraps of food 163 **o'er-eaten**/sickened with over indulgence 167 **characters**/appearances 168 **fancy**/love 171 **by weight**/ in equal measure 172 **sleeve**/band (The love token that Troilus gave to Cressida, vowing her to keep, but which she has now given to Diomed.) **helm**/helmet 173 **casque**/helmet **Vulcan**/armor maker to the gods 174 **Not**/not even **spout**/water jet 176 **Constringed in mass**/compressed into a dense mass 178 **prompted**/directed, cued

Commentary: Troilus' speech, and the lines leading up to it, are a fervent denial of the *reality* he sees in favor of the *illusion* he wants to believe. The monologue addresses one of the major themes of the play. In some ways his monologue echoes Ulysses' great speech on "degree" from Act 1. Lines 140-149 lay out a chain of consequences that lead to the antithetical conclusion, "This is and is not Cressid." All of Troilus' faculties are at war. The actor can sense the consternation and confusion in Troilus' verse (lines 150-163). The whole function of the planned deception of Cressida, and the destruction of doomed love between she and Troilus, serves to hasten the action of the play towards its bloody and bitter conclusion. If one so in love as Troilus can turn to hate, the other warriors in the play will follow suit. This speech marks that turning point for Troilus: "Hark, Greek: as much as I do Cressid love,/So much by weight hate I her Diomed." Notice how the verse changes from images of "beauty" and "soul" at the start of the speech to thoughts of storm and "sword" by the end.

TWELFTH NIGHT

Orsino

Act 1, Scene 1. Illyria. Duke Orsino's palace. He opens the action of the play, pining for the love of the beautiful widow, Olivia. He delivers his soliloquy to the strains of melancholy music.

(*Music. Enter Orsino Duke of Illyria, Curio, and other lords*)

ORSINO

If music be the food of love, play on,
Give me excess of it that, surfeiting,°
The appetite° may sicken and so die.
That strain again, it had a dying fall.°
5   O, it came o'er my ear like the sweet sound
That breathes upon a bank of violets,
Stealing and giving odor. Enough, no more,
'Tis not so sweet now as it was before.
(*Music ceases*)
O spirit of love, how quick and fresh° art thou
10   That, notwithstanding thy capacity
Receiveth° as the sea, naught enters there,°
Of what validity° and pitch° so e'er,
But falls into abatement° and low price°
Even in a minute! So full of shapes° is fancy°
15   That it alone is high fantastical.
[CURIO   Will you go hunt, my lord?]
ORSINO   What, Curio?
[CURIO   The hart.]
ORSINO
Why so I do, the noblest that I have.
O, when mine eyes did see Olivia first
Methought she purged the air of pestilence;
20   That instant was I turned into a hart,°

And my desires, like fell° and cruel hounds,
E'er since pursue me.

2 **surfeiting**/over-indulging 3 **appetite**/i.e., the lover's appetite for music
4 **fall**/cadence 9 **quick and fresh**/lively and eager 10-11 **capacity
Receiveth**/power of receiving or containing 11 **naught enters there**/i.e.,
nothing enters the lover's capacity 12 **validity**/value **pitch**/height 13
abatement/diminution   (Orsino uses images drawn from musical
phrasing.) **price**/esteem 14 **shapes**/imaginary forms **fancy**/inclination of
love 20 **hart**/deer (pun on "heart") 21 **fell**/fierce

Commentary: Even before Orsino begins his languishing soliloquy, mood-establishing music has been playing in the background.
The audience for the speech is Orsino's servants, who are referred
to, but say almost nothing. Notice how the Duke feeds on the sounds
to get his fill of melancholy and is then sickened from
overindulging. His listening is a kind of hunger. He interrupts his
own melancholy moods with a series of commands: "play on," "Give
me excess," and "Enough, no more." He both imitates the sounds and
interrupts them. And his speech is full of such harmony and discord.
What the actor should notice about Orsino is how hard he tries to
convince himself that he is in love. His likening himself to a
wounded "hart" shows how extravagant and "high fantastical"
this young lord can become. For him, melancholy love is a kind of
costume he will wear throughout the play until "true love", in the
guise of Viola, comes along to expose and win him.

TWELFTH NIGHT

Malvolio

Act 2, Scene 5. Illyria. Olivia's garden. Sir Toby Belch and Maria have set a trap for the officious Malvolio, Olivia's puritanical house steward. Through the device of an ambiguously worded letter, they hope that Malvolio's ambition and self-love will lead to his own foolish ruin as he digests and translates the contents of the false letter.

MALVOLIO *(Sees the letter)* What employment° have
    we here? *(Taking up the letter)* By my life, this is
    my lady's hand.° These be her very c's, her u's, and
    her t's,° and thus make she her great
5   P's.° It is, in contempt of question,° her hand.
    (Reads) "To the unknown beloved, this, and my
    good wishes." Her very phrases! *(Opening the*
    letter) By your leave,° wax°—soft,° and the
    impressure° her Lucrece,° with which she uses to
10   seal—'tis my lady. To whom should this be?°
        "Jove knows I love,
            But who?
        Lips do not move,
            No man must know."
15   "No man must know." What follows? The
    numbers altered.° "No man must know." If this
    should be thee, Malvolio?
        "I may command where I adore,
            But silence, like a Lucrece knife,
20   With bloodless stroke my heart doth gore.
            M.O.A.I.° doth sway my life."
    "M.O.A.I.° doth sway my life." Nay, but first let me
    see,° let me see, let me see. "I may command
    where I adore." Why, she may command me. I

25 serve her, she is my lady. Why, this is evident in
    any formal capacity.° There is no obstruction° in
    this. And the end—what should that alphabetical
    position° portend? If I could make that resemble
    something in me. Softly—"M.O.A.I." "M."
30 Malvolio—"M"—why, that begins my name. "M."
    But then there is no consonancy in the sequel.°
    That suffers under probation.° "A." should follow,
    but "O" does. And then "I" comes behind.
    "M.O.A.I." This simulation° is not as the former;
35 and yet to crush° this a little, it would bow° to me,
    for every one of these letters are in my name. Soft,
    here follows prose:° "If this fall into thy hand,
    revolve.° In my stars° I am above thee, but be not
    afraid of greatness. Some are born great, some
40 achieve greatness, and some have greatness thrust
    upon 'em. Thy fates open their hands,° let thy
    blood and spirit embrace them, and to inure°
    thyself to what thou art like to be, cast° thy humble
    slough,° and appear fresh.° Be opposite° with a
45 kinsman, surly with servants. Let thy tongue tang°
    arguments of state; put thyself into the trick of
    singularity.° She thus advises thee that sighs for
    thee. Remember who commended thy yellow
    stockings, and wished to see thee ever cross-
50 gartered.° I say remember, go to, thou art made° if
    thou desirest to be so; if not, let me see thee a
    steward still,° the fellow of servants, and not
    worthy to touch Fortune's fingers. Farewell. She
    that would alter services° with thee,
55   The Fortunate Unhappy."
    Daylight and champaign° discovers not more. This
    is open.° I will be proud,° I will read politic°
    authors, I will baffle° Sir Toby, I will wash off gross°
    acquaintance, I will be point-device° the very man.

60 I do not now fool myself, to let imagination jade°
    me; for every reason excites to this,° that my lady
    loves me. She did commend my yellow stockings
    of late, she did praise my leg, being cross-gartered,
    and in this she manifests herself to my love, and
65 with a kind of injunction drives me to these habits
    of her liking. I thank my stars, I am happy. I will
    be strange,° stout,° in yellow stockings, and cross-
    gartered, even with the swiftness of putting on.
    Jove and my stars be praised. Here is yet a
70 postscript. "Thou canst not choose but know who I
    am. If thou entertainest° my love, let it appear in
    thy smiling,° thy smiles become thee well.
    Therefore in my presence still smile, dear my
    sweet, I prithee." Jove,° I thank thee. I will smile, I
75 will do everything that thou will have me.

1 **employment**/business 3 **hand**/handwriting 3-4 **c's...t's**/(He unwittingly spells out *cut*, bawdy slang for the female sexual organ) 5 **P's**/(continues the sexual puns) **contempt of question**/without question 8 **By your leave**/with your permission (a request he makes to the seal on the letter) **wax**/the seal itself **soft**/wait a moment 9 **impressure**/image of the waxen seal **Lucrece**/i.e., the figure of the chaste Roman matron, Lucretia, who stabbed herself after being raped by Tarquin 10 **To...be?**/i.e., who is this letter meant for (there is no salutation, the letter just begins with a verse) 16 **numbers altered**/i.e., the meter of the verse has changed (an example of Malvolio's pedantry) 21-22 **M.O.A.I.**/(He pronounces rather than spells out the letters, adding a comic complication to the rhyming verse.) 22-23 **let me see**/(After having been thrown by the puzzle of "M.O.A.I.", he presses on to figure out another line.) 25-26 **evident...capacity**/i.e., clear by any normal understanding 26 **obstruction**/obstacle 27-28 **alpha-betical position**/arrangement of letters 31 **no...sequel**/i.e., no agreement in what follows 32 **probation**/examination, scrutiny 34 **simulation**/hidden meaning 35 **crush**/force the meaning **bow**/yield itself 37 **prose**/(the letter's verse has now changed to prose) 38 **revolve**/reflect **stars**/fortune, high orbit 41 **open their hands**/i.e., are ready to receive you 42 **inure**/accustom 43 **cast**/cast off 43-44 **humble slough**/lowly demeanor (i.e., the way a snake "sloughs" off its old skin) 44 **fresh**/newly born, youthful **opposite**/hostile, quarrelsome 45 **tang**/clang sharply 46-47 **trick of singularity**/affectations or habits of eccentricity 49-50 **cross-gartered**/i.e., with garters fastened above and below the knees (a ludicrous style of fashion) 50 **made**/i.e., your fortune is secured 52 **still**/evermore 54 **alter services**/exchange places 56 **champaign**/open country 56-57 **This is open**/i.e., the meaning of this is clear 57 **proud**/lofty **politic**/political 58 **baffle**/publicly disgrace **gross**/low 59 **point-device**/extremely precise (in all ways that the letter asks) 60 **jade**/trick 61 **excites to this**/urges this

232

conclusion 67 **strange**/imperious   **stout**/haughty 71 **entertainest**/
acceptest 72 **smiling**/i.e., smiling face (Malvolio normally wears a sour
expression; his name means "I wish ill") 74 **Jove**/i.e., God

Commentary: [All of the separate parts of Malvolio's speech
have been joined together and re-numbered to make one whole
soliloquy. See 2.5.82-179 for the speech in its complete context.] All
of Malvolio's isolation, pomposity and vanity are on full display in
this soliloquy. Closed and cautious at the start, he is a completely
open character at the end. The soliloquy itself is broken up with the
hilarity and reactions of hidden onstage characters. But Malvolio
thinks he is alone. The discovery of the letter is followed by a close
perusal of its contents and the ferreting out of its hidden meaning.
For Malvolio, the letter contains a secret wish: Olivia loves him
and wishes him to be her husband and master of the house. Notice
the detailed scrutiny Malvolio employs to arrive at these ludicrous
conclusions. He is a comic character blinded by his own, high self-
regard. He doesn't even notice that he is turning into a fool,
tethered in cross-garters and yellow stockings, with an ill-suited
smile on his face. As a Puritan, Malvolio is usually dressed in black,
with a somber mien. This speech, through the device of the letter,
releases in him a new emotion, joy. And in lines 49-66 he speaks
with a hopeful freedom and abandon that liberates him from the
shackles of his usual melancholy gloom.

TWELFTH NIGHT

Sebastian

Act 4, Scene 3. Illyria. Olivia's garden. Sebastian, the twin brother of Viola (who looks like him when dressed as the boy Cesario), has just met and will soon marry the Lady Olivia, who mistakes him for Cesario. In a daze, Sebastian steps from Olivia's house and delivers this speech in amazement.

SEBASTIAN

This° is the air, that° is the glorious sun.
This pearl° she gave me, I do feel't and see't,
And though 'tis wonder° that enwraps me thus,
Yet 'tis not madness. Where's Antonio° then?
5 I could not find him at the Elephant,°
Yet there he was, and there I found this credit,°
That he did range° the town to seek me out.
His counsel now might do me golden service,
For though my soul° disputes well with my sense
10 That this may be some error but no madness,
Yet doth this accident° and flood of fortune
So far exceed all instance,° all discourse,°
That I am ready to distrust mine eyes
And wrangle with my reason that persuades me
15 To any other trust° but that I am mad,
Or else the lady's mad. Yet if 'twere so
She could not sway° her house, command her
      followers,
Take and give back affairs and their dispatch
With such a smooth, discreet,° and stable bearing
20 As I perceive she does. There's something in't
That is deceivable.° But here the lady comes.

1 This/(indicates the air around him) that/(another indication) 2 This pearl/(he holds up the pearl as material evidence) 3 wonder/amazement

4 **Antonio**/a sea captain, friend of Sebastian who rescues and brings him to
Illyria 5 **Elephant**/i.e., a tavern where they were to meet 6 **credit**/report 7
range/roam 9 **soul**/rational self 11 **accident**/chance occurrence 12
instance/precedence **discourse**/reasoning 15 **trust**/belief 17 **sway**/rule
19 **discreet**/judicious 21 **deceivable**/deceptive

Commentary: Sebastian's soliloquy begins in awe. Is he in the
midst of a dream or reality? He tries to regain his balance and
conquer his bafflement. The sibilant sounds in the verse heighten
the shock sensation he is feeling. Reason battles with good fortune.
Like all romantic heroes, Sebastian tests his senses to be sure they
are in working order (lines 1-4). The actor must remember that the
character Sebastian has been plunked down in Illyria late in the
play, long after Olivia's attachment to "Cesario" has passed the
point of fancy and turned into passion. His naiveté is the one
characteristic he can play with fully. He needs to know a little
more than what his senses tell him. Not a well-rounded character,
Sebastian is more a plot device who introduces a comic complication
in the person of a "twin."

SELECTED BIBLIOGRAPHY
OF TITLES IN PRINT

Barton, John. *Playing Shakespeare*. London and New York: Methuen, 1984. Possibly the best book available on this subject, but most useful when read in conjunction with seeing the video films upon which it is based.

Brown, John Russell. *Discovering Shakespeare: A New Guide to the Plays*. London: Macmillan, 1981. An excellent short introduction to Shakespeare's plays in the theatre.

_____. *Shakespeare's Dramatic Style*. London: Heinemann, 1970. Explores the working of the text in *Romeo and Juliet, As you Like It, Julius Caesar, Twelfth Night* and *Macbeth*.

Goldman, Michael. *Acting and Action in Shakespearean Tragedy*. Princeton, NJ: Princeton University Press, 1985. Academic in tone, useful nonetheless for its sometimes penetrating ideas.

Joseph, Bertram. *Acting Shakespeare*. New York: Theatre Arts Books, 1960. One of the first books to treat the subject of acting Shakespeare, there are still useful ideas here.

_____. *A Shakespeare Workbook (Two Volumes)*. New York: Theatre Arts Books, 1980. Goes through a number of plays and speeches, working through specific points of text.

MacLeish, Kenneth. *Longman Guide to Shakespeare's Characters*. London: Longman, 1985. A fun and usable Who's Who of Shakespeare. Best for exploring character.

OTHER VALUABLE TEXTS IN PRINT

Berry, Cicely. *The Actor and His Text*. London, 1987.

Brubaker, E.S. *Shakespeare Aloud: A Guide to His Verse on Stage*. Pennsylvania, 1976.

Cook, Judith. *Shakespeare's Players*. London, 1983.

David, Richard. *Shakespeare in the Theatre*. London, 1978.

Frye, Northrop. *Northrop Frye on Shakespeare*. New Haven and London, 1986.

Gibson, William. *Shakespeare's Game*. New York, 1978.

Granville-Barker, Harley. *Prefaces to Shakespeare, Volume I*. New Jersey, 1946.

Granville-Barker, Harley. *Prefaces to Shakespeare, Volume II*. New Jersey, 1947.

Gurr, Andrew. *The Shakespearean Stage, 1574-1642*. Cambridge, 1980.

Kott, Jan. *Shakespeare Our Contemporary*. New York, 1964.

Magee, Judy. *You Don't Have To Be British To Do Shakespeare*. New York, 1985.

Onions, C.T. *A Shakespeare Glossary*. Oxford, 1986.

Sher, Antony. *Year of the King*. New York, 1987.

Spurgeon, Caroline. *Shakespeare's Imagery and What It Tells Us*. Cambridge, 1935.

Styan, J.L. *Shakespeare's Stagecraft*. Cambridge, 1967.

* * *

Although there are many editions of Shakespeare's plays available, the best are perhaps the recently published *Complete Plays* (Oxford University Press, 1986) and the separate editions published by Methuen (Arden Series), Penguin, and Signet. All have excellent notes. A fine standard edition is also the much used *Riverside Shakespeare*.

The books we have cited are generally available at first-rate general bookshops, college bookshops, and we trust at all performing arts bookshops. They may all be ordered by mail from Applause Theatre Books, 211 West 71 Street, New York, NY 10023, (212) 595-4735.

SHAKESCENES: SHAKESPEARE FOR TWO

The Shakespeare Scenebook

EDITED AND WITH AN INTRODUCTION
BY JOHN RUSSELL BROWN

Thirty-five scenes are presented in newly edited
texts, with notes which clarify meanings, topical
references, puns, ambiguities, etc. Each scene has
been chosen for its independent life requiring only
the simplest of stage properties and the barest of
spaces. A brief description of characters and situation
prefaces each scene and is followed by a commentary
which discusses its major acting challenges and
opportunities.

paper ▮ ISBN 1-55783-049-5

ONE ON ONE

BEST MONOLOGUES FOR THE 90'S
Edited by Jack Temchin

You have finally met your match in Jack Temchin's new collection, **One on One**. Somewhere among the 150 monologues Temchin has recruited, a voice may beckon to you—strange and alluring—waiting for your own voice to give it presence on stage.

"The sadtruth about most monologue books,"says Temchin. "is that they don't give actors enough credit. I've compiled my book for serious actors with a passionate appetite for the unknown."

Among the selections:
David Mamer OLEANNA
Richard Greenberg THE AMERICAN PLAN
Brian Friel DANCING AT LUGHNASA
John Patrick Shanley THE BIG FUNK
Terrence McNally LIPS TOGETHER, TEETH APART
Neil SimonLOST IN YONKERS
David Hirson LA BETE
Herb Gardner CONVERSATIONS
WITH MY FATHER
Ariel Dorfman DEATH AND THE MAIDEN
Alan Ayckborn A SMALL FAMILY BUSINESS

paper
MEN: ISBN 1-55783-151-3•WOMEN: ISBN: 1-55783152-1

MONOLOGUE WORKSHOP

From Search to Discovery
in Audition and Performance
by Jack Poggi

To those for whom the monologue has always been synonymous with terror, *The Monologue Workshop* will prove an indispensable ally. Jack Poggi's new book answers the long-felt need among actors for top-notch guidance in finding, rehearsing and performing monologues. For those who find themselves groping for speech just hours before their "big break," this book is their guide to salvation.

The Monologue Workshop supplies the tools to discover new pieces before they become over-familiar, excavate older material that has been neglected, and adapt material from non-dramatic sources (novels, short stories, letters, diaries, autobiographies, even newspaper columns). There are also chapters on writing original monologues and creating solo performances in the style of Lily Tomlin and Eric Bogosian.

Besides the wealth of practical advice he offers, Poggi transforms the monologue experience from a terrifying ordeal into an exhilarating opportunity. Jack Poggi, as many working actors will attest, is the actor's partner in a process they had always thought was without one.

paper•ISBN 1-55783-031-2